Puzzle Films

For Edward Branigan

Puzzle Films

*Complex Storytelling in
Contemporary Cinema*

Edited by Warren Buckland

WILEY-BLACKWELL

A John Wiley & Sons, Ltd., Publication

This edition first published 2009

© 2009 by Blackwell Publishing Ltd
except for editorial material and organization © 2009 by Warren Buckland

Blackwell Publishing was acquired by John Wiley & Sons in February 2007.
Blackwell's publishing program has been merged with Wiley's global Scientific,
Technical, and Medical business to form Wiley-Blackwell.

Registered Office
John Wiley & Sons Ltd, The Atrium, Southern Gate, Chichester,
West Sussex, PO19 8SQ, United Kingdom

Editorial Offices
350 Main Street, Malden, MA 02148-5020, USA
9600 Garsington Road, Oxford, OX4 2DQ, UK
The Atrium, Southern Gate, Chichester, West Sussex, PO19 8SQ, UK

For details of our global editorial offices, for customer services, and for information about how
to apply for permission to reuse the copyright material in this book please see our website at
www.wiley.com/wiley-blackwell.

The right of Warren Buckland to be identified as the author of the editorial material in this
work has been asserted in accordance with the Copyright, Designs and Patents Act 1988.

Library of Congress Cataloging-in-Publication Data is available for this title

ISBN: 978-1-4051-6861-8 (hardback)
ISBN: 978-1-4051-6862-5 (paperback)

A catalogue record for this book is available from the British Library.

Set in 10.5/13pt Minion by Graphicraft Limited, Hong Kong
Printed in Singapore by Markono Print Media Pte Ltd

001   2009

Contents

List of Contributors

Daniel Barratt is a Postdoctoral Research Fellow at the Center for Visual Cognition, University of Copenhagen, Denmark, and is currently working on a project on visual attention, emotion, and media. He has a PhD in cognitive film theory from the University of Kent, UK (awarded 2005); his thesis addresses the paradox of fiction by describing a multi-level model of the film viewer's emotion system. He has guest edited (with Jonathan Frome) the recent issue of the journal *Film Studies: An International Review* based on papers from the 2004 CCSMI conference (published Summer 2006).

Gary Bettinson is Lecturer in Film Studies at the University of Lancaster, UK. He has published articles in *Asian Cinema* and *Film Studies: An International Review.*

Warren Buckland is Reader in Film Studies at Oxford Brookes University, UK. He is the author of *Directed by Steven Spielberg* (2006); *Studying Contemporary American Film* (2002, with Thomas Elsaesser); *The Cognitive Semiotics of Film* (2000); *Film Studies* (1998; 3rd edition, 2008); and *The Film Spectator* (ed., 1995). He also edits the journal the *New Review of Film and Television Studies.*

Allan Cameron is a researcher and lecturer at the Australian Film Television and Radio School, and an honorary fellow in screen studies at the University of Melbourne. He is the author of *Modular Narratives in Contemporary Cinema* (Palgrave Macmillan, 2008). His articles on complex narrative and Hong Kong cinema have also appeared, respectively, in *The Velvet Light Trap* and *Jump Cut.*

Sean Cubitt is Professor and Director of the Program in Media and Com-
munications at the University of Melbourne, Australia, and Honorary
Professor of Duncan of Jordanstone College of the University of Dundee,
UK. He is the author of *Timeshift: On Video Culture* (1991); *Videography:
Video Media as Art and Culture* (1993); *Digital Aesthetics* (1998); *Simula-
tion and Social Theory* (2001); *The Cinema Effect* (2004); and *EcoMedia*
(2005). He is co-editor of *Aliens R Us: Postcolonial Science Fiction* with
Ziauddin Sardar (2002); *The Third Text Reader* with Rasheed Araeen and
Ziauddin Sardar (2002), and *How to Study the Event Film: The Lord of
the Rings* with Thierry Jutel, Barry King, and Harriet Margolis (2007).
He is editor in Chief of the Leonardo Book Series for MIT Press and
Leonardo/ISAST.

Marshall Deutelbaum is Professor Emeritus of English at Purdue
University, Indiana, USA. His areas of interest are film narrative and visual
logic. He is at work (with Leland Poague) on a revised edition of *A
Hitchcock Reader*; his essay "The Deceptive Design of Hong Sangsoo's
Virgin Stripped Bare by Her Bachelors" appeared in the *New Review of Film
and Television Studies*.

Chris Dzialo is a PhD student in the Department of Film & Media Studies
at the University of California, Santa Barbara, USA.

Thomas Elsaesser is Emeritus Professor of Film and Television Studies at
the University of Amsterdam, The Netherlands. His essays on European
cinema, film history and media archaeology, American cinema and contemporary media theory have been translated in more than 15 languages
and published in over 200 collections. He has been visiting professor and
research fellow at UC Berkeley, IFK Vienna, Sackler Institute Tel Aviv, NYU,
and Yale. In 2006 he was Ingmar Bergman professor at the University of
Stockholm, Sweden, and was Leverhulme Professor at Churchill College,
Cambridge, UK, in 2007. Most recent books as (co-) editor include:
Cinema Futures: Cain, Abel or Cable? (1998); *The BFI Companion to
German Cinema* (1999); *The Last Great American Picture Show* (2004); and
Harun Farocki – Working on the Sightlines (2004). His books as author include
Fassbinder's Germany: History, Identity, Subject (1996); *Weimar Cinema and
After* (2000); *Metropolis* (2000); *Studying Contemporary American Film*
(2002, with Warren Buckland); *Filmgeschichte und Frühes Kino* (2002); *Terror,
Mythes et Representation* (2005); *European Cinema: Face to Face with*

Hollywood (2005); *Filmtheorie: eine Einführung* (2007, with Malte Hagener; English edition and Italian translation forthcoming) and *Hollywood Heute* (2008).

Yunda Eddie Feng graduated with an MA in Film Studies from Chapman University. He currently lives in Austin, Texas.

Stefano Ghislotti teaches the history of cinema at the University of Bergamo, Italy. In 1996 he co-authored with Stefano Rosso the collective book *Vietnam e ritorno* (*Vietnam and Back*). In 2000 with Benvenuto Cuminetti he co-authored *Il cinema nella scrittura* (*Cinema in Writing*). In 2003 he published *Riflessi interiori. Il film nella mente dello spettatore* (*Inner Reflections. The Film in the Mind of the Viewer*). He is currently writing a book about mnemonic structures in films.

Eleftheria Thanouli teaches film studies at the Aristotle University of Thessaloniki, Greece.

Michael Wedel is an assistant professor at the Media Studies Department of the University of Amsterdam, The Netherlands. He is the author of *Der deutsche Musikfilm: Archäologie eines Genres* (2007), and is co-editor of *The BFI Companion to German Cinema* (1999), *Kino der Kaiserzeit: Zwischen Tradition und Moderne* (2002), and *Die Spur durch den Spiegel: Der Film in der Kultur der Moderne* (2004). His essays on early cinema, German film history, and contemporary Hollywood have appeared in a number of edited collections and in journals such as *Film History* and *New German Critique*.

Introduction: Puzzle Plots

Warren Buckland

People from all cultures understand their experiences and identities by engaging the stories of others, and by constructing their own stories. But in today's culture dominated by new media, experiences are becoming increasingly ambiguous and fragmented; correspondingly, the stories that attempt to represent those experiences have become opaque and complex. These complex stories overturn folk-psychological ways of understanding and instead represent radically new experiences and identities, which are usually coded as disturbing and traumatic.

This volume examines the influence of this new storytelling epoch on contemporary cinema. It identifies and analyzes "Contemporary Puzzle Films" – a popular cycle of films from the 1990s that rejects classical storytelling techniques and replaces them with complex storytelling. I spend the first part of this introduction examining the concept of the "complex plot" as found in Aristotle's *Poetics*, before pointing out how puzzle films go beyond Aristotle's sense of complexity. Other studies have begun to identify and analyze these films, positioning them on a continuum that ranges from "similar to" to "distant from" classical storytelling (see Eig [2003], the papers in Staiger [ed., 2006],[1] Bordwell [2002, 2006, pp. 72–103], Branigan [2006], and Denby [2007]). In a similar vein, Jan Simons has also used complexity theory and game theory to analyze the films of Lars von Trier (Simons 2007).

David Bordwell's "Film Futures" (2002) is representative of these studies. Bordwell subsumes complex storytelling under Aristotle's conception of plot. This may, at first, seem uncontroversial, because Aristotle does identify both simple and complex plot structures (*Poetics*, ch. 10).[2] However, I argue in this volume that the complexity of puzzle films far exceeds Aristotle's meaning of complex plot. Yet Bordwell does not feel the need to go beyond Aristotle's conception of complexity.

All poetic arts, according to Aristotle, emerge out of general principles of mimesis, or imitation. "Plot" refers to the "arrangement" of events that are imitated. For a plot to be successful, the events it selects, combines, and arranges must appear probable and even necessary rather than contingent and haphazard (which is the case with episodic plots – the worst of all plot structures, according to Aristotle). Probability and necessity form the basis of mimesis and classicism.

Simple plots are mimetic (and therefore classical) because they involve the arrangement of events into a single, continuous action organized and unified into a beginning (initiation of the action), middle (involving a complication of the action), and end (marked by the resolution of the complicating action). Audiences find such a plot easy to comprehend.

Aristotle characterizes complex plots as simple plots with the additional qualities of "reversal" and "recognition" (*Poetics*, ch. 11). A reversal (more specifically, a reversal of good fortunes) is an action or event that runs counter to a character's (usually the hero's) situation and the spectator's expectations. A tragic error suddenly befalls the hero, which has huge unforeseen consequences for him or her. Recognition names the moment when the hero discovers that he or she is subjected to a reversal. Aristotle argues that a plot becomes stronger if recognition and reversal take place at the same time. The moment Oedipus discovers that he has killed his father and married his mother is the ultimate moment of realization and reversal of fortunes to befall any character in the history of drama.

Reversal and recognition introduce a new line of causality into the plot: in addition to the actions and events motivated and caused by characters, there's the plot's additional line of causality that exists over and above the characters. Reversal and recognition are not obviously carried out by characters; they are imposed on the characters and radically alter their destiny. The addition of a second line of causality that introduces reversal and recognition is what, for Aristotle, makes the complex plot complex.

Yet, for Aristotle, complex plots are *still* classical, mimetic, and unified, because reversal and recognition are eventually made to appear probable and necessary. This may seem paradoxical, because of the huge disruption that recognition and reversal cause. To understand Aristotle's reasoning, we need to investigate what he means by "complex."

The term Aristotle uses for complex is *peplegmenos*, which literally means "interwoven." In a successful complex plot, the second line of causality (which introduces recognition and reversal) is interwoven into the first, the characters' plotline. By using the term "interwoven" Aristotle understands that, while the second plot initially disrupts the first by radically altering the hero's destiny, the second plot is eventually integrated into the first, resulting in a unified, classical plot once more, in which reversal and recognition appear to be probable and even necessary actions. Oedipus's recognition and reversal eventually appear inevitable, a necessary part of his plotline (the oracle even predicted Oedipus's misfortunes at the beginning of the drama). Once we grasp his misfortune as a plot necessity, we feel pity and fear toward the unfortunate character. These emotions elicit a cathartic reaction in the audience.

The use of the term "complex" in *Puzzle Films: Complex Storytelling in Contemporary Cinema* extends far beyond Aristotle's term *peplegmenos*. The "puzzle plot" is, I would argue, the third type of plot that comes after the complex plot. A puzzle plot is intricate in the sense that the arrangement of events is not just complex, but complicated and perplexing; the events are not simply interwoven, but *entangled*.

In regard to puzzle films, Bordwell follows Aristotle in interweaving the complex, multiple plotlines back into a single, unified classical plot. He only considers one additional quality of the puzzle film – forking path plots – which he finds he can easily subsume under Aristotle's classicism:

> [T]hese forking path films [call] forth folk-psychological inferences and [are] designed for quick comprehension. (2002, p. 91)

> [In forking path films] narrative patterning obligingly highlights a single crucial incident and traces out its *inevitable* implications. (92; emphasis added)

> [Forking paths illustrate] alternative but *integral* courses of events – something fairly easy to imagine in our own lives and to follow on the screen. (92; emphasis added)

> [Forking path films] call upon skills we already possess, notably our ability to *bind sequences together* in the most *plausible* way in terms of time, space, and causality. (96; emphases added)

Thomas Elsaesser (in this volume) notes that the result of Bordwell's argument "is that the para-normal features are given normal explanations, and the narratives are restored to their 'proper' functioning."

Edward Branigan points out in his discussion of Bordwell's paper: "it may be possible to imagine more radical kinds of forking-path films" (2002, pp. 106–7). Branigan distinguishes the more conservative forking-path films that Bordwell discusses from the more radical films by calling the latter multiple draft films.[3]

In reading Bordwell's account of forking-path plots, I am reminded of attempts by generative stylistics in the 1960s to "describe" (that is, reduce) complex literature to simple sentences and transformational rules. Following Noam Chomsky's transformational generative grammar, Richard Ohmann (1969) defines transformational rules as manipulations of a sentence that produce a new (usually more complex) sentence by reordering, combining, adding, and deleting grammatical components:

> Since the complexity of a sentence is the product of the generalized transformations it has gone through, a breakdown of the sentence into its component simple sentences and the generalized transformations applied (in the order of application) will be an account of its complexity. (1969, p. 139)

More simply put, a complex sentence is made up of one or more simple sentences plus transformational rules. A complex sentence can therefore, in this model, be accounted for and understood in terms of its simple sentences in addition to the transformational rules that combined these simple sentences together to generate the complex sentence.

Ohmann analyses 10 lines from William Faulkner's "The Bear" (here I reproduce the first three lines only):

> ... the desk and the shelf above it on which rested the ledgers in which McCaslin recorded the slow outward trickle of food and supplies and equipment which returned each fall as cotton made and ginned and sold ... (in Ohmann, p. 141)

Ohmann argues that Faulkner's prose in this passage consists predominately of simple sentences plus three transformational rules: the relative clause transformation; the conjunction transformation; and the comparative transformation (141–2). Ohmann reduces the Faulkner passage back to its simple sentences by removing the transformational rules, which yields:

> ... the desk. The shelf was above it. The ledgers rested on the shelf. The ledgers were old. McCaslin recorded the trickle of food in the ledgers. McCaslin recorded the trickle of supplies in the ledgers. McCaslin recorded the trickle of equipment in the ledgers. The trickle was slow. The trickle was outward. The trickle returned each fall as cotton. The cotton was made. The cotton was ginned. The cotton was sold. (Ohmann, p. 142)

I cannot help thinking that there's something missing from Ohmann's rewriting of Faulkner – and I'm not only referring to the transformational rules.

But Ohmann suggests that Faulkner is really very similar to Hemingway; he just uses a few more transformational rules than Hemingway does.

Bordwell attempts something similar to Ohmann in relation to forking-path/multiple draft/puzzle films. He reduces these films down to a classical framework to preserve their stability and coherence – but at the expense of their intricacy and perplexity. See, for example, his reading of *Memento* (2006, pp. 78–80). When Bordwell wants to fit the film into the classical paradigm, he downplays its narration and the spectator's experience. For example, *Memento* may actually consist of "the classical four-part pattern" (2006, p. 80), but the film's presentation obscures the logic of that pattern. And when a film does not conform to classical norms (such as redundancy), Bordwell regards the director to be amiss: "If complex storytelling demands high redundancy, Lynch [in *Lost Highway* and *Mulholland Dr.*] has been derelict in his duty" (2006, p. 89).

The premise of this volume is that the majority of forking-path/multiple draft/puzzle films are distinct in that they break the boundaries of the classical, unified mimetic plot. The puzzle film is made up of non-classical characters who perform non-classical actions and events. Puzzle film constitutes a post-classical mode of filmic representation and experience not delimited by mimesis.

For example, there is no way that the end of *Lost Highway* (1997) (a film I analyze scene by scene in this volume), in which Fred Madison is positioned outside his house *and* inside it at the same time, can be subsumed under classical conceptions of mimesis, probability, or necessity. This action (and many others in the film) is startling precisely because it is improbable. *Run Lola Run*'s (1998) three alternative plotlines break down any sense of mimesis or necessity; the film can be subsumed under the concept of probability only when we accept that it realizes or materializes three alternative probabilities, rather than (as is customary in the traditional mimetic plot) only one probability. Michael Wedel analyzes *Run Lola Run* and discusses Bordwell's forking-paths argument in this volume. In *The Sixth Sense* (1999), Dr Malcolm Crowe's realization at the end of the film that he has in fact been dead from scene 2 onward seems at first to conform to a standard moment of recognition in Aristotle's sense. However, this recognition does not lead the audience to feel catharsis, but to a sense that the film's director, Shyamalan, has pulled a "fast one" on the audience. Daniel Barratt asks in his analysis of the film in this volume: How does the director keep the audience "blind" to the film's narrative twist? It is the film's twist that drove audiences back to the cinemas to see the film again, rather than walk away from their first viewing feeling cathartic. And, although it is in part possible to motivate the backward movement of *Memento* (2000) (a film Stefano Ghislotti analyzes in this volume) by arguing that it imitates Leonard's lack of a short-term memory – for he cannot remember what happened two minutes previously, so the spectator does not (initially) see what happened two minutes previously – this mimetic reading soon breaks down, because the spectator gradually builds up a memory of what happens in the plot's *future* events, whereas Leonard never builds up a memory (of either past or future events). Hence there is no reconciliation or interweaving between the character's plot and the secondary plot. Furthermore, Leonard never experiences a reversal or revelation – or, if he does, he soon forgets about it, and writing it down leads more often than not to confusion rather than clarification (as his murder of Teddy demonstrates, since we are dubious that he is "the one").

How do puzzle plots go beyond Aristotle's definition of the complex plot? The chapters in this volume demonstrate that puzzle films embrace non-linearity, time loops, and fragmented spatio-temporal reality. These films blur the boundaries between different levels of reality, are riddled with gaps, deception, labyrinthine structures, ambiguity, and overt coincidences. They are populated with characters who are schizophrenic, lose their memory, are unreliable narrators, or are dead (but without us – or them – realizing). In the end, the complexity of puzzle films operates on two levels: narrative and narration. It emphasizes the complex *telling* (plot, narration) of a simple or complex *story* (narrative).

The term "puzzle film" names a mode of filmmaking that cuts across traditional filmmaking practices, all of which are becoming increasingly difficult to define: so-called American "independent" cinema, the European and international art film, and certain modes of avant-garde filmmaking. Rather than try to redefine these practices, this volume unites them on the basis of their shared storytelling complexity. This "unity" is of course outweighed by the diversity of each film. This volume investigates the three key sites of film production where complex storytelling is prevalent: North America, Europe, and Asia.

Outline of Chapters

Several contributors to *Puzzle Films* use David Bordwell's *Narration in the Fiction Film* (1985) to guide them through their chosen puzzle films. I will briefly outline his theory before summarizing the chapters.

Long before he began writing about forking-path films, Bordwell developed a cognitive theory of comprehension using the concepts of schemata, cues, and inferences. This theory is not limited to classical films; as the contributors to this volume demonstrate, it is sufficiently flexible to cover puzzle films.[4] When watching a film, which cognitivists posit as being inherently incomplete, spectators use schemata to organize it into a coherent mental representation. Schemata are activated by cues in the data. Gaps in the film are the most evident cues, for they are simply the missing data that spectators need to fill in. Films cue spectators to generate inferences to fill in the gaps.[5] When comprehending a narrative film, one schema in particular guides our inferences – the Aristotelian-based canonical story format:

> Nearly all story-comprehension researchers agree that the most common template structure can be articulated as a "canonical" story format, something like this: introduction of setting and characters – explanation of a state of affairs – complicating action – ensuing events – outcome – ending. (Bordwell 1985, p. 35)

As a film progresses, spectators experience the events and actions as they are arranged by the plot (or what Bordwell calls the *syuzhet*, following the Russian Formalists). Plot or *syuzhet* belongs to the level of narration to the extent that these terms refer to *how* events are presented on screen. Spectators rearrange events, disambiguate their relations and order, and in doing so, gradually construct a story (or *fabula*). This is the level of the narrative, of *what* happens.

Because the film's story is a mental representation the spectator constructs during his or her experience of the film's plot, the story is in a constant state of change, owing to the spectator's ongoing generation of new inferences, strengthening of existing hypotheses, and abandonment of existing inferences. A film may deliberately lead spectators to generate incorrect inferences or the film may deliberately challenge the canonical story format: "If the film does not correspond to the canonic story, the spectator must adjust his or her expectations and posit, however tentatively, new explanations for what is presented" (Bordwell 1985, p. 36). This process of readjustment is precisely what the spectator must go through in relation to puzzle films.

Bordwell is an "atheistic" narratologist because he does not recognize the role of an external "master of ceremonies" controlling the story events. In other words, he does not posit the existence of external narrative agents (external to the story): "To give every film a narrator or implied author is to indulge in an anthropomorphic fiction. . . . [This strategy takes] the process of narration to be grounded in the classic communication diagram: a message is passed from sender to receiver" (Bordwell 1985, p. 62). In place of this communication model, Bordwell argues that narration "presupposes a perceiver, but not any sender, of a message" (Bordwell 1985, p. 62).

Edward Branigan's cognitive model of narration (1992) presupposes both a sender and receiver of a film – in fact several senders and receivers, including narrators, characters, and focalizers. Spectators comprehend characters as agents who exist on the level of narrative; the character is therefore an agent who directly experiences narrative events and who acts and is acted upon in the narrative world. A character whose experiences of the narrative world are then conveyed to spectators become focalizers.

Branigan further distinguishes two types of focalization, each representing a different level of a character's experiences: external focalization, which represents a character's visual and aural awareness of narrative events (the spectator sees what the character sees, but not from the character's position in the narrative; the spectator shares the character's attention, rather than their experience); and internal focalization, which represents a character's private and subjective experiences.

In opposition to characters and focalizers, narrators do not exist in the narrative; they exist outside it on the level of narration. This means they have the ability to influence the shape and direction of the narrative.

From these distinctions, we can label and identify any shot in a narrative film in terms of the agents who control it and the level(s) on which it operates.

Thomas Elsaesser's "The Mind-Game Film" offers a seminal and wide-ranging historical and theoretical overview of a category of films that overlap considerably with the puzzle film – the mind-game film. Indeed, we could argue that the puzzle film is the mind-game film seen from one theoretical perspective – narratology. Elsaesser does not limit himself to one perspective, but instead examines the mind-game film from several perspectives – not only narratology, but also psychology and psychopathology, history and politics – in order to identify its multiple and diverse distinctive characteristics. He notes that mind-game films "address not just the usual (genre) issues of adolescent identity-crises, sexuality, gender, the oedipal family, and the dysfunctional community, but also epistemological problems (how do we know what we know) and ontological doubts (about other worlds, other minds) that are in the mainstream of the kinds of philosophical inquiry focused on human consciousness, the mind and the brain, multiple realities or possible worlds." Similarly, he argues that mind-game films "imply and implicate spectators in a manner not covered by the classical theories of identification."

The remaining chapters focus on a mind-game/puzzle film (or small group of films) from a narratological perspective. In my own contribution, "Making Sense of *Lost Highway*," I use Bordwell's and then Branigan's cognitive theories of narration to analyze scene by scene David Lynch's *Lost Highway*, focusing on the film's complex, intriguing, and engaging storytelling strategies.

In "'Twist Blindness': The Role of Primacy, Priming, Schemas, and Reconstructive Memory in a First-Time Viewing of *The Sixth Sense*," Daniel Barrett introduces/develops a series of new cognitive concepts into film studies – including attention, primacy, priming, reconstructive memory, and change blindness – to explain why first-time viewers of M. Night Shyamalam's *The Sixth Sense* remain "blind" to the film's narrative twist.

Stefano Ghislotti's "Narrative Comprehension Made Difficult: Film Form and Mnemonic Devices in *Memento*" examines the unique organizing principles behind the progressive, regressive, recounted, and fragmented storylines of a film many regard to be the archetypal puzzle film – *Memento* (Christopher Nolan). Ghislotti focuses specifically on the experiential difference between the original theatrical and DVD release, in which time and causality are reversed, and the alternative chronological edition provided on the special edition DVD.

Chris Dzialo studies the screenplay as a legitimate and undervalued form of cinema in itself. He examines two of Charlie Kaufman's screenplays – "Adaptation" (2002) and "Eternal Sunshine of the Spotless Mind" (2004) – and highlights their ambiguous and indeterminate articulation of time. He identifies a tension between, on the one hand, a desire to overcome time as a variable and, on the other, the demand for narrative clarity and the irreversible nature of projection time. He calls this mode of storytelling "frustrated time" narration.

Michael Wedel analyzes the narration of *Run Lola Run* and argues that it "reconfigures temporal linearity and circularity, action and causality, movement and stasis around the central problems of embodied subjectivity, spatio-temporal intervals, and hetero-topic experience." Wedel presents a substantial expansion of Bordwell's reading of *Run Lola Run* in his "Film Futures" paper, by focusing on cinematic rhythm created by sound and music – which, Wedel argues, establish another, more intricate and paradoxical temporal logic in the film.

Allan Cameron and Sean Cubitt begin by discussing the first in Andrew Lau's *Infernal Affairs* (2002–3) trilogy of films within the context of Scott Bukatman's concept of the terminal screen, before moving on to analyze how the film's morality is conveyed through its dense narrative, setting morality and narrative in opposition. They point out that the two main characters (Yan and Ming) deny each other their own truth. The authors end by discussing how the film's narrative and morality address the spectator.

Gary Bettinson charts Wong Kar-wai's manipulation of both genre and narrational conventions in *2046* (2004) and *In the Mood for Love* (2000). Whereas *In the Mood for Love* meshes melodrama and detective genres, creating a narration consisting of gaps, unreliable cues, and retardations, *2046* combines melodrama and science fiction, while its narration disorients and misdirects the spectator.

Yunda Eddie Feng begins by considering Lou Ye's *Suzhou River* (2000) and *Purple Butterfly* (2003) to be reworkings of Hitchcock's thrillers, a reworking that involves combining the thriller format with complex storytelling. Feng identifies nonlinearity and "aggressive" visual style as Lou's key complex storytelling techniques. *Suzhou River* blurs the boundary between the vision of an unseen character-narrator and that of the director. In specific terms, the film occasionally and deliberately confuses the unseen diegetic narrator's focalized shots (which he makes with his video camera) and the director's nonfocalized objective shots. Feng argues that we can only distinguish these two types of shots retrospectively, after we have seen the whole film once. *Purple Butterfly* does not conflate external and internal narration, but its dearth of exposition encourages viewers to practice active engagement in order to comprehend the narrative and to fill gaps in information.

In "The Pragmatic Poetics of Hong Sangsoo's *The Day a Pig Fell into a Well*," Marshall Deutelbaum examines Hong Sangsoo's first film, a multi-plot, multi-character film made in 1996. Deutelbaum notes that Hong's film is the result of the combination of four scripts by four writers, with each script describing a character's experience over a day. Hong revised these scripts in order to create a single story that connects the characters to one another – but without reducing the four plots to a single, coherent, mimetic plot. Rejecting critics who say the film effaces temporal linearity, Deutelbaum examines the film's complex and indirect way of signifying temporality, which he contrasts to the conventional (and mimetic) multi-plot/multi-character Hollywood film *Crash* (2004).

Eleftheria Thanouli uses Bordwell's cognitive theory to analyze Park Chan-wook's *Oldboy* (2003). She asks "what makes a film travel or 'translate' to other cultures?", "how can a filmmaker be original in the era of the 'already filmed'?", and, above all, "how can one resolve the tension between Hollywood and national cinemas in this increasing phase of globalization?" Like many contributors to this volume, she feels the need to go over the film again after first viewing, to double-check the connections among the characters in what is a "twisted narrative" transmitted through a "twisted narration." Yet, she asserts that, paradoxically, the film still remains accessible and intelligible on first viewing. Her close analysis of the film attempts to uncover the way this paradoxical viewing experience is created.

This volume could have been three times as long. Below is a list of additional puzzle films from the 1990s onward, each of which occupies a unique position on the continuum ranging from "similar to" to "distant from" classical storytelling (perhaps with *Sliding Doors* at one end and *Inland Empire* at the other, respectively). The analysis of each film will add further insight into the phenomenon of the contemporary puzzle film:

21 Grams (2003), *Abre los Ojos* (*Open your Eyes*) (1997), *Amores Perros* (2000), *Being John Malkovich* (1999), *Bin-Jip* (*Three Iron*) (2004), *Blind Chance* (*Przypadek*) (1981/released in 1987), *Butterfly Effect* (2004), *Chungking Express* (1994), *Dark City* (1998), *Donny Darko* (2001), *Fight Club* (1999), *The Game* (1997), *Go* (1999), *Inland Empire* (2006), *The Hours* (2002), *The Limey* (1999), *The Matrix* (1999), *Mulholland Dr.* (2001), *Oh!, Soojung!* (*Virgin Stripped Bare by Her Bachelors*) (2000), *Premonition* (2007), *Primer* (2004), *Pulp Fiction* (1994), *Sliding Doors* (1998), *Stay* (2005), *Tierra* (1996), *Time Code* (2000), *Total Recall* (1990), *The Usual Suspects* (1995), *Vanilla Sky* (2001), and *Yi ge zi tou de dan sheng* (*Too Many Ways to be No. 1*) (1997).

Notes

1   Staiger's volume was published as this book was in pre-production. The partial overlap of themes, topics, and terminology demonstrates a shared interest in identifying the primary characteristics of complex storytelling in contemporary cinema.

2   The following discussion of Aristotle is indebted to Jaskolowska (2004).

3   Bordwell does use the term "multiple draft narrative" at the end of his essay, but he defines it differently to Branigan. For Bordwell, "multiple drafts" is an alternative term for "forking-paths," whereas for Branigan "forking-paths" is a conservative subset of "multiple drafts."

4 Eleftheria Thanouli also argues this point in her delineation of post-classical narration (2006).
5 Gaps and inferences come in many shapes and sizes. There are: temporary and permanent; flaunted and suppressed; diffused and focused gaps. These prompt to spectator to generate curiosity and suspense inferences; inferences with different levels of probability; inferences that are either exclusive or non-exclusive; and inferences which operate on both the micro and macro levels of the film. See Meir Sternberg (1978) and Bordwell (1985).

Bibliography

Aristotle, 1987. *Poetics* (trans. R. Janko). Indianapolis: Hackett Publishing.

Bordwell, D. 1985. *Narration in the Fiction Film*. Madison: University of Wisconsin Press.

Bordwell, D. 2002. "Film futures." *SubStance*, 97: 88–104.

Bordwell, D. 2006. *The Way Hollywood Tells It: Stories and Style in Modern Movies*. Berkeley: University of California Press.

Branigan, E. 1992. *Narrative Comprehension and Film*. New York: Routledge.

Branigan, E. 2002. "Nearly true: Forking paths, forking interpretations. A response to David Bordwell's 'Film futures'." *SubStance*, 97: 105–14.

Denby, D. 2007. "The new disorder: Adventures in film narrative." *The New Yorker*, March 3.

Eig, J. 2003. "A beautiful mind(fuck): Hollywood structures of identity." *Jump Cut: A Review of Contemporary Media*, 46. Available at: http://www.ejumpcut.org/archive/jc46.2003/eig.mindfilms/text.html (accessed March 1, 2007).

Jaskolowska, J. I. 2004. "Aristotle's *Poetics*: Reason, necessity, and plot." PhD Thesis, The Catholic University of America, Washington, DC.

Ohmann, R. 1969. "Generative grammars and the concept of literary style," in G. A. Love and M. Payne (eds.), *Contemporary Essays on Style: Rhetoric, Linguistics, and Criticism*. Glenview, IL: Scott, Foresman and Company. (First published in 1964.)

Simons, J. 2007. *Playing the Waves: Lars von Trier's Game Cinema*. Amsterdam: Amsterdam University Press.

Staiger, J. (ed.) 2006. "Complex narratives." Special issue of *Film Criticism*, 31, 1/2. With papers by Charles Ramírez Berg, Elliot Panek, Michael Z. Newman, Walter Metz, Hsuan L. Hsu, Robert Davis, and Riccardo de los Rois.

Sternberg, M. 1978. *Expositional Modes and Temporal Ordering in Fiction*. Bloomington: Indiana University Press.

Thanouli, E. 2006. "Post-classical narration: A new paradigm in contemporary cinema." *New Review of Film and Television Studies*, 4, 3: 183–96.

1

The Mind-Game Film

Thomas Elsaesser

Playing Games

In December 2006, Lars von Trier's *The Boss of It All* was released. The film is a comedy about the head of an IT company hiring a failed actor to play the "boss of it all," in order to cover up a sell-out. Von Trier announced that there were a number of ("five to seven") out-of-place objects scattered throughout, called Lookeys: "For the casual observer, [they are] just a glitch or a mistake. For the initiated, [they are] a riddle to be solved. All Lookeys can be decoded by a system that is unique. [. . .] It's a basic mind game, played with movies" (in Brown 2006). Von Trier went on to offer a prize to the first spectator to spot all the Lookeys and uncover the rules by which they were generated.

"Mind-game, played with movies" fits quite well a group of films I found myself increasingly intrigued by, not only because of their often weird details and the fact that they are brain-teasers as well as fun to watch, but also because they seemed to cross the usual boundaries of mainstream Hollywood, independent, auteur film and international art cinema. I also realized I was not alone: while the films I have in mind generally attract minority audiences, their appeal manifests itself as a "cult" following. Spectators can get passionately involved in the worlds that the films create – they study the characters' inner lives and back-stories and become experts in the minutiae of a scene, or adept at explaining the improbability of an event. Besides reaching movie-house audiences, several of the films have spawned their own online fan communities or forums on the imdb website. Film critics, as well as scholars from different disciplines and even social commentators and trend-watchers also get hooked, judging by the interesting things they have to say. This widespread, but diverse appeal, as well as other differences, makes me hesitate to call the films in question a genre or a sub-genre. I prefer to think of them as a phenomenon, or maybe – in deference to François Truffaut – a "certain tendency" in contemporary cinema. But if it is a tendency, it does not point in one direction only; and if it is a phenomenon, what is it symptomatic of?

First of all, a broad description of the mind-game film. It comprises movies that are "playing games," and this at two levels: there are films in which a character is being played games with, without knowing it or without knowing who it is that is playing these (often very cruel and even deadly) games with him (or her): in Jonathan Demme's *Silence of the Lambs* (1991) the serial killer "Buffalo Bill" is playing games with the police (and the women he captures) and Hannibal Lecter is playing games with Clarice Starling (and eventually, she with him). In David Fincher's *Se7en* (1995), John Doe, another serial killer, is playing games with the rookie policeman played by Brad Pitt. In Fincher's *The Game* (1997), Michael Douglas is the one who is being played games with (possibly by his own brother). In Peter Weir's *The Truman Show* (1998), the eponymous hero leads an entire life that for everyone else is a game, a stage-managed television show, from which only Truman is excluded. Then, there are films where it is the audience that is played games with, because certain crucial information is withheld or ambiguously presented: Bryan Singer's *The Usual Suspects* (1995), Fincher's *Fight Club* (1999), Christopher Nolan's *Memento* (2000), John Woo's *Paycheck* (2003), John Maybury's *The Jacket* (2005), David Lynch's *Lost Highway* (1997), and *Mulholland Dr.* (2001) fall in this category. The information may be withheld from both characters and audience, as in M. Night Shyamalan's *The Sixth Sense* (1999) and Alejandro Amenábar's *The Others* (2001), where the central protagonists are already "dead, except [they] don't know it yet," to quote one of the opening lines of Sam Mendes' *American Beauty* (1999). Sometimes, the "masters" of the game reveal themselves (*The Truman Show, Se7en*), but mostly they do not, and at other times, a puppet master is caught up in his own game, as in Spike Jonze/Charlie Kaufman's *Being John Malkovich* (1999), the hypochondriac writer in the same team's *Adaptation* (2002), or the two magicians in Nolan's *The Prestige* (2006).

Other films of the mind-game tendency put the emphasis on "mind": they feature central characters whose mental condition is extreme, unstable, or pathological; yet instead of being examples of case studies, their ways of seeing, interaction with other characters, and their "being in the world" are presented as normal. The films thus once more "play games" with the audience's (and the characters') perception of reality: they oblige one to choose between seemingly equally valid, but ultimately incompatible "realities" or "multiverses": Ron Howard's *A Beautiful Mind* (2001), David Cronenberg's *Spider* (2002), Richard Kelly's *Donnie Darko* (2001), or the Wachowski Brothers' *The Matrix* (1999). The nature of consciousness and memory, the reality of other minds, and the existence of possible/parallel worlds are equally at issue in films like Richard Linklater's *Waking Life* (2001), Shane Carruth's *Primer* (2004), Michael Gondry/Charlie Kaufman's *Eternal Sunshine of the Spotless Mind* (2004), Cameron Crowe's *Vanilla Sky* (2001, a remake of Amenábar's *Abre los Ojos*, 1997), and Peter Howitt's *Sliding Doors* (1998).

The last two titles indicate that the tendency is not confined to Hollywood or North American directors. To varying degrees and in sometimes surprisingly different ways, "mind-game" films are also being made in Germany, Denmark, Britain, Spain, South Korea, Hong Kong, and Japan: Tom Tykwer's *Run Lola Run* (1998), Lars von Trier's *Breaking the Waves* (1996), Julio Medem's *Tierra* (*Earth*) (1996), Pedro Almodovar's *Habla con ella* (*Talk to Her*) (2002), Kim Kii Duk's *Bin-Jip* (*Three Iron*) (2004), Wong Kar-wai's *Chungking Express* (1994), *In the Mood for Love* (2000), and *2046* (2004). Park Chan-wook's *Oldboy* (2003), Michael Haneke's *Funny Games* (1997), *Code Inconnu* (2000), and *Caché* (2005), with their sadomasochistic undertow of revenge and guilt, also qualify, along with many others, some of which are discussed and analyzed in this volume.

While several mind-game films have affinities with genres such as the horror film (*The Silence of the Lambs*), science fiction (*The Matrix, eXistenZ* [1999]), the teen film (*Donnie Darko*), time travel films (*The Village* [2004]), and film noir (*Lost Highway, Memento*), they address not just the usual (genre) issues of adolescent identity-crises, sexuality, gender, the oedipal family, and the dysfunctional community, but also epistemological problems (how do we know what we know) and ontological doubts (about other worlds, other minds) that are in the mainstream of the kinds of philosophical inquiry focused on human consciousness, the mind and the brain, multiple realities or possible worlds.

Yet one overriding common feature of mind-game films is a delight in disorienting or misleading spectators (besides carefully hidden or altogether withheld information, there are the frequent plot twists and trick endings). Another feature is that spectators on the whole do not mind being "played with": on the contrary, they rise to the challenge. The fact that audiences are set conundrums, or are sprung "traps for mind and eye," that they are – as with von Trier's Lookeys – confronted with odd objects or puzzling details that do not "add up" – even though the overall experience "makes sense" – would indicate we are dealing with a phenomenon that spectators recognize as relevant to their own worlds. Mind-game films thus transcend not only genre, but also authorial signature (even though recognized auteurs are prominent) and national cinema (even though a Europe–East Asia–American independents triangle can be discerned). If read symptomatically, from the point of view of reception, what is at stake are new forms of spectator-engagement and new forms of audience-address (although "new" here functions merely as a diacritical marker of difference: the genealogy of the mind-game film includes such venerable master-magicians of surprise, suspense, and the double-take as Fritz Lang, Luis Buñuel, Alfred Hitchcock, and Orson Welles, as well as 1950s/1960s "art cinema" films by Akira Kurosawa, Alain Resnais, and Ingmar Bergman).

As such, mind-game films could be seen as indicative of a "crisis" in the spectator–film relation, in the sense that the traditional "suspension of disbelief" or the classical spectator positions of "voyeur," "witness," "observer" and their related cinematic regimes or techniques (point-of-view shot, "suture," restricted/omniscient narration, "fly on the wall" transparency, *mise-en-scène* of the long take/depth of field) are no longer deemed appropriate, compelling, or challenging enough. It would not be the first time that the "institution cinema" experiments with spectator-address, in the face of technical, economic, or demographic changes. Lars von Trier's Lookeys, for instance, and the idea of offering prizes to the audience for correct guesses, deliberately confuse film viewing with game-shows on television, in order to provoke a different, more direct form of participation: the cinematic equivalent of the phone-in. But in the early- to mid-1910s, when the so-called "cinema of attractions" was said to give way to the "cinema of narrative integration," a German director, Joe May, initiated a successful, if brief vogue for so-called "Preisrätselfilme" or prize-puzzle-films as a sub-genre of the (Danish-inspired) detective film, where clues were planted without being revealed at the end. Instead, prizes were offered to spectators who identified them (Pehla 1991).

On the other hand, besides the transition from "early" to "classical" cinema, drastic changes in audience-address (at least in mainstream cinema) have been relatively rare, and are usually coded generically (comedy and the musical allowed for frontal staging and direct address, which would not have been common in Westerns or thrillers). If mind-game films are indeed harbingers of such changes in audience-address and spectator-engagement, then the underlying transformations of the "institution cinema" would presumably have to be correspondingly momentous. Some candidates suggest themselves, such as the changes brought by digitization, but perhaps it is better to first consider some alternative definitions and explanations.

A List of Common Motifs

Taking a step back: what goes on in mind-game films, what stories do they tell, what characters do they depict, and why should they be so popular *now*? Even though this is not an exhaustive catalogue of typical situations, here are some of the most frequently named features of the mind-game film, by way of a map or directory of motifs:

1   A protagonist participates in, or is witness to, events whose meaning or consequences escape him: along with him, the film asks: what exactly has happened? There is a suspension of cause and effect, if not an outright reversal of linear progression (*Memento, Donnie Darko, Lost Highway*).
2   A protagonist seems deluded or mistaken about the difference between reality and his/her imagination, but rather than this inner world becoming a clearly marked "subjective" point of view of a character (as in the European art film), there is no perceptible difference either in the visual register or in terms of verisimilitude, between real and imagined, real and simulated, real and manipulated. As one commentator puts it: films like *The Matrix, Dark City* (1998), and *The Truman Show* involve "a hefty plot twist, one that forces the protagonist to question reality itself. Said reality tends to be nothing more than a simulation, and a conspiratorial simulation at that" (Sankey 2001).
3   A protagonist has a friend, mentor, or companion who turns out to be imagined (*Fight Club, A Beautiful Mind, Donnie Darko, Lost Highway*).
4   A protagonist has to ask himself: "who am I and what is my reality?" (the Philip K. Dick adaptations *Blade Runner* [1982], *Total Recall* [1990], *Paycheck* and *Minority Report* [2002]), and even "am I still alive or already dead" (*Angel Heart* [1987], *Jacob's Ladder* [1990], *The Sixth Sense, The Others*).
5   Not only is the hero unable to distinguish between different worlds: he or she is often not even aware that there might be parallel universes, and neither is the audience – until a moment in the film when it

turns out that the narrative and plot have been based on a mistaken cognitive or perceptual premise (*Fight Club, The Sixth Sense, A Beautiful Mind*). The point in the story at which it undergoes such drastic revision, where the ground is pulled from under the audience's feet, is commented on by one of the fans as follows: "You want that big, juicy, brain-blasting, oh-my-god-everything-has-changed feeling," to which another blogger replied: "Yes – but the 'oh-my-god-everything-has-changed' feeling in *The Sixth Sense* is reinforced by the 'gotcha' feeling of replayed scenes from earlier in the movie that you now understand differently. The viewer gets to have it both ways: have the oh-my-god feeling and watch the protagonist experience it too."

6   A character is persuaded by his – or more often, her – family, friends, or the community that she is deluded about the existence or disappearance, usually of a child – a self-delusion brought upon by trauma, excessive grief, or other emotional disturbance. He/she insists on maintaining this delusion against all odds, and is usually proven right, by uncovering a conspiracy, either of a very sophisticated, diabolical kind, or on the contrary, consisting of a very "scientific," bureaucratic, or routine "test" or "measure" ordered by the powers that be (*Minority Report, The Forgotten* [2004], *The Village* [2004], *Flight Plan* [2005]).

From such *ad hoc* definitions and the folk/fan wisdom, it is evident that the mind-game film can usefully be analyzed under several headings: for instance, one can foreground issues of narrative and narratology (by concentrating on the unreliable narrators, the multiple time-lines, unusual point of view structures, unmarked flashbacks, problems in focalization and perspectivism, unexpected causal reversals and narrative loops); one can highlight questions of psychology and psychopathology (characters suffering from amnesia, schizophrenia, paranoia, "second sight" or clairvoyance); philosophers of mind can find conundrums about the relation of body, brain, and consciousness that challenge concepts of "identity," or ask what it means to be "human" as we share our lives with ever smaller machines and ever more "intelligent" objects. Mathematicians can elucidate game theory, explicitly thematized in *A Beautiful Mind* and implicitly instantiated in David Mamet's *The Spanish Prisoner* (1997), or they can comment on the role of contingency, chance, stochastic series, and explain the "butterfly" effects of chaos theory, the "sensitive dependence on initial conditions" thesis, (positive) feedback loops as opposed to linear causality (in films like *The Butterfly Effect* [2004] or *Donnie Darko*). Several films raise matters of *ontology* and parallel worlds, while skepticism and doubt, but also their obverse: belief and trust, are often the *epistemological* issues at stake. Not all of these approaches or entry-points can be discussed here, and I shall limit myself to three: the case for "complex storytelling" (and the possible disjuncture between "narrative" and "database," "narrative logic" and "game logic"), the idea of identity crises and personality disorders as "productive pathologies," and the "social uses" of mind-game films as helping either to "discipline and control" or to "teach and train."

The Mind-Game Film: A Case of Complex Storytelling?

There is clear evidence that cinematic storytelling has in general become more intricate, complex, unsettling, and this not only in the traditionally difficult categories of European auteur and art films, but right across the spectrum of mainstream cinema, event-movies/blockbusters, indie-films, not forgetting (HBO-financed) television. Several of the features named as typical of the mind-game film are grist to the mill of professionally trained (literary) narratologists: single or multiple diegesis, unreliable narration and missing or unclaimed point-of-view shots, episodic or multi-stranded narratives, embedded or "nested" (story-within-story/film-within-film) narratives, and frame-tales that reverse what is inside the frame (going back to *The Cabinet of Dr Caligari* [1919]). As a consequence, the films I group under the mind-game tendency are generating a broad literature focusing on the narratological issues raised, with corresponding terminologies: some talk of "forking-path" narratives (David Bordwell 2002; see below) or "multiple-draft" narratives (Bordwell; Edward Branigan 2002), others refer to them as (psychological) puzzle films (Elliot Panek 2006), twist films (George Wilson 2006), complex narratives (Janet Staiger 2006), or try to define them as special cases of "modular narratives" (Allan Cameron 2006). Jason Mittell (2006) has also studied the complex puzzle narrative in contemporary television.

Let us assume that the mind-game film sets the viewer a number of *narratological problems or puzzles*: Mind-game films at the narrative level, offer – with their plot twists and narrational double-takes – a range of strategies that could be summarized by saying that they suspend the common contract between the film and its viewers, which is that films do not "lie" to the spectator, but are truthful and self-consistent within the premises of their diegetic worlds, that permit, of course, "virtual" worlds, impossible situations, and improbable events. Audiences, for instance, felt cheated by a film like *The Usual Suspects* (1995), because it involved not only an unreliable narrator, Keyser, but also a mendacious point-of-view shot, implying the presence of a witness in a crucial scene, when there was none. *Bona fide* mind-game films by contrast maintain a basic consistency and self-consistency or they enact the very condition their hero suffers from, in the structure of the film itself, as in *Memento*, where the film, as it were, wipes out its own memory, by being told in short segments that precede each other, rather than follow each other. Films such as *The Matrix*, *Donnie Darko*, and *Fight Club* present their parallel worlds without marking them off as different by superimposition, soft focus, or any of the other conventional means by which films indicate switches of register or reference. The question then becomes: do the films "lie," or is it the very opposition of truth and lie, between the actual and the virtual, the subjective and the objective, that is at stake? The disorientation of the spectator extends to the reality-status of what was being shown, and unlike other forms of deception, illusionism, and make-believe, the mind-game film does not involve a matter of ocular (mis-)perception, nor does it have to do with perspectivism; it is neither a matter of the human eye missing something (such as the body in Antonioni's *Blow Up* [1966], which is then revealed via the mechanical camera), nor are we presented with several versions of the same event, as in Kurosawa's *Rashomon* (1950).

Film scholars who have turned to narratology to explain these films can point to precursors of the complex storytelling mode and of multiple point-of-view narration, such as Bergman's *Persona* (1966), the unreliable narration from Hitchcock's *Stage Fright* (1950), with its "lying" flashback, Fritz Lang's *Woman in the Window* (1944) and *Beyond a Reasonable Doubt* (1956), or Alain Resnais' *Hiroshima mon amour* (1959) and *Last Year in Marienbad* (1961), not to mention Orson Welles' *Citizen Kane* (1941) and *F for Fake* (1974) or almost the entire oeuvre of Luis Buñuel, mind-game player par excellence, who needed to invoke neither external agents nor aberrant psychology to persuade the audience of multiple universes, held together by chance and contingency, between which characters may switch on a mere whim or when perceiving a seemingly banal object. In literature, too, there is no shortage of precursors: Boccaccio, Cervantes, Lawrence Sterne, tracing a line to Chesterton, Borges, Gide, Nabokov, and Calvino (each one a master of the shaggy dog story of mutual/multiple embeddedness), as well as the classic modernists from Flaubert to Proust, Virgina Woolf, and Joyce, or Conrad, Mann, and Faulkner.

Narratologists tend to perceive mind-game films either as occasions for refining existing classifications or as challenges to prove that there is nothing new under the sun when it comes to storytelling. A head-on exercise in demystification of mind-game films has been undertaken by David Bordwell (2002). Under the name of "Forking Path Narratives" he discusses, among others, Tom Tykwer's *Run Lola Run*, Krzysztof Kieslowski's *Blind Chance*, Peter Howitt's *Sliding Doors*, and Wai Ka-Fai's *Too Many Ways to be No. 1* (1997) (while in another publication, Kristin Thompson set out to prove just how "classical" films like *Groundhog Day* [1993] are, appearances to the contrary [Thompson 1999]). Bordwell's main line of argument, for instance, is that the paths (or narrative trajectories) are still linear once they have forked, that the forks are signposted and foreshadowed, that forks are made to intersect eventually, that all paths are not equal: there is a hierarchy, and the last one taken presupposes all others. And finally, that there are still deadline structures (such as in *Donnie Darko* or *Run Lola Run*), which hold the narrative universe together and inflect it with a linear causality.

The perspective taken by Bordwell, Thompson, as well as Murray Smith (2001) and others is that this is a challenge to theory that can be "mastered" simply by extending classical narratology to include some of the recent work in cognitive psychology, about how the mind organizes visual cues, how perception, identification, and mental schema function. The result is that the para-normal features are given normal explanations, and the narratives are restored to their "proper" functioning.

The problem with such approaches is that they tend to reduce the films to business as usual, making one wonder why the writer or director went to such trouble in the first place. Surely, in these films (as indeed, some earlier ones as well), the most intriguing and innovative feature is this insistence on temporality as a separate dimension of consciousness and identity, the play on nonlinear sequence or inverted causality, on chance and contingency, on synchronicity and simultaneity and their effects on characters, agency, and human relations: we are in worlds that often look just like ours, but where multiple time-lines coexist, where the narrative engenders its own loops or Möbius strips, where there may well be a beginning, a middle, and an end, but they certainly are not presented in that order, and thus the spectator's own meaning-making activity involves constant retroactive revision, new reality-checks, displacements, and reorganization not only of temporal sequence, but of mental space, and the presumption of a possible switch in cause and effect.

A countervailing strategy in the field of narrative analysis has been to consider the mind-game films as leftovers of classical narrative, during a period of transition, when the default value of cinematic storytelling is rapidly becoming that of the interactive video-game and the computer simulation game. In practice, there clearly are crossovers, as many Hollywood block-busters (from *Die Hard* [1988] to *King Kong* [2005]) have lucrative par-allel lives as computer games, and stories originating as games have found their way into cinemas, such as *Resident Evil* (2002), *Doom* (2005), and *Silent Hill* (2006). The crossover "graphic novel" has also been a recent phenomenon much remarked upon, after the box office success of *Ghost World* (2001), *V for Vendetta* (2005), *Sin City* (2005), and *300* (2006). But the assump-tion of video-game architecture now determining narrative is as much an oversimplification as the earlier voiced complaint that special effects were driving out narrative and plot in the blockbuster film. Both assertions should certainly leave the theoretician dissatisfied: the literature on whether games are narratives at all, or need to be seen as an entirely different species, is vast and vastly divided, and the arguments for blockbusters still being intricately plotted, as well as multimodal with respect to video-game logic, have also been made (Elsaesser and Buckland 2002, chapter 5; King and Krzywinska 2002; Simons 2007).

Narrative versus Database

The popularity and profitability of computer games has nonetheless given rise, among film and humanities scholars, to a renewed interest in mathematical game theory. Especially "new media" theorists have begun to rethink the logic of traditional narratives, arguing that the storytelling we know and are familiar with from Homer to Homer Simpson may itself be a historic-ally specific and technology-dependent – and thus a doubly variable – way of storing information and of organizing direct sensory as well as symbolic data. It would therefore be not altogether unreasonable to assume that new technologies of storage, retrieval, and sorting, such as the ones provided so readily and relatively cheaply by the computer or internet servers, will in due course engender and enable new forms of "narrative," which is to say, other ways of sequencing and "linking" data than that of the story, cen-tered on single characters, and with a beginning, a middle, and an ending.

For contemporary cinema, the challenge might be: What is the equival-ent, or rather what sorting principles can replace or complement narrative?

Because narrative, considered as a universally prevailing basic ordering principle, does have peculiarities: it enforces a linearity and teleology; it operates a logic of sequential implication (*post hoc ergo propter hoc*), and it tends to rely on causally motivated chains of events, propelled by identifiable agents, usually human beings. That is fine as far as it goes, but if one considers it purely under the aspect of its ordering function, it also looks very self-limiting and possibly even unsuitable for a whole range of tasks at hand.

These new tasks or challenges to narrative can be defined in three directions: one leads us toward the rhizome, archive, the database, as foreseen in the writings of Vannevar Bush and Ted Nelson, the Cold War 1950s geniuses of hypertext architecture and cyberspace. The hotspots and network nodes that now link the web are clearly breaks with narrative linearity, and the literate community has adapted surprisingly quickly to the labyrinth pathways and navigational principles behind such architectures. The second way, in which a complement to (modernist) narrative might be conceived, is in upping the ante in terms of convolution and involution, layering and *mise-en-abyme*, i.e., accommodating seriality, multiple options, and open-endedness within a broadly telic and goal-oriented storytelling format. Narrative accommodates quite well its own enunciative double-takes, its own reflexive bootstrapping and metaleptic strategies, but computer and internet-driven demands for more "dynamic," "real-time" feedback and response are putting pressure even on (post-)modernist narrative. The third direction would reassess the present state and future potential of the material object and symbolic form which has largely shaped linear narrative in both word and image: the printed book.

From an evolutionary–anthropological perspective, human beings have developed in the course of their history two symbolic systems of representation: the visual-mimetic and the verbal-symbolic. Both received a major boost/underwent a quantum leap in fifteenth/sixteenth-century Europe: the linearization of the verbal system ("the word"), with printing and the book, and the spatialization of the visual mimetic system ("the image"), with perspectival projection and portable, oil-based, easel painting. The twentieth/twenty-first century may come to be seen has having effected a similarly epochal shift in these representational systems, around the computer, wireless telephony, and digitization. Even if the philosophical implications and political consequences of this shift are not yet as clear as those of the Renaissance and Humanist Enlightenment, it is safe to say that fixed perspective and the "window on the world" of easel painting (and cinema) is competing with the multiple screen/monitor/interface (with its virtual windows, refreshed images, embedded links, and different forms of graphics, topographies, and visualizations) and that the book is also in full mutation, as written texts become both searchable and alterable, as well as dynamically linked with images, diagrams, and graphics. The consequence is that narrative (as the traditionally most efficient organizing principle of connecting disparate information to a user) has to contend and rival with the archive and the database and their forms of organization and user-contact. Such "automated" user-contact, for instance, would be the "digital footprints" web-users leave behind, and the "data-mining" that connects their activity to the textual body or viewed object, often played back to them as their "choices" and "preferences."

Mind-Game Films as Examples of "Productive Pathologies"

What one can say about mind-game films with respect to narratology is thus that they are different from their literary forebears that play with narrative *mise-en-abyme*, unreliable narrators, and the multiple embedding of points of view, in that the latter emphasize, not a ratching up of auto-reflexivity and self-reference, but instead a "lowering" of self-consciousness and a different form of recursiveness, by, in some cases, knocking out part of the conscious mind altogether, and replacing it with "automated" feedback: this is signaled by protagonists suffering from various personality disorders, among which schizophrenia or amnesia are the two favored forms of dis-ordering identity and dis-associating character, agency, and motivation, and thus of motivating a "reboot" of consciousness and the sensory-motor system.

Some critics (Stewart 2005) have pointed out a certain nihilism in Hollywood's manipulation of referentiality and temporality in these films. While there are cases where this may be so, I would argue also for the possibility of a properly philosophical nihilism about the conceptual and perceptual impasses which our image worlds have burdened us with. At the same time, I see a certain radical ambivalence in the way these films present their characters as suffering from particular pathologies, for – as indicated – mind-game films tend to revolve around mentally or psychologically unstable characters, whose aberrations fall into three major types: paranoia, schizophrenia, and amnesia. Even though the films identify them as "conditions," the fact that these characters' point of view is usually privileged over all others (and thus functions as the spectator's guide) is more than a "trick": it points to a peculiar aspect of their mental state, namely that it suspends our usual categories of sane/insane, as well as those of victim and agent. As to the latter, the pathologies are often connected to a personal past: mostly a traumatic incident that keeps returning or insists on manifesting itself in the present, such as the violent death of Lenny's wife in *Memento*, the death of John Anderton's son in *Minority Report*, or a childhood injustice that comes to haunt the hero in *Caché*. This would call for a psychoanalytic approach, and indeed, once one begins to assess the different traumata from this perspective, one can see the mind-game protagonists' plight as the pathologies of individual lives, but just as forcefully, opening out to contemporary issues of identity, recognition by others, and subjectivity in general, so that the pathologies prevailing in the films reveal other dimensions as well, as follows.

Paranoia

Recent paranoia films include Hollywood films where women – mothers – grieve for a child, or are haunted by the loss of children. Often it is not clear whether these children were ever there, or whether husbands, therapists, or doctors are merely trying to persuade them they never existed. Examples are *The Forgotten*, *Flight Plan*, *The Others*, *What Lies Beneath* (2000), *The Village*, and even Spielberg's *Minority Report*. Usually some conspiracy – instigated by a powerful father figure – lies at the bottom of it.

In many ways the paranoia mind-game film is a revival of a classical genre, derived from the Victorian Gothic tale, such as Henry James's *The Turn of the Screw*, or Daphne du Maurier's *Rebecca*, still the two most frequently used templates. Feminist critics have exhaustively studied these "paranoid woman's films," ranging from *Rebecca* (1940), *Gaslight* (1944), *Experiment Perilous* (1944) to *The Locket* (1946), *Two Mrs Carrolls* (1947), *Secret Beyond the Door* (1948), and *Caught* (1949) (Doane 1987). In all of them, women fear for their sanity because of the mixed messages they get from the world around them, or are driven insane by husbands whom they no longer think they can trust, until they are either disabused of their delusions, or in the case that their worst fears are confirmed, until they are rescued by another male, usually younger and more "modern," but male nonetheless. *Flight Plan* knowingly reverses the stereotype by making the younger man the villain, not the racial or ethnic other, and the unwittingly colluding therapist is a woman, rather than an instance of paternal authority.

Yet paranoia, one can argue, is also the appropriate – or even "productive" – pathology of our contemporary network society. Being able to discover new connections, where ordinary people operate only by analogy or anti-thesis; being able to rely on bodily "intuition" as much as on ocular per-ception; or being able to think "laterally" and respond hyper-sensitively to changes in the environment may turn out to be assets and not just an affliction. The "creative potential" of conspiracy theories lies in the way they help deal with impersonal bureaucratic systems, based on protocols and routines, and practicing mysterious forms of inclusion and exclusion, rather than implementing transparent laws and explicit prohibitions. Par-anoia might also be seen as a response to the crisis in subject-formation, which instead of following the Oedipal trajectory of law versus desire and accepting "castration" as entry point, engages with the symbolic order by constant dis-articulation and vigilance toward its systemic intentions and disembodied intelligence. Paranoia and conspiracy theories, by shifting perspectives and generating horizons with higher degrees of complexity, can lead to new kinds of knowledge.

Schizophrenia

Classical films featuring protagonists with mental problems, such as Hitchcock's *Spellbound* (1943) or Nicholas Ray's *Bigger Than Life* (1956), tended to focus on the family and on patriarchal authority as the root cause of the affliction. A loving and understanding partner was seen as the best cure. In this respect, the films of Roman Polanski marked a change: in *Repulsion* (1965), for instance, the spectator observes and sides with Carol's terrified realization of how predatorily and casually aggressively the male world around her behaves, before beginning to suspect her to be not only unusually sensitive but mentally unbalanced. As in several other films by Polanski, one is invited, indeed seduced into entering another mind, and seeing the world from his or her perspective, before being led on a downward spiral to murder and/or suicide (as in *The Tenant* [1976], *Death and the Maiden* [1994], or *Bitter Moon* [1992]). Yet however shocking the dénouement, the spectator is usually allowed to withdraw into a relatively safe zone of fascinated, spellbound, or horrified observa-tion, rather than being caught entirely unawares or left in mental and moral limbo.

   Mental illness in a mind-game film is generally not signaled in the way it is in Polanski. Usually the frame of "normality" against which a character's behavior can be measured is absent, and even the revelation of his or her condition does not provide a stable external reference point. In David Cronenberg's *Spider* (2002), the protagonist is schizophrenic, a condition made clear both by plot and behavior, but the fusion of memory and delusional fantasy engenders its own kind of unframed vision, increasing the spectatorial discomfort, as we realize the nature of the delusional labyrinth we have come to share. It provides the film with an unreliable narrator, whose unstable mind and oedipal obsessions create a state of tension and suspension, without endowing the hero with special insight, as does *Rain Man* (1989), a film that rewards the autistic Raymond (Dustin Hoffman) with a photographic memory and a phenomenal ability with numbers. By contrast, *A Beautiful Mind* begins with a character who, while shy and withdrawn, seems different only by degrees from the Princeton freshmen he shares his time with. Awkward social behavior is here compensated by a mind – at once more acute and more dissociative – that makes some astonishing discoveries, which begin as relatively harmless, like spotting patterns and resemblances where no one would suspect them (between neckties and cut-glass fruit-bowls), or being able to translate the random scurrying of pigeons for breadcrumbs in the quad into mathematical formulas. The apotheosis of this paradox of the supremely gifted misfit comes in a scene where he and his friends are trying to seduce some girls in a pub, and John Nash comes up with a formula that guarantees success, but which inadvertently lays the foundations for a whole new branch of mathematics – game theory – to which the "Nash equilibrium" makes a major contribution. During the first half of the film, as John is inducted into the rarefied and highly competitive world of Princeton's mathematics department, he has a room-mate, whom we only much later realize is a figment of his troubled mind, aggravated by his involvement in the shadowy world of the Rand Corporation and Cold War espionage. Yet *A Beautiful Mind* is about mind-games (as played by mathematicians and US government agencies), more than it is itself a mind-game film. For that it would need to maintain the premise of the first half, where we share John Nash's "deluded" world and assume it to be normal. Instead, the plot gradually dismantles the layers of invisible framing, so central to the mind-game film, turning an initial pleasure in sharing the exhilaration of a brilliant mind and his special insights into patterns, where ordinary mortals see nothing but chaos or contingency, into the disappointment at having been "had," followed perhaps by pity for Nash, his schizoid delusions and marriage-destroying self-deceptions, from which the true devotion of his wife eventually rescues him. *Donnie Darko*, on the other hand, is a more achieved mind-game film, even though the hero's schizophrenia is clearly signposted from the start. At first, Donnie's "weirdness" is more like a probe, by which the nuclear family, the school dynamics, and the small-town suburban community are tested and found wanting. On the margins of this world, a wise but mad old lady and a frightening figure in a bunny suit called Frank emerge as ambiguous figures of authority and agency, but not necessarily of wisdom and salvation. However, the character of Donnie Darko remains darkly mysterious in his motivation, perception, and possibly preemptive action, even given the ample clues and references to the supernatural, string theory, and books about black holes. Indeed, they almost seem to be planted in the film, in order to divert attention from some of the more "unframed" events that structure the narrative, such as the airplane engine that drops out of nowhere on his parents' roof, or the figures he encounters during his nightly sleepwalking. Donnie "keeps it low," meaning that he stays matter-of-fact even in the face of the most extraordinary encounters and events, so that nothing gives us access to his mind other than the reality that we experience in his presence. Without endorsing R. D. Laing's motto "schizophrenia isn't always a breakdown; sometimes it's a breakthrough," *Donnie Darko* presents its hero's condition as a pathology with a special kind of use: at the very least as a different way of connecting mind and sensation/perception, but possibly as the redemptive and saving grace in a world in denial of its fallen state.

Amnesia

Memento's Leonard Shelby has become the archetypal example of the character who suffers from a loss of memory. His condition not only damages his personality and subjectivity, but also utterly transforms the way he views and interacts with the world. While, to all appearances, Leonard struggles to regain his memory, in order to avenge the death of his wife, the very fact that the film "runs backward" allows also an inverse reading of his intentions and goals. Considered as a productive pathology, Leonard's amnesia would remind one of the importance of forgetting, rather than remembering. By the "stripping" of long-term memory into traumatic programming, i.e., the way that repetitive tasks are inscribed in the body, and by the manner in which revenge becomes a meaningless concept, the film foregrounds the idea of "programming," as opposed to remembering: it points to the importance of the change from a society based on law/

prohibition (so strong in analyses of myths and narratives) to one organizing itself around procedures and protocols (in systems analysis, engineering, and information sciences). As one can see from the uses that the other protagonists in *Memento* – especially Teddy and Natalie – make of Leonard, in order to further their own ends and objectives, the amnesiac hero is in his pathology programmable like a weapon: he is like a smart bomb, a repeat-action projectile on autopilot. To this extent, Leonard represents not the old-fashioned film noir detective, but the new multitasking personality (dissociative, reactive: not rapid reaction, but random reaction force), with a subjectivity programmable not through ideology and false consciousness, but programmed by a fantasy, or self-programmed through the body (where the body functions as a technology of recording, storage, and replay: the somatic or pathologized body as an advanced "neural" or " biological" medium, in its mental instability and volatility potentially more efficient than the current generation of electronic media, at least for certain tasks.

Schizophrenia, paranoia, amnesia and the risk society

What used to be private detectives looking for clues down those mean streets in film noir appear now to be insurance agents assessing risk on behalf of their corporate employers in the neo-noir films of the 1990s. Not since *Double Indemnity* (1944) has this profession played such a prominent role in the movies, when we think that Leonard Shelby, the hero of *Memento*, is an insurance man, and so is Jack, played by Edward Norton, the hero of *Fight Club*, who also works for an insurance company as a risk assessor and loss adjuster. In Leonard's case, his job is directly related to his memory disorder, insofar as the disavowal of his guilt-feelings regarding his role in the death of his wife converge with his guilt-feelings regarding one of his clients, the wife of amnesiac Sammy Jankis, with whom Leonard increasingly comes to be identified. In Jack's case, guilt-feelings are a no less prominent motor of his behavior that finds in the split self and alter ego Tyler Durden its most stabilizing form. But "trauma-theory" is only one path to access the mind of mind-game protagonists. If we understand these illnesses as anthropomorphized versions of mathematical code and automated programs, then they seem to liberate and create new connections, establish new networks, but these are not "open" and "free." They are contained and constrained within a protocol, whose subjective dimensions have not yet been fully understood, not least because of the way they model the future at the same time as they preempt it, and thus potentially short-circuit the very connections they seek to establish: hence the allegorical (and tragic) figure of the "risk-insurer," who risks becoming a self-fulfilling prophet.

In each pathology of subjectivity, I would argue, the mental condition is such that it exceeds the clinical case-story. Indeed, the point of giving such subjectivities-in-action the format of a mind-game film would be to draw the audience into the protagonists' world in ways that would be impossible if the narrative distanced itself or contextualized the hero via his or her (medical) condition. In other words, the hypothesis would be that mind-game films imply and implicate spectators in a manner not covered by the classical theories of identification, or even of alignment and engagement, because the "default values" of normal human interaction are no longer "in place," meaning that the film is able to question and suspend both the inner and outer framing of the story.

Disavowal

Finally, there is disavowal, not only on the part of the protagonists, but also at the level of reception. I noted earlier on that internet fan communities are particularly aware of the mind-game film (which features there under the different label of the "mind-fuck film" [Eig 2003]). But the fan sites and internet forums for mind-game films also seem to operate according to their own mind-game principle: irrespective of how implausible the causes or "magical" the agents are that the film deploys, the status as artifice is disavowed. Instead, the world depicted is taken as real: as if this is the rule of the game, the condition of participating in the postings. No more "representation," no insistence on "cultural constructions": the discussions take for granted the ability to live in fictional or rather virtual worlds, often enough amplified and extended by links to recommendations or other forms of advertising. The directors themselves, as integral parts of the film's marketing, provide additional clues (notably David Lynch, but as we saw, also Lars von Trier with his Lookeys), to suggest that the featured world can be opened up, expanded, making the films into occasions for further para-textual or hypertextual activity. As a node that sustains and distributes a particular form of (floating) discourse, a given film allows fans to engage with each other, by suspending their "reality-check," while nonetheless endowing the text with a plethora of clues, on which paranoia can feed, networks can proliferate, and conspiracy theories can blossom.

Discipline and Control, Teach and Train?

On the one hand, thus, we are dealing with pathologies (of subjectivity, of consciousness, of memory and identity): indications of crisis and uncertainty in the relation of the self with itself and with the world (and by extension: of the spectator with the screen). On the other hand, these apparently damaged minds and bodies are capable of displaying remarkable faculties at times, being in touch with agents from another world (*The Sixth Sense*), intuiting imminent disaster (*Donnie Darko*), or starting popular protest movements (*Fight Club*). Their disability functions as empowerment, and their minds, by seemingly losing control, gain a different kind of relation to the man-made, routinized, or automated surroundings, but also to the more "cosmic" energies, which usually center on the new physics of time travel, curved spaces, stochastic systems, and warps in the universe. In other words, these pathologies are presented to the spectator in some sense as *productive pathologies*.

This would indicate that "trauma" is not only something that connects a character to his or her past, but also opens up to a future. It suggests a Foucault-inspired approach: Foucault sought to explain mental pathologies in terms of bodily regimes, discourses, and institutional practices, which go beyond the individual instance, and inscribe pathology "productively" – in terms of the micro-politics of power – into society at large. Given the resonance that his theories have had in most humanities fields, we should perhaps read the mind-game film also across the paradigms of "discipline" and "control." For instance, seen from the Deleuzian interpretation of Foucault's shift from "disciplinary" to "control" societies (Deleuze 1992), these pathologies of the self are a way of making the body and the senses ready for the new surveillance society. They inscribe "index and trace" in the form of *Aufschreibsysteme* (systems of inscription) on the individual body, much the way that Kafka depicts the governor in *The Penal Colony* being inscribed by his own machine, or the way Leonard in *Memento* has his body tattooed, in order to remember not to forget, much the way he uses his Polaroids. A line could even be drawn from Walter Benjamin's theories of the technical media and the body (around concepts of "shock" and the "optical unconscious"), which (in German philosophy) leads to thinkers like Friedrich Kittler, Klaus Theweleit, and Peter Sloterdijk, with their interest in extending "materialities of communication" to writing and literature (their examples are drawn, besides Kafka, from modernist writers such as Rainer Maria Rilke and Gottfried Benn, not usually associated with the "technical media"). Kittler's *Grammophone, Film, Typewriter* (1999) would be the most systematic attempt, in this vein, to analyze the physiological effects of media-practices, including those of writing, recording, and imaging. Mind-game films would thus be the narratives of such "inscription systems" under the conditions of generalized surveillance and real-time, permanent feedback.

For French philosophy, on the other hand, in the wake of Foucault's *Madness and Civilization* (originally 1961) and following on from Gilles Deleuze and Felix Guattari's *Anti-Oedipus: Capitalism and Schizophrenia* (originally 1972), madness, rather than signifying, as it had done for the Romantics, exceptional talent and genius, becomes a way of "socializing" subjectivity in bourgeois society and under the conditions of liberal market economics. Read "politically" in the light of Foucault, mind-game films would show how perceptual or somatic faculties released or manifest by illness are equally "socialized": they either represent the (individual) solution to a (collective) problem – rather than constituting the problem, as in the case study – or the illness is made to work, fitting a body (through its mind no longer "in control") around a new set of social tasks and political relations. In this way "aberrant" mental states signify the effects of the new disciplinary machines of which they are the early warning systems, heralding the next step after internalizing (bourgeois) self-discipline and self-monitoring, where it would no longer be the mind – not even the Freudian mind, with its unconscious and superego competing for control – that is in charge, but instead, where the senses, the sensations, affects, and the body are the ones that are being directly addressed, stimulated, and appealed to, and thus "organized" and "controlled," in order to fit the subject into the contemporary world and the social matrix of "affective labor" (Hardt and Negri 2001).

While this recalls once more Walter Benjamin, and his theory of the cinema as a disciplinary machine, "training the senses" for modernity and urban life, it also provides a bridging argument to an apparently quite different school of thinking about reordering and realigning our somatic responses with the sensory overload of contemporary life. According to Benjamin, shocks to the body are buffered by the cinema, in that films duplicate, repeat, and thereby make pleasurable in the form of humor (slapstick, Charles Chaplin) the terrors of a world where the human body is exposed and subjected to the logic of abstract systems or machines, be they bureaucratic or technological. Cinema thus rehearses and readies the human sensorium for the tasks of "distracted attention," especially with respect to the perceptual organization of the visual field at the place of work and in everyday life (for instance, when crossing a street with traffic, as in Harold Lloyd or Buster Keaton films).

Thus, on the one hand, Benjamin's thinking seamlessly precedes (and in its historical reference, follows) that of Foucault about the body and the senses in the "classical age," except that for Foucault, the micro-systems of power (of the eighteenth and nineteenth centuries) had ways of inscribing themselves directly onto the body, in the form of sexual mores, rules of hygiene, or the rigid time-tabling of the working day, rather than "mediated" by modern audio and visual entertainment forms. On the other hand, within an apparently quite different ideological context, because given a positive turn, one finds a similar argument made by the American social analyst Steven Johnson, in his book *Everything Bad Is Good for You* (2005). There, Johnson develops a theory about the "post-industrial" role for the modern media, by arguing that computer games, and especially contemporary American television, notably some of the HBO-produced or inspired programs such as *The X-Files*, *The Sopranos*, *24*, or *Lost* (as well as "weird" movies: more or less the same titles I cite as mind-game films), are "good" for the young, because they train new cognitive skills and teach appropriate ways of responding to and interacting with automated systems of surveillance and control, such as increasingly predominate on the work-floor and in offices, as well as in the home and in interpersonal discourse. Johnson, in other words, takes a pragmatic and proactive view of the new control society, making the best case for America's mass media fulfilling their historic role in adapting the working population to the social technologies that promise their economic survival, maintain civic cohesion, and assure America's hegemonic position in the world. Trend-watcher Malcolm Gladwell's review of Johnson's book, tellingly entitled "Brain Candy" (a possible alternative for mind-game), sums up the case as follows:

> To watch an episode of "Dallas" today is to be stunned by its glacial pace – by the arduous attempts to establish social relationships, by the excruciating simplicity of the plotline, by how obvious it was. A single episode of "The Sopranos," by contrast, might follow five narrative threads, involving a dozen characters who weave in and out of the plot. [. . .] The extraordinary amount of money now being made in the television aftermarket – DVD sales

and syndication – means that the creators of television shows now have an incentive to make programming that can sustain two or three or four viewings. Even reality shows like "Survivor," Johnson argues, engage the viewer in a way that television rarely has in the past: When we watch these shows, the part of our brain that monitors the emotional lives of the people around us – the part that tracks subtle shifts in intonation and gesture and facial expression – scrutinizes the action on the screen, looking for clues . . . How can the greater cognitive demands that television makes on us now, he wonders, not *matter*? [. . .] Johnson's response [to the sceptics] is to imagine what cultural critics might have said had video games been invented hundreds of years ago, and only recently had something called the book been marketed aggressively to children:

"Reading books chronically understimulates the senses. Unlike the longstanding tradition of gameplaying – which engages the child in a vivid, three-dimensional world filled with moving images and musical soundscapes, navigated and controlled with complex muscular movements – books are simply a barren string of words on the page [. . .]. Books are also tragically isolating. While games have for many years engaged the young in complex social relationships with their peers, building and exploring worlds together, books force the child to sequester him or herself in a quiet space, shut off from interaction with other children [. . .]. But perhaps the most dangerous property of these books is the fact that they follow a fixed linear path. You can't control their narratives in any fashion – you simply sit back and have the story dictated to you [. . .]. This risks instilling a general passivity in our children, making them feel as though they're powerless to change their circumstances. Reading is not an active, participatory process; it's a submissive one." (Gladwell 2005)

While tongue-in-cheek and deliberately provocative, the argument put forward here by both Johnson and Gladwell about television watching, game playing, and movie going is clear. The counterintuitive and counterfactual example of the book being invented *after* the video-game is a useful reminder of the role as "symbolic form," which (technical) systems of representation occupy in human history. But above all, it confirms that media consumption has become part of the "affective labor" required in modern ("control") societies, in order to properly participate in the self-regulating mechanisms of ideological reproduction, for which retraining and learning are now a lifelong obligation. Undergoing tests – including the "tests" put up by mind-game films – thus constitutes a veritable "ethics" of the (post-bourgeois) self: to remain flexible, adaptive, and interactive, and above all, to know the "rules of the game."

The Rules of the Game

This may explain why mind-game films are at once so popular and give rise to such a flurry of hermeneutic activity. The films are experienced as pleasurable, but also perceived to be relevant. What is, however, remarkable is that this relevance is not mimetic (based on "realism") or therapeutic ("cathartic" in Aristotle's sense). We noted the extraordinary diversity of the commentators, from internet fan communities to philosophers, from literary scholars to trend-analysts, from high theory to social analysis: not only does everyone have something to say, they say it at a meta-level, of which one extreme is to treat the mind-game films as "symptomatic" and the other, to treat them as "literal": this, too, is a form of meta-commentary. Postings on fan-sites are usually grouped under FAQs, so that, for instance, for *Silence of the Lambs*, one finds questions like: "Buffalo Bill's House: How many rooms were in that basement?" "Who did everyone find scarier, Jame Gumb or Hannibal Lecter?" "What order should I watch these in?" "What is the song that is playing when Buffalo Bill is dancing in front of his video camera?" "What does Hannibal Lecter mean when he says that 'Anthrax Island' was 'a nice touch'" "What is [on] Buffalo Bill's tattoo?"

In other words, the FAQs either ignore the fictional contract and treat the film as an extension of real life, to which factual information is relevant, or they tend to use the film as the start of a database, to which all sorts of other data – trivia, fine detail, esoteric knowledge – can be added, collected, and shared. What they do not seem to be engaged in is (symbolic or allegorical, intentionalist or symptomatic) *interpretation*. This is surprising, given the patently impossible or at least highly implausible "realities" the films deal with, and since this fan-base is rarely a credulous new-age cult community, but made up of very savvy media-consumers, one has to assume that such "taking for real" is one of the rules of the game that permit participation. The film is thus part-text, part-archive, part-point of departure, part-node in a rhizomatic, expandable network of inter-tribal communication.

The narratologist, too, is not interested in interpretation, but concerned with definition and the general rules by which certain effects are generated or validated. George Wilson, elaborating a theory of what he calls "perspectively impersonal, but subjectively inflected" film sequences in *Fight Club* and *The Others*, concludes:

> It would be interesting to inquire why cinematic assaults on the norm of
> narrational transparency have become so common around the turn of the
> century. I do not know the answer, and I am not sure how such an inquiry,
> responsibly conducted, should proceed. No doubt a certain amount of
> copycatting has gone on, and perhaps some kind of postmodern skepticism
> about the duplicity of reality and the photographic image has drifted over
> Hollywood. In any event, my present aim has been to say something fairly
> systematic about what some of these subversions of cinematic transparency
> amount to. (Wilson 2006, p. 93)

By contrast, high theory and social commentary could be said to be nothing but interpretation. They take the films as symptomatic for broader
changes in the field of (bourgeois, Oedipal) subjectivity, of (theories of)
consciousness and identity (as I did above, with "productive pathologies"
and Slavoj Žižek has done in his readings of Lynch [2000] and Kieslowski
[2001]), they promote the cinema – across such films – as examples of
"doing philosophy" (Mulhall 2002; Smith and Wartenberg 2006), or they
ask: what are these films (good) for (and answer in the way that Johnson,
Gladwell, or Douglas Rushkoff [1995] has done). Yet, these too, like the
other communities, have their "structuring absences," which define the rules
of the game. What is left out (or only hinted at in Johnson), for instance,
are the material conditions and economic implications of the mind-game
film. But these are not "repressed" truths that somehow need to be
brought to light; rather, the material conditions and the hermeneutic
games are each the recto of a verso, where both sides cannot be visible at
the same time.

In this case, moving from the recto to the verso means to shift from
reception to production, and to consider, however briefly, what the rules
of the game now are for, say, Hollywood film production, but also for other
filmmaking nations (another symptomatic feature of the mind-game
films, in that they are, as indicated, not limited to Hollywood, but appear
a typical product also of Hollywood's alter ego, in respect to production, distribution, and marketing: the international film festival circuit
[Elsaesser 2005]).

Hollywood has always had to produce "texts" that are highly ambiguous, or permeable, when it comes to meaning-making: movies had to permit multiple entry-points without thereby becoming incoherent. This is
what David Bordwell has called the "excessively obvious" nature of the classical film, and why he and others, such as Edward Branigan, have insisted
on comprehension (along with transparency, linearity, and closure) as the

abiding virtues of Hollywood, while others – with equal justification – have pointed to the lacunary, redundant, and circular nature of the same classical cinema. One might call it a policy of "access for all" ("a Hollywood film is a party to which everyone can bring a bottle" is how the director Robert Zemeckis once phrased it), and no small achievement, when one considers that multiple entry-point means: audiences of different gender, different age-groups, different ethnic or national identities, different educational backgrounds, but also quite literally, audiences that "enter" a film at different times during a given performance (on television) or at different points in history (the "classic" or "cult" film). Films have also had to perform well on different media-platforms, at least since the 1960s: as theatrical releases, as television re-runs, as pre-recorded videotapes. Since the 1990s, the marketplace has expanded (it has become global, rather than merely US-domestic, European, Japanese, and Australian) and the platforms have diversified: besides the ones named, one needs to add: a film's internet site, the movie trailer, the video-game, and the DVD. And while scholars can draw up useful binary distinctions – between special effects and intricate plotting, between cinema of attraction and narrative integration, between narrative structure and game logic, between linearity and seriality, between "optical vision" and "haptical vision," between classical and post-classical cinema, between "home entertainment" and "event-movie," between private realm and public space – Hollywood has no such luxury. As the phrase goes: in order to exist at all, it has to be "a major presence in all the world's markets," but also, one can add, "a major presence in all the world's modes of representation." This is no longer only "no small achievement," but a truly daunting challenge, when one considers the proliferation of reception contexts and media-platforms. What once was "excessively obvious" must now be "excessively enigmatic," but in ways that still teach (as Hollywood has always done) its audiences the "rules of the game" of how a Hollywood film wants to be understood, except that now, it seems, at least as far as the mind-game film is concerned, the rules of the game are what the films are also "about," even more overtly than before.

My conclusion would therefore be something like this: the new contract between spectator and film is no longer based solely on ocular verification, identification, voyeuristic perspectivism, and "spectatorship" as such, but on the particular rules that obtain for and, in a sense, are the conditions for spectatorship: the (meta-)contact established by the different interpretative communities with the films, across the "rules of the game" that each community deems relevant and by which it defines itself: its "felicity conditions," as linguists might say. What makes the mind-game films noteworthy in this respect is the "avant-garde" or "pilot" or "prototype" function they play within the "institution cinema" at this juncture, where they, besides providing "mind-games," "brain-candy," and, often enough, spectacular special effects, set out to train, elaborate, and, yes, "test" the textual forms, narrative tropes, and story motifs that can serve such a renegotiation of the rules of the game. Mind-game films, we could say, break one set of rules (realism, transparency, linearity) in order to make room for a new set, and their formal features – whether we examine them from a narratological angle, from an ontological, epistemological, psycho-pathological, or pedagogical perspective (for all of which they provide credible "entry-points") – represent a compromise formation, which is itself flexible, adaptable, differential, and versatile: not unlike its ideal (implied) spectators, if we follow the arguments I have presented here. In addition, they fulfill the material conditions of multiple entry, as well as of multiple platforms. To take just one example: for a feature film to be not only recordable, storable, and playable as a DVD, but in some sense, particularly "DVD-enabled," it would have to be a film that requires or repays multiple viewings; that rewards the attentive viewer with special or hidden clues; that is constructed as a spiral or loop; that benefits from back-stories (bonuses) or para-textual information; that can sustain a-chronological perusal or even thrives on it. All these conditions chart the type of textual organization which responds to the conditions of distribution, reception, consumption, cinephilia, connoisseurship, and spectatorship appropriate for the multi-platform film, which can seduce a theater-going public with its special effects and spectacle values, engage the volatile fan-communities on the internet by becoming a sort of "node" for the exchange of information and the trade in trivia and esoterica in social networking situations, as well as "work" as a DVD and possibly even as a game. It will not come as a surprise, if I have described several salient features of the mind-game film, now looked at from the point of production.

We seem indeed to have come full circle. Initially, I posited that the main effect of the mind-game film is to disorient the audience, and put up for discussion the spectator–screen relationship. The notable emergence (some would argue: reemergence) of mind-game films since the mid-1990s would be one sign of this "crisis," to which they are the solution at a meta-level. After exploring some of these meta-levels, and showing why there might be too many explanations of the phenomenon, only some of which complement each other, while others could prove incompatible, I can now conclude that as a solution, the mind-game films set out to aggravate the crisis, in that the switches between epistemological assumptions, narrational habits, and ontological premises draw attention to themselves, or rather, to the "rules of the game." These rules, in addition to what has already been said about them, favor pattern recognition (over identification of individual incidents), and require cinematic images to be read as picture puzzles, data-archives, or "rebus-pictures" (rather than as indexical, realistic representations).[1]

Thus, what appears as ambiguity or "Gestalt-switch" at the level of perception, reception, and interpretation is merely confirmation of strategy at the level of production and marketing: with the mind-game film, the "institution cinema" is working on "access for all," and in particular, on crafting a multi-platform, adaptable cinema film, capable of combining the advantages of the "book" with the usefulness of the "video-game:" what I have called the DVD-enabled movie, whose theatrical release or presence on the international film festival circuit prepares for its culturally more durable and economically more profitable afterlife in another aggregate form. Which would lead one to conclude that the mind-game films make "mind-games" out of the very condition of their own (im)possibility: they teach their audiences the new rules of the game, at the same time as they are yet learning them themselves.

It is for this reason that I want to insist on treating these films as a "phenomenon" and a "certain tendency." It may be true that many, if not all, can – in due course and given sufficient determination – be disambiguated by narratological means, forcing the analyst to refine his tools, and in the process, forcing the films to yield their secrets. Yet given their often cult status, the interest they have elicited from pop culture fans, philosophers, public intellectuals, and even people who usually do not write/think about movies, it is probably equally sensible to treat them as symptomatic for wider changes in the culture's way with moving images and virtual worlds. Mind-game films may show how the cinema itself has mutated: rather than "reflecting" reality, or oscillating and alternating between illusionism/realism, these films create their own referentiality, but what they refer to, above all, are "the rules of the game". This means that, indeed, we cannot be sure if contemporary cinema is "part of the problem" (Foucault, Deleuze) or already "part of the solution" (Johnson, Gladwell) in the reorientation of the body and senses, as we learn to live symbiotically with machines and "things," as well as with hybrid forms of intelligence embedded in our many automated systems. In this respect, the cinema – even more than a machine of the visible – may have become a mode of performative agency, as well as a form of thinking: that is why I believe these films are mind-game films, and not merely complex narratives, or rather: why complex narratives are only one of the games they play with our minds.

Note

1   A picture puzzle contains enigmatic details or special twists, which is to say that something is revealed that was always there, but hidden in another more conventional configuration, and which in order to be recognized, requires a kind of resetting of perceptual or cognitive default values. A picture puzzle is also an image which via a different organization of the separate parts allows different figures to be recognized; it is an image which contains figures (usually animals, objects, bodies) which cannot be identified at first glance and require for their recognition an adjustment on the part of the viewer; finally, it can be a correctly constructed image, but whose perspectival representation proves to be impossible, such as one finds in gestalt-switches or Escher's drawings.

Bibliography

Bordwell, D. 2002. "Film futures." *Substance*, 97: 88–104.
Branigan, E. 2002. "Nearly true: Forking paths, forking interpretations. A response to David Bordwell's 'Film futures'." *SubStance*, 97: 105–14.
Brown, M. 2006. "Lookey here: Lars von Trier is at it again." *The Guardian*, Friday December 8. Online at: http://film.guardian.co.uk/News_Story/Guardian/0,,1967275,00.html?82%3A+Film+news (accessed April 20, 2007).
Cameron, A. 2006. "Contingency, order, and the modular narrative: *21 Grams* and *Irreversible*." *The Velvet Light Trap*, 58: 65–78.
Deleuze, G. 1992. "Postscript on the societies of control." *October*, 59: 3–7.
Doane, M. A. 1987. *The Desire to Desire. The Woman's Film of the 1940s*. Bloomington: Indiana University Press.
Eig, J. 2003. "A beautiful mind(fuck): Hollywood structures of identity," *Jump Cut*, 46. Online at: http://www.ejumpcut.org/archive/jc46.2003/eig.mindfilms/index.html (accessed April 20, 2007).
Elsaesser, T. 2005. "Film festival networks: The new topographies of cinema in Europe," in *European Cinema: Face to Face with Hollywood*. Amsterdam: Amsterdam University Press.
Gladwell, M. 2005. "Brain candy: Is pop culture dumbing us down or smartening us up?" *The New Yorker*, May 16. Online at: http://www.newyorker.com/archive/2005/05/16/050516crbo_books (accessed April 20, 2007).

Hardt, M., and Negri, A. 2001. *Empire*, new edn. Cambridge, MA: Harvard University Press.

Johnson, S. 2005. *Everything Bad Is Good for You*. New York: Riverhead Books.

King, G., and Krzywinska, T. (eds.) 2002. *ScreenPlay: Cinema/Videogames/ Interfaces*. London: I.B. Taurus.

Kittler, F. 1999. *Gramophone, Film, Typewriter*. Stanford, CA: Stanford University Press.

Mittell, J. 2006. "Narrative complexity in contemporary American television." *The Velvet Light Trap*, 58: 29–40.

Mulhall, S. 2002. *On Film*. New York: Routledge.

Panek, E. 2006. "The poet and the detective: Defining the psychological puzzle film." *Film Criticism*, 31, 1/2: 62–88.

Pehla, K. 1991. "Joe May und seine Detektive. Der Serienfilm als Kinoerlebnis," in H-M. Bock and C. Lenssen (eds.), *Joe May. Regisseur und Produzent*. München: edition text + kritik.

Rushkoff, D. 1995. *Playing the Future: What We Can Learn From Digital Kids*. New York: Riverhead Books.

Sankey, D. 2001. Blog entry at: http://d.sankey.ca/blog/131/mindfuck-films (accessed September 5, 2006).

Simons, J. 2007. *Playing the Waves. Lars von Trier's Game Cinema*. Amsterdam: Amsterdam University Press.

Smith, M. 2001. "Parallel lines," in J. Hillier (ed.), *American Independent Cinema: A Sight and Sound Reader*. London: BFI Publishing, pp. 155–61.

Smith, M., and Wartenberg, T. 2006. *Thinking Through Cinema: Film as Philosophy*. Oxford: Blackwell.

Staiger, J. 2006. "Complex narratives, an introduction." *Film Criticism*, 31, 1/2: 2–4.

Stewart, G. 2005. "VR ca. Y2K." Unpublished paper presented at the *Time@20: The Afterimage of Gilles Deleuze's Film Philosophy* Symposium, Harvard University, 6–7 May.

Thompson, K. 1999. *Storytelling in the New Hollywood: Understanding Classical Narrative Technique*. Cambridge, MA: Harvard University Press.

Wilson, G. 2006. "Transparency and twist in narrative fiction film." *Journal of Aesthetics and Art Criticism*, 61, 1: 81–95. (Also in Smith and Wartenberg 2006.)

Žižek, S. 2000. *The Art of the Ridiculous Sublime: On David Lynch's* Lost Highway. Washington: University of Washington Press.

Žižek, S. 2001. *The Fright of Real Tears: Krzystof Kieslowski between Theory and Post-theory*. London: British Film Institute.

2

Making Sense of *Lost Highway*

Warren Buckland

The operatic version of David Lynch's 1997 film *Lost Highway*, which premiered in the US in February 2007, is nothing more than a pared down, abbreviated version of the film. Rather than translating the film into operatic terms, the opera tried to imitate the film, and failed spectacularly. It attempted to offer condensed versions of the film's main scenes, stripping them down to their minimal signs, taking away from the film everything that makes it complex, intriguing, and engaging. At best, the opera was trying to prompt the audience to recognize the scenes in the film, and thereby hoping we would provide the action on stage with its content. The opera is, in other words, purely derivative; Olga Neuwirth's strange and innovative music, Elfriede Jelinek's libretto, and the liveness of the performance did not (with one exception) add anything to the story the film tells. (Lynch's film already has strange and innovative dialogue, sound, and music, which he partly mixed himself.) The simplistic set design was angled upward to look like a German Expressionist set, with a bed in the middle (doubling up as a car) and a screen to one side, on which video images and Fred Madison's hallucinations were shown. The front of the entire stage was completely covered with a translucent screen, upon which various images were projected (close-ups of characters or video noise), which basically said to the audience – this is where opera breaks down, so we're going to rely on film techniques. The projected images were filmed for this performance, except David Lynch's iconic image of the speeding roadway shot from a low angle at night, which appeared several times on the front screen. Only once was this screen used in an innovative manner. At the end of the story, Fred Madison kills Dick Laurent in the desert. The mystery man films the murder, and what he records is projected onto the front screen – creating a double point of view. But this innovation was far too little too late to save the opera. Only Raphael Sacks's performance as Mr Eddy/Dick Laurent added something to the story – his acting brought out Laurent's schizo-phrenic behavior, turning him into an even more scary and amusing character at the same time.

In the following analysis I will be using David Bordwell's (1985) and then Edward Branigan's (1992) cognitive theories of narration to examine what makes the film version of *Lost Highway* complex, intriguing, and engaging.

Lost Highway: Scene by Scene

The credit sequence of *Lost Highway* consists of a shot of a camera attached to the front of a car traveling very fast along a highway at night. The car's headlights illuminate the road. The credits appear from the middle of the screen, travel rapidly toward the camera, and pause moment-arily (the letters appear to stick to the film screen) before disappearing "behind" the camera and spectator.

In the opening scene we are introduced to Fred Madison (Bill Pullman) at home. Because of his frequent appearance in the opening scenes, we assume that Fred is the film's main protagonist. The scene opens with Fred sitting in the dark on the edge of his bed. He is smoking a cigarette and looking at himself in the mirror. The front door intercom buzzes, and he hears the message "Dick Laurent is dead." He goes over to the window in another part of the house to look out, but he sees no one. As he heads toward the window we hear the off-screen sound of tires screeching and a police siren.

Bordwell argues that a film's beginning is crucial because the spectator's hypotheses need to establish a foothold in the film early on. The intercom message leads the spectator to generate at least two hypotheses, focused around the questions: Who rang the bell? And, who is Dick Laurent? These two hypotheses are generated in response to the gaps in the narrative that the narration has constructed. Firstly, knowledge about the narrative is severely limited. But this limitation is motivated because the narration is linked to Fred's level of awareness and experience of narrative events: the spectator sees and hears what Fred sees and hears. The knowledge is therefore deep and restricted, and the narration is being communicative, because it gives the spectator access to this knowledge. (We shall see later in this chapter that Edward Branigan discusses character awareness and experience in terms of the concept of focalization.) The gaps in the nar-rative are, firstly, spatial. The restricted narration does not show us the identity of the person outside and does not show us the source of the off-screen sounds. This spatial gap in the narrative is evident to the spectator, and is therefore a flaunted (rather than a suppressed) gap. It is also a clearly delineated gap, and is therefore specific (rather than diffuse). Finally, it is temporary (rather than permanent) because it is eventually filled in at the end of the film. The hypotheses we generate about this spatial gap are a suspense, non-exclusive hypotheses operating at the film's macro level – suspense because we assume the gap will be resolved in the future (so we anticipate the filling in of this gap at a later time in the film's unfolding); it is non-exclusive because it could have been anyone (we cannot generate an hypothesis suspecting a particular person); and it operates on the macro level because it spans the entire film. The scale of probability–improbability usually refers to the hypotheses we generate. But in this case, the way the narration fills in this gap at the end of the film is highly improbable. Although our hypotheses were non-exclusive, it is highly unlikely that any spectator would generate the hypothesis that Fred is *also* outside the house pressing his own doorbell!

The lack of information on Dick Laurent's identity is a temporary, flaunted, focused gap that leads the spectator to generate an exclusive, curiosity hypothesis that operates on the macro level (for his identity is not immediately resolved). In a more conventional film (one that follows the conventions of the canonical story format), the spectator's narrative schema would condition her to expect the next scene to contain exposition explaining who Dick Laurent is.

The screeching tires and the police siren are not coded as prominent cues, and many spectators may not perceive them as cues, but as part of the film's "reality effect" – that is, background noise that one may expect to hear, rather than a significant narrative event. In summary, the opening scene enables the narrative schema to gain a foothold in the film, since the spectator generates hypotheses in response to the gaps the narration has constructed, and is anticipating events in future scenes.

The first scene ends on an establishing shot, a very long shot of the front of Fred's house in the early morning light. After a fade, the second scene begins by repeating this exterior establishing shot, except this time it is night. Inside the house, we see Fred packing a saxophone into its case, and talking to Renee (Patricia Arquette), who wants to stay home and read rather than go to the club with him. This seemingly simple scene nonetheless keeps the spectator busy. It appears to follow the canonical story format by continuing to introduce the setting and characters, and by explaining a state of affairs. On the basis of the two exterior establishing shots (shown back to back), we generate the hypothesis that the film has now progressed from morning to evening of the same day. In other words, using our narrative schema, we establish a linear temporal relation between the two scenes. Secondly, information about Fred is conveyed indirectly: we assume he is a musician, and we find out from his talk with Renee that the two of them are married (RENEE: "I like to laugh, Fred." FRED: "That's why I married you.") The deadpan way the two characters interact, plus the sparse dialogue, may suggest that the marriage is at a stalemate, to the point where Fred's sax playing bores Renee, and she invents improbable reasons for wanting to stay home (she does not appear to be the type of person who will spend her evenings at home reading).

In contrast to the end of scene 1, scene 2 ends abruptly, as we cut from the quiet interior of the Madisons' house to an image of the exterior of the Luna lounge and the very loud sound of sax music. This sudden break from scene 2 jolts the spectator, not only because of the contrast in sound and image, but also because there is no reference to the two gaps in scene 1. Fred does not mention the message he received on the intercom, and therefore we are no closer to finding out who the messenger was, or who Dick Laurent is. Reference to these cues would have strengthened the causal relationship between scenes 1 and 2. As it is, the two scenes are linked more tenuously – visually (the visual repetition of the establishing shot), and linearly (the progression from day to night), rather than causally. The narration is marked by a lack of redundancy between scenes.

In scene 3 Fred is shown playing his sax and phoning his wife during an intermission. But no one answers the phone at home; the house appears empty. In scene 4 Fred returns home to find his wife asleep in bed. These two scenes introduce a discrepancy between Renee's words and actions. In combination with the way Fred and Renee interact in scene 2, the discrepancy enables the spectator to group these actions together and call them a complicating action, the next stage of the canonical story format. The complicating action can be called "unhappy marriage," with the probability of infidelity on Renee's part. The spectator's hypothesis of infidelity is a near exclusive hypothesis – one with only a few alternatives, and is generated on the basis of Renee's absence from the house in scene 3 (a flaunted, focused gap in the film's narrative). The infidelity hypothesis is the most probable, but because the narration is restricted to Fred's perspective, the spectator does not gain any more information than Fred knows to confirm or disconfirm this hypothesis.

Scene 5, the next morning. Renee picks up the newspaper outside, and discovers a video tape on the steps, with no addresser, addressee, or message. After watching the tape, which shows the outside of their house plus a closer shot of the front door, the Madisons are understandably perplexed, and Renee generates the weak, improbable hypothesis that a realtor may have made the tape. This scene again presents another flaunted, focused gap in the narrative (which can be formulated into the following question: Who made the tape?), and its only link to the previous scenes is a continuity of characters and settings. There is no narrative continuity between this scene and the film's previous scenes. But the narration does seem to establish an internal norm, whereby it selects very specific portions of the narrative to show – namely, actions and events performed early in the morning or late at night.

Scene 6. Renee and Fred in bed at night (the film therefore continues to follow the internal norm of only showing actions performed in the morning or at night). We see several of Fred's memory images – of him at the Luna lounge playing his sax, and seeing Renee at the club leave with another man (we later find out that he is Andy). Fred and Renee then make love, and afterwards Fred recounts a dream he had the previous night. We then cut to several of the dream images: Fred looking around the house at night, hearing Renee call out to him, and a shot of Renee in bed being frightened by a rapidly approaching, off-screen agent. The spectator shares this agent's vision as he approaches Renee, but we do not see who it is. Renee looks into the camera and screams (her look into the camera makes the narration mildly self-conscious). Fred is then shown waking up, and looking at Renee. But another face is superimposed upon her (we later find out that it belongs to the "mystery man").

In this scene the narration continues to be restricted and deep, and seems communicative, as we gain access to Fred's memory and dream images. But the status of the memory images is ambiguous. To make sense of these images, we can generate the probable hypothesis that they refer to a narrative event that took place before the film begins, and that Fred is generating these images to fill in the gap in scene 3. We can paraphrase these images in the following way: "Last night Renee was probably with the guy who accompanied her to the Luna lounge on a previous occasion."

The dream images are also ambiguous. Above we noted that the narration in this scene is restricted and deep, and *appears* to be communicative. But a close analysis of later scenes in the film makes the film analyst realize that the narration in this scene is in fact being very uncommunicative, but that its uncommunicative status is disguised. At this stage in the film, we are used to a communicative narration, with flaunted gaps. But in the dream sequence, we (or, at least, the film analyst) retrospectively realize that the narration contains suppressed gaps and is uncommunicative. This is why later scenes in the film jolt us.

Furthermore, Fred does not question Renee about her whereabouts the previous evening (although in the script he does[1]). He only mentions the dream he had the previous night. Therefore, the link between this scene and previous scenes is only temporal, rather than causal (although the memory images of the club do at least refer us back to the location of scene 3). Owing to this lack of causal cues, the spectator tries to generate weak hypotheses to connect the mystery narrative (who is Dick Laurent?) to the romance narrative (perhaps the guy in the club is Dick Laurent, etc.).

Other events in this scene are even more vague. As Renee and Fred make love, the screen suddenly turns white for a moment (a white fade) and the action is slowed down. Although these make the narration self-conscious (both devices challenge the conventions of standard speed and black fades), it is unclear what these devices are meant to cue, other than the director's intervention (thereby defining the *mise en scène* as mannerist). Furthermore, the moment Fred wakes up and sees the mystery man's face superimposed upon Renee's face still constitutes part of Fred's dream he had the previous evening. In other words, *the scene ends inside Fred's dream*; the narration does not return to the image of Fred in bed narrating the dream. But one thing at least is clear from this scene: Renee and Fred make love dispassionately, which strengthens the hypothesis that their marriage is in crisis.

Scene 7: the following morning. Renee finds another video tape on the steps. But this one shows more than the previous tape by filming inside the house, and ending on Fred and Renee asleep in bed. Renee then calls the police. The second video tape adds to the "complicating action" chunk of the by now strained canonical story format.

In scene 8, two detectives watch the second video tape, and look around the house for possible signs of a break-in. Information is planted in the dialogue to facilitate the spectator's hypothesis-generating process. Fred tells the detectives he hates video cameras, because he likes to remember things his own way, not necessarily the way they happen. Many critics who reviewed *Lost Highway* saw this line as a nodal point on which to focus the previous scenes, as a key to the film's meaning – namely, many of the narration's twists can be motivated psychologically, as Fred's distorted view of events. The spectator also has the opportunity to test out this reading of the film in the next scene.

Scene 9: party at Andy's house, late at night. (Andy was shown previously in Fred's memory images – in scene 6 – of Renee and Andy leaving the Luna lounge while Fred plays his sax.) The canonical story format is challenged, and begins to break down in this scene. In the previous scene, Fred and Renee did not talk about going to a party at Andy's house. If they had done so, it would have strengthened the causal relation between the scenes. More radically, Fred is shown drinking two whiskies and then talking to "the mystery man" (Robert Blake), whose face we have already seen superimposed over Renee's face in Fred's dream (recounted in scene 6). The mystery man says to Fred that they have met before (although Fred does not remember), and then defies Newtonian space-time physics by suggesting that he is in Fred's house at that very moment (that is, he is in two places at once). The mystery man "confirms" this by persuading Fred to phone his home, where indeed the mystery man also answers! In terms of them meeting before, we tend to side with the mystery man; firstly because of the comment Fred made in scene 8 (he likes to remember things his own way, not necessarily the way they happened); and secondly, because the mystery man appeared in Fred's recounted dream in scene 6 (his face is superimposed over Renee's face).

By challenging one of the fundamental background assumptions of the canonical story format (a character cannot be in two places at once), scene 9 begins to open up inferential possibilities, as we have to try to explain or motivate this fundamental discrepancy in the film's narrative. Is Fred simply delusional, and are we sharing his delusions? This assumes that the narration continues to be highly communicative by conveying Fred's deep experiences.

When Fred asks Andy who the mystery man is, he responds that he is a friend of Dick Laurent, to which Fred replies: "Dick Laurent is dead, isn't he?" Troubled by this news, Andy protests that Dick Laurent can't be dead. (He also says to Fred "I didn't think you knew Dick," which is an odd thing to say immediately after telling Fred that the mystery man is a friend of Dick Laurent.) The mention of Dick Laurent's name finally brings into sharper focus one of the gaps opened up in scene 1. Through its linear progression from scene to scene, the narration is now finally beginning to refer back to gaps in previous scenes.

Scene 10: Fred and Renee in the car on the way back from Andy's party. Renee describes how she met Andy (RENEE: "I met him at this place called

Moke's . . . We became friends . . . He told me about a job. . . .") This is one
of the few fragments of exposition the spectator has received from the narration, which means that it is impossible to slot it into a context and make
more sense of it. Instead, it remains a fragment of exposition. But from
Fred's reaction, we understand that he dislikes Andy, possibly because he
thinks Renee is having an affair with him.

Scene 11. At home, Fred checks around the house. He switches off the
alarm, hears the telephone ring (but does not answer it), and he and Renee
then prepare for bed. The events that follow refer back to Fred's recounted
dream in scene 6. What is extraordinary is that parts of Fred's dream are
now repeated and "played out" as non-dream events. As Fred wanders around
the house, we hear Renee call out Fred's name in exactly the same way she
did in the dream. In a few images we also see Fred moving around the house
in the same way he did in his dream. In the bathroom, he looks intensely
at himself in the mirror. He then walks toward the camera, blocking our
view entirely (a self-conscious moment of narration). In the next shot, the
camera is positioned outside a door.

This scene challenges the canonical story format further, since it distorts
the notion of linear progression (unless we read the dream as a premonition). At the end of the scene, the narration is also uncommunicative, because
it creates a gap in the narrative as the camera is positioned outside a closed
door. But on the basis of a shot in Fred's dream – of an unseen agent attack-
ing Renee in bed, together with the hypothesis that Renee is having an affair
– we can generate a near exclusive, probable hypothesis that Fred is attack-
ing Renee.

This hypothesis is confirmed in scene 12. Fred finds a third video tape
on the doorstep, plays it, and sees, in addition to the initial footage on the
second tape, a series of shots depicting him murdering and dismember-
ing Renee. He acknowledges the video camera filming him, by looking directly
into it (making the narration self-conscious). But for Fred watching the
tape, the images are horrifying, and in desperation, he calls out to Renee.
He is suddenly punched in the face by one of the detectives who visited
the house in scene 8. There is a flaunted ellipsis in the narrative at this
moment in the film, as Fred is now being questioned about Renee's
murder (scene 13). The narration is both communicative and uncommunicative, since it shows us (via the video camera images) Fred murdering Renee, but it is uncommunicative in supplying information about
who recorded the video tapes, who Dick Laurent is, the mystery man's ability to be in two places at once, and the identity between Fred's recounted

dream and Renee's murder the following evening. More generally, the film is marked by a lack of synchronization between its narrative and unfolding narration.

Retrospectively, we can now reevaluate the film so far as a detective film, which Bordwell (1985, p. 64) defines as having the following characteristics: a crime (cause of crime, commission of crime, concealment of crime, discovery of crime) and investigation (beginning of investigation, phases of investigation, elucidation of crime). We can characterize the film as enacting a crime, with emphasis on its concealment and discovery, with a very condensed investigation (at this stage consisting of identification of criminal and consequences of identification). We hypothesize that Fred is the causal agent, motivated by jealousy, who carried out the murder soon after Andy's party.

The policeman throws his punch directly at the camera, suggesting the narration's continued alignment with Fred. It also makes the narration self-conscious, not only because the action is directed at the camera, but also because it reminds a cine-literate spectator of similar moments in Hitchcock's films – most notably, *Strangers on a Train* (1951) and *North by Northwest* (1959), where punches are similarly directed at the camera. In another Hitchcockian moment, Fred's trial is not shown, but is reduced to the voiceover of the judge pronouncing sentence, as Fred is led to his cell. This goes beyond Hitchcock's rapid depiction of Margot Wendice's trial in *Dial M for Murder* (1954). (In *Lost Highway*, a scene taking place in the courtroom is in the script, but has been omitted from the final cut.)

There follows a quick series of scenes (sometimes consisting of three or four shots) as Fred is taken to his cell (scene 14), which is intercut with video images of Renee's murder (coded as Fred's memory images). Scene 15 continues with this theme, as Fred tries to figure out what is happening to him. In scene 16 he collapses in the prison courtyard, complaining of a headache. In scene 17 the prison doctor forces him to swallow some sleeping pills, and in scene 18, he has a vision of an exploding cabin in the desert, although the explosion is shown backward (making the narration self-conscious). The mystery man then comes out of and goes back into the cabin. The iconography reminds the cine-literate spectator of the exploding beach house at the end of *Kiss Me Deadly* (Robert Aldrich 1955) – a film that also begins with a shot from a camera attached to the front of a car traveling very fast along a highway at night. During these scenes in the prison, it becomes evident that Fred is not a rational, goal-driven agent who causally motivates narrative events, since he is unable to remember or explain his actions. But his state of mind motivates the lack of synchronization between the narrative and narration.

The events in the second half of scene 18 and in the following scenes completely defy and undermine the canonical story format. Scene 18 ends on the following shots:

- Fred's cell; there is a sudden flash of bright light, and light bulb in his cell goes dim (perhaps representing the effects of an electrocution on the rest of the prison);
- the highway at night, repeating the image of the credit sequence; but this time, the car stops in front of a young man (whom we later find out is Pete Dayton);
- cut in closer to Pete, with a superimposed shot of his girlfriend Sheila, and Pete's parents; Sheila is screaming Pete's name;
- big close-up of Pete's eyes, superimposed over an image of the light in Fred's prison cell;
- Fred frantically rocking from side to side in his prison cell, screaming and covered in blood (this image seems to be strongly influenced by Francis Bacon's portraits, to the extent that it can be read as a filmic equivalent to Bacon's still images);
- shot of the prison ceiling; the camera tilts down to Fred;
- cut to an image of what looks like an open wound, and the camera moves toward it.

Working along the lines of a surreal logic, the narration presents a series of fragmented narrative events, which retrospectively we infer signifies Fred's transformation into Pete. (The version of this event in the script is more explicit about the transformation.)

Scenes 19 to 25 depict a prison guard discovering Pete in Fred's cell, Pete's identification, his release, and his home and work life. It is as if the film has "started again" or, more accurately, we seem to be watching the second half of another film, because the narration has identified Pete as the film's main protagonist, and has introduced a new setting and additional characters. This sudden jolt in the film's narrative is caused by the fact that the previous protagonist, whom we were given privileged access to, and from whom the camera rarely departed, has suddenly and inextricably disappeared from the narrative.

This jolt is far more radical than superficially similar scenes in other films – such as the murder in *Psycho* (1960) of Marion Crane, the film's primary protagonist up to that point. In *Psycho*, the transfer from Marion to Norman takes place within a stable narrative. In *Lost Highway*, the narrative has been severely disrupted, creating a flaunted, but diffuse permanent gap that is never filled in. But to attempt to fill in this gap, the spectator needs to generate the two mutually exclusive hypotheses: Is Pete the same person as Fred? That is, are two actors playing the same character? Or are the two actors playing two different characters? However, the narration does not contain sufficient cues to enable us to choose one hypothesis over the other.

After the spectacular transfer of agency from Fred to Pete, we start to question the communicative status of the narration. It seems to hide more than it shows. As we continue to watch the film unfold, the unresolved issues remain, because the film does not address or even acknowledge them – that is, until scene 24, when Pete's girlfriend Sheila mentions to Pete that he has been acting strangely since "the events" of the previous evening. Also, the narration continues to follow the internal norm established at the beginning of the film – to depict events taking place early in the morning or late at night. In scene 25 Pete returns to work (as a mechanic), and in scene 26 repairs the car of a gangster, Mr Eddy. The scene ends with Mr Eddy driving away from the garage where Pete works, and two cops who are following Pete identify Mr Eddy as Dick Laurent. One of the gaps presented in the narrative at the beginning of the film (who is Dick Laurent?) is now brought into clearer focus, although it raises another question: why is Mr Eddy also called Dick Laurent? From this moment onward, the narration makes additional and more frequent references to the first part of the film, enabling the spectator to focus other gaps and refine hypotheses.

At the beginning of scene 27, Pete looks at himself in the mirror in the same way as Fred looked at himself just before he murdered Renee. But in this part of the film, Pete takes Sheila out on a date.

Scene 28. At work the following morning, Pete hears sax music on the radio – identical to the music Fred played at the Luna lounge. The music distresses Pete, and he switches it off. A few moments later, he meets Mr Eddy's girlfriend, Alice, played by Patricia Arquette, who also played Fred's wife Renee. But, as Renee, Arquette looked vampish; as Alice, she conforms to the stereotype of the blonde femme fatale. Hypotheses we generated when Fred transformed into Pete recur here, but inverted. Now we need to ask: Are Renee and Alice the same character in disguise (because they are played by the same actress)? Or is Patricia Arquette playing two characters?

Scenes 29 to 32 depict the affair that Pete develops with Alice. In scene 33, after Alice had to break off a date with Pete, we see Pete in his room, experiencing hallucinations and hearing strange sounds. The narration is restricted, deep, and communicative because the spectator directly shares these experiences (the camera goes out of focus, we see Pete's hallucinations of Alice, and so on). In scene 34 Pete decides to go and see Sheila, and in scene 35, Pete's parents talk to him. They know what happened to him, but refuse to tell him everything. They tell him that he came home with Sheila and "a man," but say no more. This scene is interrupted by a montage sequence repeating the shot, in scene 18, of Pete's parents and Sheila screaming, although this time it is not superimposed over an image of Pete. This is followed by a shot of the open wound, and a video image of Renee's mutilated body. These shots are coded as Pete's memory images, whereas previously, they were coded as Fred's.

In following scenes, Mr Eddy threatens Pete, and Alice devises a plan whereby she and Pete will rob Andy and run away together. In scene 39 Alice tells Pete how she met Mr Eddy. She uses the same line that Renee used to describe to Fred (scene 10) how she met Andy (ALICE: "I met him at this place called Moke's . . . We became friends . . . He told me about a job. . . .")

Scene 40. Pete breaks up with Sheila, and then takes a phone call from Mr Eddy-Dick Laurent and the mystery man (confirming Andy's comment in scene 9 that the mystery man is a friend of Dick Laurent). When the mystery man talks to Pete, he uses the same phrases as he did in scene 9, when speaking to Fred at Andy's party ("We've met before, haven't we?" etc.). He then indirectly threatens Pete.

In scene 41, Pete carries out Alice's plan to rob Andy, but in the process Andy is killed. Pete finds at Andy's house a photo of Mr Eddy, Renee, Alice, and Andy standing together. Pete asks Alice "Are both of them you?," echoing an hypothesis the spectator generates when first seeing Alice in scene 29. Pete then goes upstairs to clean up, but the corridor in Andy's house looks like a hotel corridor. Furthermore, we see flashes of light in the corridor, as we did in Fred's prison cell.

In scene 42 Pete and Alice drive to the desert to sell Andy's valuables to the mystery man at his cabin. Shots of the highway at night, and the shot of the burning cabin are repeated. In scene 43, Alice and Pete make love in the desert. Alice then goes inside the cabin, and Pete gets up. However, he has now inexplicably transformed back into Fred. But before we have time to adjust to Fred's sudden return to the narrative, the narration presents a series of unusual shots and scenes. Fred looks into his car and sees the mystery man inside, staring back. We then hear the mystery man's voice off-screen, and he suddenly appears in the entrance of his cabin. He then goes inside the cabin in the same way he did in Fred's memory image in scene 18. Fred enters the cabin where he sees the mystery man, but no Alice. Fred asks him where Alice is, and he replies that her name is Renee. Despite the photograph in Andy's apartment, Renee and Alice may be the same person (although this still does not explain her disappearance after entering the cabin). The mystery man then confronts Fred about his name, and begins to film him using a video camera. As Fred runs out of the cabin into his car, several of the shots are from the mystery man's perspective filmed through the video camera, and the resulting images are the same as the three tapes sent to the Madisons' home. We can now fill in one of the gaps generated in the first part of the film, for we have conclusive evidence that the mystery man made the video tapes. Moreover, the hypotheses about the relation between Alice and Renee, and Fred and Pete, are brought into focus, but they are not resolved, for the "solutions" the narration presents are highly improbable.

Scene 44. Fred drives along the highway, and shots of the highway at night are repeated. Scene 45 takes place at the Lost Highway motel. Fred wanders along the corridors in the same way Pete did in Andy's house. Fred enters an empty room, while Renee and Dick Laurent make love in another room. Another gap in the narrative is filled in, as we realize that Renee is having an affair with Dick Laurent, not Andy. (Andy therefore presents the spectator with a false lead.) In scene 46, Renee leaves the hotel and Fred knocks out Dick Laurent, watched by the mystery man. In scene 47 Fred takes Laurent to the desert where he kills him, with the help of the mystery man. In fact, the mystery man suddenly appears just at the right moment, to hand Fred a knife. The mystery man then shoots Laurent, but a few moments later he suddenly disappears, leaving Fred with the gun in his hand.

In an attempt to make sense of what is happening in these scenes, we can return to the opening scenes, when we generated the hypothesis that Renee may be having an affair. We now see that Fred has followed her to the Lost Highway motel, and discovers that she is having an affair with Dick Laurent, whom Fred subsequently kills. The mystery man and Alice now seem to be figments of Fred's imagination. However, if we accept this, then it generates more questions and additional gaps in the narration, such as: Who made the three video tapes?

Scene 48. The police are at Andy's house. The two detectives who questioned Fred look at the photo – but Alice is missing, strengthening the hypothesis that Alice is a figment of Fred's imagination. The two detectives realize that Pete Dayton's prints are all over the place, so they head toward Fred's house. For this scene, then, the film has "flipped back" to the Pete Dayton side of the narrative, but has erased Alice from it. The police have generated the hypothesis that Pete/Fred has murdered Andy, possibly because Fred thought that Andy was having an affair with Renee. In terms of the film's narrative, perhaps Fred followed Renee to Andy's place first, killed Andy, and then followed her to the Lost Highway motel, where he subsequently kills Dick Laurent. At some point in the narrative, he also kills Renee. (Obviously, in this reconstruction of narrative events, he does not kill her after going to Andy's party, because Andy is already dead.)

Scene 49. Outside Fred's house. Fred has just returned from the desert, and presses the intercom and leaves the message "Dick Laurent is dead." The two cops then turn up, and give chase. Scene 50: the film ends with the police chasing Fred as he continues to drive along the highway at night. He appears to undergo another transformation, but we are left with an image of the highway at night.

The gap opened up in scene 1 is now filled – it is Fred who rings his own door bell and who leaves the message that Laurent is dead! The off-screen sounds of screeching tires and the police siren are similarly repeated, but now as on-screen sounds. The final scenes fill in most of the gaps the narration has generated, but they do not lead to a resolution, because the "answers" they present pose additional questions since they are improbable answers.

Irresolvable Ambiguities and Inconsistencies

From this cognitive reading of *Lost Highway*, we can discern several irresolvable ambiguities and inconsistencies. Firstly, concerning character stability: in scene 9, at Andy's party, the mystery man is in two places at once. Fred is also in two places at once: in scene 1, he is inside his own house receiving the message on the intercom that "Dick Laurent is dead" and in scene 49, which returns to scene 1, Fred is outside his house delivering the message. Other instabilities of character include Fred's transformation into Pete at the end of scene 18, and his transformation back again in scene 43; in scene 12 it appears that Renee is murdered, but in scene 28 she seems to return to the film's narrative. The spectator needs to ask if Fred and Pete are the same character played by two different actors, or are they different characters? And are Renee and Alice two different characters played by the same actress, or the same character in disguise? And why is Mr Eddy also called Dick Laurent? Other irresolvable ambiguities include: in scene 6, in Fred's dream images, he sees the mystery man's face superimposed over Renee's face; but in scene 9, when the mystery man introduces himself, Fred cannot remember meeting him before. Scene 35 repeats the video images of Renee's murder, and a shot of the open wound; when they first appeared in scenes 15 and 18 (respectively), they were coded as Fred's memories, but now they are coded as Pete's memories. Furthermore, the photo in Andy's apartment is shown in scene 41 and repeated in scene 48, but Alice is missing when the photo is shown again. Finally, there are ambiguities concerning the linear, temporal ordering of events: the events in scene 6 (Fred's recounted dream) are repeated (as non-dream events) in scene 11; and Fred's visions in scene 18, of an the exploding cabin from which the mystery man appears and disappears, are repeated in scenes 42 and 43, although they are not coded as Fred's visions. But how can Fred's dreams and visions so accurately predict forthcoming events – unless those events have already happened? This suggests that the narrative of *Lost Highway* is organized like a loop – or better, a Möbius strip – rather than linearly. If this is the case, then scene 18, in Fred's prison cell, represents the twist in the möbius strip, the twist where the topside is transferred to the underside. Scenes 1 and 49 are the moments where the two edges of the Möbius strip are connected together, with Fred represented outside his house on one side, and inside the house on the other side. Moreover, to travel around the entire length of the Möbius strip, one needs to go around it twice – first on one side (from the intercom message to Fred's transformation in his cell), then on the other side (from Pete being released from prison to his transformation back into Fred), before we are returned to the moment where the two sides are joined (Fred conveying the intercom message to himself). The metaphor of the Möbius strip appears to accurately represent the structure of *Lost Highway*.

It is important to remember when discussing such ambiguous moments that our aim is not to disambiguate them, for this is a reductionist move that attempts to explain them away. Instead, we should attempt to explain how the ambiguities are produced, and what effects they achieve. Either these scenes contain too few cues, or too many cues that contradict one another; or there are too many flaunted and suppressed gaps;

or maybe the cue is a permanent gap. All these cues may lead the spectator to generate non-exclusive, diffuse hypotheses that are not brought into focus, or are "resolved" in an improbable manner. Lynch's films are open to analysis as long as we do not try to reduce these ambiguous moments to a rational logic, but recognize that a non-rational but meaningful energy governs them. *Lost Highway* also prevents spectators from automatically applying schemata to it, since it goes beyond the commonsense, rational logic embedded in these schemata; instead, spectators become aware of the schemata's conventions, and work hard to apply them in new and unforeseen ways (spectators unwilling to do this stop watching the film).

Point of View and Focalization

I shall now reanalyze key scenes from the perspective of Edward Branigan's (1992) cognitive theory of narration – especially the various agents and levels of narration he outlines. The focus of the following analysis is therefore: What narrative agent (if any) motivates the selected images? And: What level of narration can they best be described as operating upon?

After the Madisons view the first video that has been sent to them (scene 5), the film cuts to the hallway leading up to the Madisons' bedroom. This hallway is draped by a distinctive red curtain (a characteristic feature of Lynch's films). What is the status of this shot? Is it simply a transitional shot between scenes? It seems to be a nonfocalized shot – that is, a shot not controlled by any narrative agent in the film's diegesis, but controlled by an agent outside the diegesis – the narrator.

In scene 6, Fred's recounted dream consists of the following shots, which also raise intriguing questions in terms of agency and levels:

- We see Fred walking around the house and hear Renee calling out to him; we also hear Fred's voiceover recounting the dream. All of the recounted dream shots are therefore internally focalized (depth) shots.
- Image of fire (with exaggerated sound, rendering the fire uncanny). (This shot is part of the dream – that is, internal focalization [depth]; but *within* the dream, it is non-focalized.)
- Fred and voice of Renee.
- A puff of smoke rises from the stairway (as with the red curtain, smoke is another characteristic symbol in Lynch's films). This shot is coded as

Fred's optical point-of-view (pov) shot. In other words, within his
recounted dream we have a pov shot.

- Fred in hallway (there is an ellipsis, since he have moved location
  between cuts).
- Hallway. Again, this is a pov shot.
- Fred.
- Hallway and red curtain, and bedroom (coded as Fred's pov).

Here we have a repetition of the red curtain, but this time it is coded as
Fred's pov. Whereas previously the shot could be read as a transitional shot,
which means that it is non-focalized (objective, or belonging to the narrator), here Fred has now appropriated this image, as it is focalized around
his vision *and* is part of his recounted dream.

With Fred still recounting or narrating the dream in voiceover, the
camera quickly moves toward Renee, and she screams. Fred then "wakes up"
– but this seems to be part of the dream. (This is the conclusion we reached
in the "Bordwellian" analysis of this scene.) In Branigan's terms, is this image
of Fred waking up an internally focalized (depth) image (that is, part
of the recounted dream), or has Fred stopped recounting the dream?
There are insufficient (or conflicting) data in the image to enable us to decide
one way or the other. The voiceover has ended, and the film has returned
to Fred and Renee in bed, the place where Fred began narrating the
dream. This suggests that Fred has stopped narrating the dream. However,
there is no continuity between this shot of Renee and Fred in bed and
the shot of Fred beginning to narrate the dream. This is discontinuous because
both of them are now asleep, and Fred is waking up from the dream. He
then sees the mystery man's face imposed over Renee's face. This means
that he is not only narrating the dream to Renee, but is also telling her
that he woke up and did not recognize her. The film is inherently ambiguous about which description is correct. Furthermore, there are no other
cues in the film indicating that Fred stops narrating the dream. If the
second description is correct, it means that the dream remains open-
ended – we don't know when and where it ends.

The second video (first shown in scene 7) also deserves closer scrutiny.
As Renee and Fred watch the second video, Renee turns to Fred and calls
his name. Fred looks at the TV screen. Cut to a shot of the hallway. This
is a complex shot to describe. Firstly, it is Fred's pov shot as represented
in his dream. But another narrative agent has also appropriated it – this
time the agent who has made the video (the mystery man). But as Fred

watches this shot on screen, it becomes his pov shot again! He is therefore watching his pov shot within his dream now being manifest in reality via the video. There are multiple layers of agency attached to this shot (as there are with many shots; however, here the presence of the various agents becomes apparent). Perhaps part of Fred's fear is that he feels someone has got inside his head and is now reproducing his dream on video. Cut to a close-up of Fred's eyes, and then cut back to the video image, now showing the red curtain, a shot used twice before, but this time it is attributable to the mystery man (or the mystery man appropriates it from Fred, who appropriated it from the narrator). The video then shows Renee and Fred in bed.

When Fred comments in the next scene that he does not own a video camera because he prefers to remember events his own way, not necessarily the way they happened, this comment seems (as we saw in the "Bordwellian" analysis of this scene) to be a nodal point on which to focus the previous scenes. Yet by looking at the previous scenes more closely, through the lens of Branigan's theory, we come to realize that *the video images appropriate Fred's pov shots*. In other words, there is no conflict between what Fred sees and remembers, and what we see on video; yet Fred's comment serves to distinguish video images from his experience.

Later we can attribute the video images to the mystery man. The fluctuating attribution of agency to these shots gives us textual evidence to link the mystery man to Fred. Furthermore, we argued that the shot of the red curtain, when it is first seen, is a non-focalized shot (that is, is attributable to the narrator); on its second appearance, Fred has appropriated it; and on the third occasion, the mystery man appropriates it. We can use this description to link the narrator to Fred and the mystery man, and perhaps go even further and link the narrator with the historical director, Lynch. It is easy to make wild assertions (or hypotheses) about the relation between Fred, the mystery man, the narrator, and Lynch; what we need is textual evidence to support these hypotheses, so that we can attach or ground these assertions in the film itself.

In scene 11, of Fred in the house after Andy's party, the shot of the red curtain is repeated for the fourth time, which could be the pov shot of an unseen agent, who then seems to confront Fred. Could it be the mystery man with his video camera recording what's going to happen in the house? (If so, then do we identify the narrator's-Lynch's camera with the mystery man's video camera?) Otherwise, it could be a non-focalized shot. When preparing for bed, Fred looks at himself in the mirror in the same way he looked at the camera a moment ago. Renee then calls out, in the

same way she did in Fred's dream. We then have a shot of the living room
with two shadows (are they replacing the image of the blazing fire in Fred's
dream?). Is this the mystery man following Fred with his video camera,
ready to record what's going to happen next? Instead of finding out what
happens next, the spectator is positioned outside a door. We then cut to
the next morning, where Fred picks up the third video tape, which fills
in the ellipsis of the previous scene. The dream can also be added to fill
in this ellipsis, since we see Fred approaching Renee as she sleeps in bed.

Conclusions

My reanalysis of key scenes and shots from the first half of *Lost Highway*
only begins to demonstrate Branigan's theory of agents and levels of film
narration. But from this short analysis, its ability to make more and finer
distinctions than Bordwell's theory makes it a powerful tool, particularly
in analyzing moments of ambiguity, in more detail and with more sub-
tlety. The spectator's hypotheses can be formulated more clearly, and
exclusive hypotheses can be related to one another more precisely (by linking each to a particular agent and level of narration). Whereas Bordwell's
theory offers a methodology that reads a film as a linear or horizontal string
of cues that spectators try to identify, Branigan develops a methodology
that reads a film both horizontally *and* vertically, which enables the analyst to recognize the complexity of an individual shot or scene. A notable
example from *Lost Highway* is the shot of the hallway in the second video,
which Fred is watching. Branigan's method of analysis not only revealed
the complexity of this shot, but also supplied the tools to analyze it in detail.

Adapted from Warren Buckland's chapter "Cognitive Theories of
Narration (*Lost Highway*)," in Thomas Elsaesser and Warren Buckland
(2002), *Studying Contemporary American Film: A Guide to Movie Analysis*,
pp. 168–94.

Note

1   See Lynch and Gifford (1997, pp. 11–12). At breakfast, Fred questions Renee
    (who is reading a book), after they have looked at the first video tape. This
    scene has been deleted and replaced with the single shot of the red curtain.

Bibliography

Bordwell, D. 1985. *Narration in the Fiction Film*. Madison: University of Wisconsin Press.

Branigan, E. 1992. *Narrative Comprehension and Film*. New York: Routledge.

Lynch, D., and Gifford, B. 1997. *Lost Highway* (screenplay). London: Faber and Faber.

3

"Twist Blindness": The Role of Primacy, Priming, Schemas, and Reconstructive Memory in a First-Time Viewing of *The Sixth Sense*

Daniel Barratt

Introduction

The main thing which struck me when watching *The Sixth Sense* (1999) a second time round was the hospital scene in which child patient Cole Sear (Haley Joel Osment) reveals that he can "see dead people" – dead people who "don't know they're dead" – while the camera is focusing in on Dr Malcolm Crowe (Bruce Willis). In this scene, the writer and director M. Night Shyamalan effectively waves the film's celebrated narrative twist in the face of the viewer. Considering the explicit nature of both the dialogue and the method of filming – for example, Cole's statement that these dead people "walk around like regular people" is immediately followed by a close-up of Malcolm – why does the first-time viewer fail to make the connection between Cole's revelation and Malcolm's situation? With regard to this particular scene, Frank Marshall, one of the producers of the film, states: "I actually thought we had overdone it. I actually thought we're giving too much away here."[1] Presumably, however, test audiences failed to pick up on the scene's implication. In this chapter, I am interested in explaining why the average viewer does not, contrary to Marshall's fear, pick up on this type of clue first time round, thereby remaining "blind" to the film's narrative twist. This is where the notions of *primacy*, *priming*, and *schema* – referred to in the title – fit into the picture.

My second point is more speculative and relates to *The Sixth Sense*'s advertised status as "A Real 'Must See Twice' Film." At the film's conclusion, we are presented with three flashbacks: the first features Cole's revelation; the second, Malcolm sitting opposite Cole's mother Lynn (Toni Collette); and the third, Malcolm having dinner with his wife Anna (Olivia Williams). I would suggest that one of the main reasons the film demands a second viewing is that we tend to assume – on the basis of one viewing alone – that the filmmaker has, in Marshall's words, "pulled a fast one." We suspect that the flashbacks – especially the second and third involving Lynn and Anna – are not representative and that the filmmaker has conveniently forgotten certain contradictory scenes. Contrary to our initial recollections, however, a second viewing reveals that Shyamalan *is* "honest" and "true," or at least as honest and true as he can be given that a narrative of this type is never going to be completely watertight. This is where the notion of *reconstructive memory* fits into the picture.

Methodology

My more general objective in this chapter is to explore the scope and limitations of two particular psychological faculties in film viewing. The first of these faculties can be described as *attention*. Although attention is notoriously difficult to characterize, various analogies can be drawn. One example is to compare attentive processing with either a spotlight or a zoom lens. Another, and more informative, example is to compare attentive processing with foveal vision on the grounds that it is both limited and serial – a move taken by Dirk Eitzen (1993).[2] For instance, foveal vision occupies only one or two degrees of our field of view – the size of a thumbnail held at arm's length. Likewise, we are only capable of focusing on (or "foveating") one aspect of the world at any given time. The second psychological faculty of interest is *memory*. Contrary to popular belief, memory is not photographic in nature. Perhaps the closest approximation to a photographic capacity is sensory memory: here, auditory and visual traces are held in a sensory buffer, but only for a period of milliseconds to seconds. Meanwhile, the capacity of short-term (or working) memory is thought to equal seven items "plus or minus two"; however, retaining these items for any degree of time requires both deliberate rehearsal and the absence of distraction (Miller 1956; Baddeley 1995). Significantly, the capacity of long-term memory – the type of memory to which we refer in everyday conversation – is even less robust.

Although attention and memory can be treated as separate psychological faculties – and although they are often discussed in separate chapters

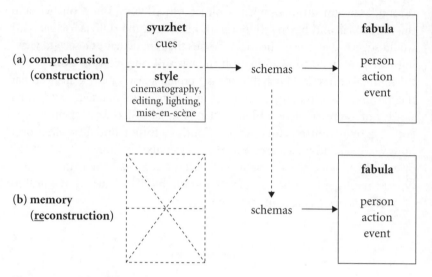

Figure 3.1 Comprehension and memory

in psychology textbooks – it should be acknowledged that they are perhaps best thought of as opposite sides of the same coin: how we memorize a scene at time t_2 is a direct indication of how we attended to that scene at time t_1.

The scope and limitations of attention and memory are frequently exploited by filmmakers: M. Night Shyamalam's *The Sixth Sense* is a prime example of this. How, though, does Shyamalan specifically ensure that a first-time viewer will remain "blind" to the film's narrative twist? A possible answer to this question is that he relies, at least implicitly, on a number of extremely powerful effects and procedures which are at play in everyday cognition. In this section, I intend to outline these effects and procedures before going on to discuss their possible role in a first-time viewing of the film.[3]

(a) Attention and memory: the role of schematic (re)construction

The first key question is: How do we *attend to* – and comprehend – the people and events presented by a fiction film (see Figure 3.1a)? In order to answer this question, let us follow the cognitive and narrative theory of the film scholar David Bordwell (1985, 1989). To begin with, we need to cite the fundamental distinction between *fabula* and *syuzhet*. The fabula is the story of the film: a cause-and-effect chain of events which occurs within a given space and time. The syuzhet, on the other hand, is the film's plot: that is, the sequence of information which is actually presented, potentially in an alternative order and with numerous omissions. Employing a constructivist psychology, Bordwell argues that the film viewer *constructs* the fabula from the syuzhet by employing *schemas* (Bartlett 1932). Schemas, from our perspective, are conceptual frameworks which model different aspects of the world: persons, actions, events, and so forth. An agent-based schema, for instance, comprises a cluster of characteristics typically associated with a given type of person; the schema for doctor includes such characteristics as "educated at medical school," "intelligent," "trustworthy," and "caring." Significantly, a schema of this nature allows the viewer to "go beyond the information given" and "fill in the gaps": if we are told that the character of Malcolm Crowe is a doctor, then we can draw the inference that he is intelligent and we can generate the hypothesis that he is caring.

In addition, we need to cite the fundamental distinction between *syuzhet* and *style*, which corresponds roughly to the distinction between content and form. Whereas the syuzhet refers to the narrative in terms of key scenes and actions, the style refers to the way in which the narrative is filmed – notable examples of stylistic techniques include cinematography, editing, lighting, and *mise-en-scène*. The significant point is that the style interacts with the syuzhet in a number of ways: for instance, filming Malcolm from a low camera angle (an element of form) will contribute to the impression that he has a high social status (an element of content).

The second key question is: How do we *remember* the people and events in fiction film (see Figure 3.1b)? In this chapter, I intend to develop the above theory by stressing the role of memory – a faculty cited by Bordwell (1985, p. 37) but not described in any detail.[4] Considering that memory is not photographic in nature, the specific details of a given scene are usually discarded. In the way that we construct the fabula by employing certain schemas, we *reconstruct* our memories of the fabula by employing those very same schemas once again; both the syuzhet and the style (the precise content and the precise form) drop out of the equation. Significantly, if our memories are liable to schematic elaboration, then they are also liable to schematic distortion, a consequence investigated by Elizabeth Loftus (1975) and others in relation to the reliability of eyewitness testimony. The phenomenon of schematic distortion can be demonstrated by appealing to the simple example of the "restaurant script" (Bower, Black, and Turner 1979, p. 179). If subjects are presented with a story which states that a character, say Anna Crowe, paid a bill and left a restaurant, they will also tend to recall (after a short interval) that Anna ordered and ate a meal, details which are *not* specified in the original text but *are* included in the script for visiting a restaurant.

(b) Filmmaking strategies: the roles of primacy and priming, information, and emotion

How can the filmmaker maximize the application and efficacy of these schemas? To begin with, it should be noted that the viewer's mind-brain contains various "assumptions" about the nature of the world. These assumptions are so fundamental that we take them for granted; indeed, Bordwell (1985, p. 37) states that we only notice them when they are violated. In terms of perception, assumptions concern the basic properties of physical objects. For instance, our perceptual systems "assume" that objects are solid, bounded, and evenly lit, that they tend to move in a single direction, and that, when moving, they continually cover and uncover parts of the background. In terms of cognition, assumptions form the default settings of various schemas. When it comes to "personhood," these assumptions are akin to Murray Smith's (1995, pp. 82–3) notion of recognition. For instance, we "assume" that a person who is apparently capable of walking and talking also possesses the properties of "existence," "life," and "being human," even though these properties are never explicitly acknowledged or described. With respect to *The Sixth Sense*, we "assume" that the walking and talking Malcolm is also alive and well.[5]

Considering these various assumptions, one could argue that the odds of a first-time viewer being able to foresee the film's narrative twist are stacked in Shyamalan's favor from the very outset. Nevertheless, Shyamalan is capable of maximizing the viewer's twist-blindness by employing certain methods. One method involves the *primacy effect* and the *priming procedure* (cited by Bordwell 1985, p. 38; Grodal 1997, p. 68). When we encounter new people and situations, the folk wisdom that "first impressions count" seems to be accurate. For example, consider the following two sentences (adapted from Aronson 1995, pp. 131–4):

(A)   Malcolm Crowe is intelligent, industrious, impulsive, critical, stubborn, and envious.
(B)   Malcolm Crowe is envious, stubborn, critical, impulsive, industrious, and intelligent.

Both sentences actually present the same information but in a different order; the list in sentence B is simply a reverse of the list in sentence A. According to the primacy effect, however, the ordering of the information has important consequences: subjects will tend to rate Malcolm A more positively than Malcolm B simply because sentence A lists the positive character traits first whereas sentence B lists the positive character traits last. The positive rating of Malcolm A and the negative rating of Malcolm B can be partly explained by making reference to the priming procedure: our first impression of a person or situation "primes" us to label that person or situation using a certain type of schema which biases the way in which we interpret, and attend to, subsequent information. So in sentence A, for example, the first trait "intelligent" primes the subject to label Malcolm using a certain type of positive person-schema (or stereotype) which inclines them to positively interpret ambiguous traits like "critical" and to disregard incongruent negative traits like "envious." It should be stressed that this particular example is concerned with the effect of primacy on the subject's judgment of character. With regard to the actual film, primacy firstly affects the viewer's judgment of a more basic attribute: namely, the status of Malcolm as either living or deceased. It is plausible, however, that the same principles apply and, furthermore, that these principles are exploited throughout the film, in order to establish various character relationships.

Another method is to interrupt the generation of certain inferences and hypotheses. This interruption can be achieved in at least two basic ways. The first way is by presenting the viewer with additional information to process (an *informational load*). In experimental situations, psychologists sometimes prevent the subject from entertaining certain propositions by giving them a "distracting task" such as counting backward or performing simple arithmetic. With respect to *The Sixth Sense*, a specific example would be to prevent the viewer from entertaining the proposition that "Malcolm might be dead," by encouraging them to focus on some other aspect of the film's narrative. The second way is by eliciting an emotional response (an *emotional load*). An emotion such as fear directs our processing resources toward the threatening object on the one hand, and our options for fight or flight on the other, and away from those aspects of our environment – either external or psychological – which are not central to survival. Further, emotional responses tend to persist, decaying slowly over time. In terms of *The Sixth Sense*, these facts could be exploited by presenting Malcolm's fatal shooting in conjunction with, say, a strong startle or fear response.

Finally, two general points which relate to the preceding before I go on to analyze the film itself. First, attention tends to decrease over the course of time (Aronson 1995, pp. 133–4). All other things being equal, we are usually more "discerning" at the beginning of a film (or a film sequence) than at the end. Second, human cognition tends to be conservative (ibid., pp. 150–3). In the absence of contradictory information, we usually trust our first impressions and go for the most obvious interpretation of events (by using our schematic knowledge). Both attention decrement and conservative cognition are of obvious relevance, I think, to understanding our gullibility when watching *The Sixth Sense*, a film which begins by creating a series of relatively "conservative" first impressions before waving a highly "unconservative" twist in our faces after about fifty minutes of screen-time.

Analysis

In order to obtain an overview of *The Sixth Sense*, the film can be divided roughly into four main parts and 23 key scenes (see Table 3.1). It makes sense to begin our analysis of the film by considering the introductory scene (numbered 1 in the table). It is night-time. Malcolm and his wife Anna have returned home from a ceremony in which Malcolm has been given an award by the mayor of Philadelphia. In the first scene that we are witness to, Anna fetches a bottle of red wine from the cellar. Shivering suddenly, she runs up the steps to join Malcolm in the living room. Through expository dialogue and the device of the award (a framed plaque), we learn that Malcolm is a child psychologist who is dedicated to his work and who has often put his patients before his wife. Soon afterwards, the couple go upstairs to the bedroom and discover, to their alarm, that the window has been broken (Figure 3.2). The intruder is standing in the adjacent bathroom, a half-naked and visibly distressed man (played by Donnie Wahlberg). After a nervous exchange, we learn that the man's name is Vincent Gray and that he was once a child patient of Malcolm's, a patient whom Malcolm was unable to help. Without warning, Gray removes a gun from the bathroom sink (Figure 3.3) and shoots Malcolm in the stomach, before turning the gun on himself. The scene ends with an overhead shot of Malcolm, lying on the bed and clutching his stomach (Figure 3.4).

In light of the methodology, Shyamalan is able to maximize the "twist blindness" of a first-time viewer of *The Sixth Sense* by presenting certain types of information (i.e., information easily incorporated into standard

Table 3.1 Sequence/character relationships and principle schemas

	Story	Sequence / character relationship	Principal schemas, concerns, conclusions, emotions
1	–	introductory sequence	– – –
2	–	Malcolm–Cole	schema: doctor–patient relationship
3	–	Lynn–Cole	schema: mother–child relationship
4	–	Malcolm–Lynn–Cole	schemas: doctor–parent, doctor–patient relationships
5	–	Malcolm–Anna	schema: husband–wife relationship
6	A	the case (walking to school)	concern: why is Cole disturbed?
7	B	Malcolm–Anna–rival	schema: breakup of marriage
8	A	the case (at school)	concern: why is Cole disturbed?
9	B	Malcolm–Anna	schema: breakup of marriage
10	A	the case (party, traumatic event)	concern: why is Cole disturbed?
11	A	Malcolm–Lynn–doctor	schemas: doctor–parent, parent–doctor relationships
12	B→A	revelatory sequence 1	*Malcolm is sad, Cole sees ghosts*
13	A	horror sequence 1 ("kitchen woman")	emotions: suspense, startle, fear
14	A	horror sequence 2 (hanged family)	emotions: suspense, startle, fear
15	A	horror sequence 3 ("gunshot boy")	emotions: suspense, startle, fear
16	B	Malcolm–Anna–rival	schema: breakup of marriage
17	B→A	revelatory sequence 2	*Malcolm is neglecting Anna, ghosts are asking Cole for help*
18	A	horror sequence 4 (Kyra Collins)	emotions: suspense, startle, fear
19	A	resolution 1	*Cole helps the ghost of Kyra Collins*
20	A	resolution 2 (school play)	*Cole gains acceptance from peers*
21	A	resolution 3	*Cole makes it up with Lynn*
22	B	resolution 4 (flashback sequence)	*Malcolm discovers the truth*
23	B	resolution 5	*Malcolm makes it up with Anna*

Figure 3.2   *The Sixth Sense*

Figure 3.3   *The Sixth Sense*

schemas) and by presenting this information at a particular stage in the narrative (i.e., earlier rather than later) in order to benefit from both the primacy effect and the priming procedure. More specifically, Shyamalan has to establish as early and simply as possible Malcolm's *apparent* status as a living person, and his *apparent* relationships with the two main characters besides Cole: Cole's mother Lynn and Malcolm's wife Anna. This is the function of the first part of the film.

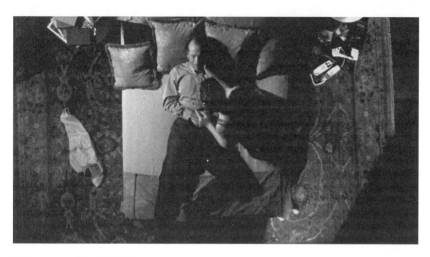

Figure 3.4 *The Sixth Sense*

Figure 3.5 *The Sixth Sense*

(a) Establishing Malcolm's apparent status as a living person

How does Shyamalan establish Malcolm's apparent status as a living person? Why do we not entertain the proposition that "Malcolm might be dead?" Given the unexpected and explosive nature of the gun-shot in the introductory scene (scene 1), it is reasonable to assume that the first-time viewer experiences a relatively strong startle response, especially in comparison with

Figure 3.6   *The Sixth Sense*

Figure 3.7   *The Sixth Sense*

a subsequent viewing of the film on television (Simons 1996). This startle response is possibly compounded by fear for Malcolm's well-being and shock at Gray's subsequent suicide. The subsequent timing is crucial. Within only 15 seconds of the first gun-shot, the scene fades to black (cue scene 2). And within only 27 seconds, the film flashes up the inter-titles "THE NEXT FALL

... SOUTH PHILADELPHIA" (Figure 3.5), and presents the viewer with a clear view of Malcolm – apparently alive and well – sitting on a bench opposite Cole's house (Figure 3.6). This view is inter-cut with a series of point-of-view shots from Malcolm's optical perspective: firstly of Malcolm's handwritten notes regarding Cole's case history, and secondly of Cole exiting the front door (Figure 3.7).

This transitional sequence (scenes 1 to 2) severely reduces our chances of foreseeing the film's narrative twist from the very outset. To use Bordwell's (1985, p. 55) terms, the gap in the narrative is not "flaunted"; rather, it is "suppressed" by a number of interrelated factors. First, we have to contend with the "emotional spill over" from our response to the gun-shot; given that emotional arousal decays slowly and soaks ups our limited processing resources, it reduces our ability to form hypotheses, especially regarding the long-term implications of the shooting. Second, we are not given a sufficient amount of time to recover from our emotional responses and form such hypotheses: for example, within only 27 seconds of the gunshot, we are presented with inter-titles and a clear view of Malcolm. Third, the film immediately presents us with an additional informational load to process: for instance, the reading of the inter-titles effectively serves as a distracting task. Fourth, when forming impressions of people and situations, primacy predominates; our first impression of Malcolm is that he is alive and well. Fifth, considering that human cognition tends to be conservative, the most obvious interpretation of events is that time has passed and that Malcolm has made a full recovery. Sixth, the narrative immediately encourages us to anticipate future events (the case of child patient Cole Sear) rather than to dwell on the event which has just occurred.

In summary, our emotional response to the shooting, the short time-gap between the shooting and the next shot of Malcolm, the informational load, and the nature of our first impression of Malcolm severely reduce the likelihood that we will seriously entertain the proposition that "Malcolm might be dead." This, in turn, reduces the likelihood that such a proposition will be committed to our long-term memory. To put the point another way, even if we did briefly entertain the proposition that "Malcolm might be dead," the emotional spill over from the introductory scene and the information load presented by the subsequent sequence would inhibit the cognitive rehearsal of this proposition; such rehearsal would be required for the successful transfer of the proposition from short-term (or working) memory to long-term memory.

(b) Establishing the apparent relationship between
Malcolm and Lynn

Having successfully established that Malcolm is apparently alive and well, the film must then establish Malcolm's *apparent* relationship with Cole's mother Lynn. The foundations of this relationship are put in place by two relatively low-key scenes. Consider the scene in the church when Malcolm officially introduces himself to Cole (2). Malcolm's first words are: "It's okay Cole, my name is Dr Malcolm Crowe. We were supposed to meet today but I missed our appointment, I'm sorry." This piece of dialogue immediately activates the schema for a certain type of institutional relationship: it is reasonable to assume that every viewer will have a fundamental understanding of the relationship between a doctor and a patient. Similarly, the following scene is set in the home of Lynn and Cole (3). Lynn dresses for work and serves Cole his breakfast at the kitchen table. This scenario brings another type of institutional schema into play: one could argue that the bond between a mother and her child is the most fundamental of all human relationships. I would suggest that both the doctor–patient and mother–child relationships are so deeply rooted in the viewer's psychology that when it comes to establishing the apparent relationship between Malcolm and Lynn (doctor–parent), Shyamalan does not need to use any dialogue whatsoever: the viewer's schematic knowledge and inferential capacities effectively do the work. Indeed, the inference in question is almost a transitive one with Cole acting as the all-important link: Malcolm is significantly related to Cole; Cole is significantly related to Lynn; therefore, Malcolm is significantly related to Lynn.

In light of this, all that Shyamalan needs to do is to briefly present Malcolm and Lynn in the same frame in order to create the impression that they have met each other. The key scene (4) is the subject of the second flashback at the film's conclusion: an establishing shot presents Malcolm and Lynn sitting down opposite each other, both apparently waiting for Cole to arrive home from school (Figure 3.8). From this point, Shyamalan uses the stylistic technique of editing to keep Malcolm and Lynn separate. When Cole arrives through the doorway mid-frame, both Malcolm and Lynn turn round. As Lynn rises to greet Cole, the film cuts forward to a three-quarter shot of the two engaging in light-hearted banter, Lynn joking that she has won the Pennsylvania Lottery and Cole joking that he hit a grand slam to win a kickball game at school. This exchange is inter-cut with two cutaway shots of Malcolm, showing Malcolm's reaction of amusement.

At the end, the camera cuts back briefly for a reestablishing three-shot: Lynn exits the scene to make some pancakes for Cole with the ambiguous phrase, "You've got one hour" aimed in the vague direction of Malcolm.

By using a combination of establishing and cutaway shots, Shyamalan creates a spatial and formal relationship between Malcolm and Lynn, while allowing the two characters to operate in their own physical and psychological space. For the entire duration of the film (excluding the flashback), Malcolm and Lynn only occupy the same frame for approximately 15 seconds, a surprisingly short length of time given that this is a relatively important relationship and the film lasts for over 100 minutes. If a first-time viewer was given a questionnaire and asked to estimate Malcolm and Lynn's shared screen-time, then it is plausible that they would approximate minutes rather than seconds. Such an over-estimation would be a consequence of reconstructive memory, a phenomenon that I will go on to describe shortly.

(c) Establishing the apparent relationship between Malcolm and Anna

The next objective is to establish the apparent relationship between Malcolm and his wife Anna. After Malcolm's first meeting with Cole, we witness a brief scene in which Malcolm arrives home, sees the kitchen table with a single place setting, and goes to the bedroom where Anna is sleeping. This scene, however, establishes little more than the spatial proximity of the two characters. Given the complexity and profundity of the husband–wife relationship, Shyamalan needs a bigger and suitably ambiguous scene: the scene in question (5) is set in an Italian restaurant and is the subject of the third flashback at the end of the film (Figure 3.9). An analysis of this scene can be used to illustrate the possible interplay between primacy, priming, schemas, and reconstructive memory.

The first key question is: How do we *attend to* – and comprehend – the scene in question? How do we construct the fabula from the syuzhet? The first element of the scene is Malcolm's apology to Anna: "I thought you meant the other Italian restaurant I asked you to marry me in." In accordance with the *primacy effect*, the opening dialogue creates an unambiguous first impression which primes us to label the scene as a certain type of social situation: namely, a wedding anniversary dinner for which one of the two parties is late. This labeling brings certain *schemas* into play: for example, we possess schemas for wedding anniversaries, lateness for

Figure 3.8   *The Sixth Sense*

Figure 3.9   *The Sixth Sense*

important social events, and so forth. In turn, these schemas incline us to make certain inferences, an obvious example being that Anna is upset because she has interpreted Malcolm's lateness as an indication that he cares more about his work than their marriage. From Shyamalan's perspective, the significant effect of these schematic constructions is that they incline us to interpret the ambiguous details of the scene in certain ways. For instance, we are inclined to interpret the lack of eye-contact and (two-way) conversation as consequences of Anna giving Malcolm the cold shoulder, rather than as consequences of Anna being unable to see Malcolm. In addition, our interpretations are reinforced by Anna apparently snatching the bill away from Malcolm's grasp, Malcolm's apology, and Anna's ambiguous statement ("Happy Anniversary") with which the scene closes.

Once again, Shyamalan relies on *style* (in addition to syuzhet). In particular, he maximizes both the primacy effect and the ambiguity of the scene through the use of camera placement and camera movement. By beginning with a head-on long shot of Malcolm, the scene primes us to focus our attention on Malcolm's face – and the all-important opening dialogue – rather than the oblivious Anna. By moving the camera round the table, Shyamalan maintains the visual interest of the scene while avoiding the shot/reverse-shot style of editing which would normally be used to film an interaction between two people. The significant point is that we cannot attend to both form and content simultaneously; although our perception of the scene is influenced by the camerawork, we tend to attribute our perceptions to the scene itself (see Kraft 1986, 1987).

The second key question (and the flip side of the coin) is: How do we *remember* the scene in the Italian restaurant? What, for example, do we actually recall when we are prompted by the flashback at the end of the film? To begin with, it should be acknowledged that the specific details of the scene will be processed at a perceptual level. Visual examples include Malcolm's brown suit, Anna's red dress, the layout of the table in the foreground, and the decor of the restaurant in the background. A significant example of content is the fact that Anna fails to register Malcolm's presence, while a significant example of style is the precise movement of the camera. Research suggests, however, that these specific details will not be committed to long-term memory. Instead, we only retain the basic properties and spatial relations of the main objects of our attention, and the basic meaning or significance of the scene as we interpreted it at the time. Furthermore, these aspects are encoded in schematic form and expressible in natural language, often as subject-predicate propositions (Branigan 1992, p. 14; May and Barnard 1995). For instance, the basic properties and spatial relations of the characters can be expressed by the proposition, "Malcolm and Anna *are sitting opposite each other*," while the basic meaning of the scene can be expressed by the proposition, "Malcolm and Anna's marriage *is on the rocks*."

Contrary to our intuitions, therefore, we do not store a recording of the scene in the precise fashion of, say, a video or a DVD. When we are prompted to recall the scene at the end of the film, our recollection does not involve us replaying a "memory video" in our mind's eye. Although it is probable that we are able to recall one or two distinctive details – for example, Anna apparently snatching the bill away from Malcolm's grasp – what primarily happens is that we reconstruct our memory of the scene using the schemas and propositions just described. Significantly, these schemas and propositions incline us to go beyond the information given by filling in the gaps with details not included in the original scene – hence, the possibility of us falsely recalling, say, an argument between the two characters. Schematic distortion can affect the accuracy of eyewitness testimony. Similarly, the schematic distortion of our eyewitness testimony of the restaurant scene and other parts of the film may account for our initial skepticism towards the flashback sequence and the film's conclusion.

(d) Telling the rest of the ghost story

Having established Malcolm's apparent status as a living person and his apparent relationships with Lynn and Anna – by exploiting the primacy effect and the priming procedure – how does Shyamalan go about telling the rest of his ghost story? And why does the fact that Malcolm never has a (two-way) conversation with his wife after the introductory scene – or indeed *any* character other than child patient Cole – not sound any alarm bells during a first-time viewing? Ed Tan (1996) argues that our primary emotion when viewing a fiction film such as *The Sixth Sense* is one of "interest," where interest is approximately synonymous with attention (although it also involves the inclination to act). In particular, interest encourages us to devote our limited processing resources to constructing the film's overt narrative; the more processing resources we devote to an obvious construction, the less processing resources we devote to a non-obvious one. Significantly, the two primary determinants of interest are "thematic structures" and "character structures" which influence our expectations regarding the outcome of the plot ("cognitive concerns") and the fate of the characters ("affective concerns") respectively.

In the second part of the film, two storylines are developed and run in parallel. The primary storyline (labeled A in Table 3.1) centers on the case of Cole. Here, the main cognitive concern is "What is the cause of Cole's anxiety?" while the main affective concern is "Will Cole recover from this anxiety?" In the first of three scenes (6), Malcolm accompanies Cole on his way to and from school. We learn that Cole is regarded as something of a freak by his peers and that Cole's father has left the family to live in another city with another woman. We also learn that Cole has engaged in the exercise of "free association writing" and that he has written "upset words." The second scene (8) takes place in the school itself. In a history lesson, the teacher (and former pupil) Stanley Cunningham asks the class what the school building was used for a hundred years previously. Timidly, Cole raises his hand and states that the building was used as a place for hanging people; when this answer is rejected, Cole has a tantrum and taunts the teacher with his schoolboy nickname of "Stuttering Stanley." In the third and climactic scene (10), Cole is invited to the birthday party of a boy from school. In a cruel prank, Cole is locked into the attic of the house by the birthday boy and an accomplice – a room which, unbeknownst to the two, houses a ghost-like presence that is only visible to Cole. Severely traumatized by the experience, Cole is taken to the hospital for a suspected seizure. By systematically increasing the number of cognitive clues (free association writing, unexplained knowledge of the past, evidence of extra-sensory perception) and by systematically increasing the affective stakes (upset words, tantrum, seizure), these three scenes encourage us to generate a series of hypotheses about Cole's condition and to refrain from assessing Malcolm's apparent status as a living person.

Meanwhile, the secondary storyline (labeled B in Table 3.1) centers on Malcolm's relationship with Anna. Here, the main cognitive concern is "Is the marriage between Malcolm and Anna breaking up?" while the main affective concern is "Can the marriage be saved?" Given that the "marriage on the rocks" schema has been successfully activated, Shyamalan no longer needs to include scenes in which Malcolm and Anna are presented in the same frame, while being in a position in which they could (plausibly) see each other; from this point onward, he uses various stylistic strategies to keep the two characters separate. In the first of two scenes (7), Sean, a young man who works at Anna's store, knocks on the front door and invites Anna out to a market, only for the invitation to be rejected. The crucial separation is achieved in both spatial and visual terms: Malcolm is sitting in his study and hears the conversation between Sean and Anna "off-screen." When Malcolm goes to the window, his hostility toward the departing Sean is clearly signaled by the dialogue. In the second scene (9), Malcolm walks into the bathroom as Anna is taking a shower. In this case, the crucial separation is achieved through an aspect of the *mise-en-scène*: namely, the frosted glass of the shower door. When Malcolm discovers a bottle of anti-depressants in the bathroom cabinet, his concern for Anna is signaled through facial expressions and a shift in the music track. Through the process of schematic construction, it is more likely that we will interpret these two ambiguous episodes as specific symptoms of a deteriorating marriage, and less likely that we will inter- pret them as consequences of the death of a spouse: Sean is regarded as a romantic rival to Malcolm (not a potential replacement for the deceased Malcolm), while Anna is seen to be depressed at the state of her relation- ship with Malcolm (not at the death of Malcolm and her life as a widow).

After Cole is taken to hospital following the traumatic incident at the birthday party, we witness one brief scene in which Malcolm and Lynn appear together (11). Lynn is interrogated by a young doctor about the cuts and bruises on Cole's body (Shyamalan's cameo role). Given that the doctor–parent schema is also successfully activated, Shyamalan does not need to present a clear shot which establishes that Malcolm is also present. Once again, stylistic strategies come to the fore. When the doctor insinu- ates that Lynn has been abusing Cole, Malcolm's presence – and his reaction of disgust – is communicated to us by means of two cutaway reaction shots, thus maintaining the visual, if not the spatial, separation of the characters.

The central scene of *The Sixth Sense* is the revelatory sequence in the hospital (12). In this sequence, the primary and secondary storylines are corroborated, elaborated, and connected, the secondary storyline effectively providing the motivation for the primary one. To begin with, Malcolm reveals the cause of his sadness: he is preoccupied with his failure to help Vincent Gray and this preoccupation has caused him to become a stranger to his wife. The crucial connection is that Malcolm hopes that he will be able to make amends, with respect to both Anna and Gray, by helping Cole. In return, Cole reveals the cause of his anxiety: he can see "dead people," dead people who "don't know they're dead" and who "walk around like regu- lar people" (Figure 3.10). After both of these revelations, our cognitive and our affective concerns become more focused. For instance, the question "What is the cause of Cole's anxiety?" is replaced by the question "Is Cole deluded in some way or does he *really* see ghosts?" Malcolm, for one, is skeptical, privately noting in his Dictaphone that he suspects that Cole is suffering from visual hallucinations, paranoia, and "some kind of school- age schizophrenia."

In the third part of the film, the questions surrounding the primary storyline are answered by a number of horror sequences, each of which is

Figure 3.10 *The Sixth Sense*

based on the appearance of a ghost. The first horror sequence (13) is representative. In the dead of night, Cole plucks up the courage to visit the bathroom in the dark. The camera is positioned outside the bathroom, looking through the open doorway toward Cole standing in front of the lavatory. The film cuts to a close shot of a thermostat on the wall, signaling that the temperature in the house is falling. The film then cuts back to the shot of Cole in the bathroom. Suddenly, a figure walks past the camera from right to left; our startle response to this movement is bolstered by a musical stinger on the soundtrack. In a state of fear, Cole follows the figure into the kitchen to see a woman who resembles his mother, standing in a pink dressing gown with her back to the camera. When the figure turns round, however, we see an entirely different woman – battered, bruised, and with red slash marks on her wrists – eliciting two further startle responses.

The three subsequent horror sequences (14, 15, and 18) follow a similar pattern: the ghostly appearances of the "gunshot boy," the hanged family in the school, and the young girl Kyra Collins all involve forewarning, entrance, and threat. Crucially, the corresponding emotions (suspense, startle, and fear) direct our processing resources toward a "primary appraisal" of the depicted situation in terms of the potential danger to both ourselves and the characters, and away from a more critical and distanced "secondary appraisal" of the supernatural aspect of the narrative. Further, because these emotions persist, decaying slowly over time, the cognitive bias is likely to continue after each sequence has ended.

Meanwhile, the questions surrounding the secondary storyline are answered by a brief scene at Anna's store (16). After Anna gives Sean a birthday present, an embrace between the two characters is interrupted by the sound of glass breaking. Rushing to the front window, Anna apparently catches sight of Malcolm's figure hurrying away down the street.

This scene overlaps aurally with a further revelatory sequence (17): a brief reprise of the sequence which occurs in the hospital, and which connects the primary and secondary storylines for a final time. In a conversation with a distressed Cole, Malcolm acknowledges that he has been neglecting Anna and that he can no longer act as Cole's doctor. In the subsequent scene, however, Malcolm listens to an old tape recording from a session with Vincent Gray. This recording reveals that Gray was also visited by ghosts, while a translation reveals that these ghosts were actually asking for help and did not intend to do any harm, a revelation which Malcolm then shares with Cole in the church setting of their first encounter. This revelation sets up the fourth and final part of the film, a subject which I will reserve for the chapter's conclusion.

In this analysis, I have concentrated on the way that we increasingly focus our attention forward and into the future (and how we construct the narrative according to two principal storylines, in conjunction with two sets of cognitive and affective concerns). What, though, would happen if we deliberately chose to look backward and into the past? At this point, it should be stressed that reconstructive memory need not be a process which only occurs after we have left the cinema; it can be an ongoing process which occurs while we are watching the film. Say that we deliberately attempted to recall Malcolm's encounter with Vincent Gray and that we questioned the function of the introductory scene with respect to the narrative. Given our construction of the primary storyline, we would be more likely to interpret the scene's function as providing Malcolm with the psychological motivation to help Cole, and less likely to interpret the scene's function as shifting Malcolm's status from "living" to "deceased." Similarly, say that we deliberately attempted to recall Malcolm's post-shooting encounters with Lynn and Anna, and that we questioned whether or not we had witnessed any (two-way) conversations between the characters. Given our construction of the secondary storyline, it is more likely that the encounters in question would be encoded in memory using the general "doctor–parent" and "marriage on the rocks" schemas, and less likely that they would be encoded as specific incidents in which (two-way) conversations do not take place. By reconstructing the narrative in memory while following it, we might go beyond the information given and fill in those conversations which the narrative does not provide.

Conclusion

How should we explain the "twist blindness" of the first-time viewer of *The Sixth Sense*? How should we explain a failure of attention exemplified by the revelatory sequence in which Cole reveals that he can "see dead people" – dead people who "don't know they're dead" – while the camera is focusing in on Malcolm? First, because we classify Malcolm as "alive" from the very outset, it is extremely unlikely that the proposition that "Malcolm might be dead" will be transferred to our long-term memory. Second, because we are continually (re)constructing the narrative and attempting to confirm our first impressions, it is extremely unlikely that we will have cause to consider the possibility that "Malcolm might be dead." For these reasons, the camera is able to focus on Malcolm during Cole's revelation without either our long-term memory or our ongoing narrative (re)construction sounding any alarm bells. During a first-time viewing of *The Sixth Sense*, we fail to make the connection between Cole's revelation and Malcolm's situation effectively because there is nothing in either our long-term memory or our ongoing narrative (re)construction for us to connect Cole's revelation *to*.

In the fourth and final part of the film, both the primary and secondary storylines are resolved. The resolution of the primary storyline confirms our narrative (re)construction. In three consecutive scenes (19 to 21), Cole overcomes his fear by helping the ghost of the young girl Kyra Collins to reveal her murderer, he makes it up with his mother Lynn by revealing his secret and passing on a message of love from Lynn's deceased mother, and he gains acceptance from his teacher and peers by taking the starring role in the school play. It is the resolution of the secondary storyline that presents the celebrated narrative twist. In the flashback sequence (22), we see Cole's revelation, Malcolm and Lynn sitting opposite each other, and Malcolm and Anna having dinner. When Malcolm says goodbye to the sleeping Anna in the closing scene (23), our surprise at the twist, and our admiration for Shyamalan's ingenuity, may be tempered by a certain skepticism. Considering the characteristics of reconstructive memory, it is plausible that this skepticism is due to the fact that we have a tendency to overestimate the number of scenes in which Malcolm appears in the same frame as either Lynn or Anna – thereby overestimating the opportunities for narrative contradiction – and that we falsely recall, say, (two-way) conversations between Malcolm and either Lynn or Anna which do not actually take place. It is partly this skepticism which prompts a second viewing.

In conclusion, Cole states that the dead people who haunt him "only see what they want to see." I would suggest that when we watch *The Sixth Sense* for the first time, we only see what we have been "primed" to see. Conversely, by the time we watch the film a second time round, the proposition that "Malcolm might be dead" has been solidified into a fact: we have had a chance to commit this fact to long-term memory and to incorporate it into our narrative (re)construction. In short, we have been "primed" to see the film in a new light.

The original version of this chapter was presented at the third conference for the Center for Cognitive Studies of the Moving Image, University of Pécs, Hungary, May 2001. An abridged version was presented at the annual Screen conference, University of Glasgow, June 2002. Thanks to Murray Smith and Edward Branigan for their comments.

Notes

1   Interviewed in the DVD Bonus Feature "Rules and Clues."
2   According to Eitzen's "parallel processing model of selective attention," automatic processing is analogous to peripheral vision on the grounds that it is unlimited, parallel, and largely beyond conscious control.
3   The use of the term "twist blindness" is partly inspired by an astonishing defect of our attention system known as *change blindness* – an inability to detect visual changes to filmic and real-world scenes that are obvious to viewers who know that they are going to happen (Levin and Simons 1997; Simons and Levin 1998). One of the main implications of change blindness is that we do not store detailed representations of our visual world in memory from one moment to the next: rather, the filmic or real-world scene serves as an "external memory store" for the specific details; we only tend to pick up and retain abstract, schematic information (Simons 2000).
4   In the field of film studies, Bordwell (1992, p. 194) discusses comprehension and memory in relation to a first-time viewing of Michael Curtiz's *Mildred Pierce* (1945), arguing that the film's flashback of the murder scene exploits the

viewer's "inability to recall certain details." Edward Branigan (1992, pp. 13–15) discusses the role of memory in his book on narrative comprehension and film, arguing that a film's narrative is typically remembered as "categories of information" expressible in natural language and that a film's "surface features" (its exact shots, dialogue, etc.) are forgotten as soon as new information is presented.

5 A related assumption is that a person or "soul" only occupies one body, an assumption which is violated by the character of Tyler Durden in David Fincher's *Fight Club* – also released in 1999.

Bibliography

Aronson, E. 1995. *The Social Animal*, 7th edn. New York: W. H. Freeman & Company.

Baddeley, A. 1995. "Working memory," in M. S. Gazzaniga (ed.), *The Cognitive Neurosciences*. Cambridge, MA: MIT Press, pp. 755–64.

Bartlett, F. C. 1932. *Remembering*. Cambridge: Cambridge University Press.

Bordwell, D. 1985. *Narration in the Fiction Film*. Madison: University of Wisconsin Press.

Bordwell, D. 1989. "A case for cognitivism." *Iris*, 9: 11–40.

Bordwell, D. 1992. "Cognition and comprehension: Viewing and forgetting in *Mildred Pierce*." *Journal of Dramatic Theory and Criticism*, 6, 2: 183–98.

Bower, G. H., Black, J. B., and Turner, T. J. 1979. "Scripts in memory for text." *Cognitive Psychology*, 11: 177–220.

Branigan, E. 1992. *Narrative Comprehension and Film*. London: Routledge.

Eitzen, D. 1993. "Attending to the fiction: A cognitive account of cinematic illusion." *Post Script: Essays in Film and the Humanities*, 13, 1: 46–60.

Grodal, T. 1997. *Moving Pictures: A New Theory of Film Genres, Feelings, and Cognition*. Oxford: Clarendon Press.

Kraft, R. N. 1986. "The role of cutting in the evaluation and retention of film." *Journal of Experimental Psychology: Learning, Memory and Cognition*, 12: 155–63.

Kraft, R. N. 1987. "The influence of camera angle on comprehension and retention of pictorial events." *Memory and Cognition*, 15: 291–307.

Levin, D. T., and Simons, D. J. 1997. "Failure to detect changes to attended objects in motion pictures." *Psychonomic Bulletin & Review*, 4, 4: 501–6.

Loftus, E. F. 1975. "Leading questions and the eyewitness report." *Cognitive Psychology*, 7: 560–72.

May, J., and Barnard, P. J. 1995. "Cinematography and interface design," in K. Nordby, P. H. Helmerson, D. J. Gilmore, and S. A. Arnesen (eds.), *Human–Computer Interaction: Interact '95*. London: Chapman & Hall, pp. 26–31.

Miller, G. 1956. "The magic number seven, plus or minus two: some limits on our capacity for processing information." *Psychological Review*, 63: 81–93.

Simons, D. J. 2000. "Current approaches to change blindness." *Visual Cognition*, 7, 1–3: 1–15.

Simons, D. J., and Levin, D. T. 1998. "Failure to detect changes to people during a real-world interaction." *Psychonomic Bulletin & Review*, 5, 4: 644–9.

Simons, R. C. 1996. *Boo!: Culture, Experience, and the Startle Reflex*. New York: Oxford University Press.

Smith, M. 1995. *Engaging Characters: Fiction, Emotion, and the Cinema*. Oxford: Clarendon Press.

Tan, E. S. H. 1996. *Emotion and the Structure of Narrative Film: Film as an Emotion Machine* (trans. B. Fasting). Mahwah, NJ: Lawrence Erlbaum.

4

Narrative Comprehension Made Difficult: Film Form and Mnemonic Devices in *Memento*

Stefano Ghislotti

Enigmatic and challenging; clever and startling; engaging and disorienting. Few recent films found so passionate and responding fans as *Memento* (Christopher Nolan, 2000). Since its release, reviews, forums, and discussions absorbed not only professional critics, but also a great number of interested viewers, all fascinated by the puzzling experience of the film. *Memento* has been dissected, analyzed, investigated, commented on; students and scholars wrote doctoral theses and essays on the subject, and the film is always referenced when the topic is that of enigmatic, brain-teasing, puzzling cinematic experiences.

For these reasons every new discourse about *Memento* should summarize a lot of questions, interventions, interpretations, which are part of its reception. Of all the issues raised by the film, one of the most intriguing is that concerning the viewers' mental activity: how one can cope with a film so intricate and difficult to understand is a very stimulating question. So is the search for an organizational schema in its intricacies.

In *Memento* multiple story lines, either progressive, regressive, recounted, or fragmented, are bound together by elements capable of recalling previous stages of the story, announcing or suggesting possible developments, showing effects whose causes are still unknown, retrospectively affecting several central features of the story, or even obliging the viewers to reconsider the story as a whole. *Memento* is a very good example of what a complex narration can be. Answering the questions we proposed can help us to figure out the relationship existing between this film's features and the mental operations we have to perform in order to understand the narrative. These kinds of "puzzle-films" have in fact the particularity of highlighting the role of the viewers, the mental abilities they have to employ, and the mental operations they have to perform. As a matter of fact, the difficulties we experience are deeply rooted in the skillful way we normally watch ordinary movies. *Memento* is difficult and challenging because we are not able to construct a coherent *fabula* during the screening. It is also attractive because the puzzle demands a solution.

Thus, what we can add to the general ideas already expressed about the film are remarks concerning unconventional narration, and the fact that if for some reasons understanding the story is difficult, we have to question the way the film is composed and the mental functions it activates. *Memento* emphasizes the fundamental role of viewers' activity in the process of film viewing, because its unusual composition hinders some basic functions of memory. Because the film moves backward, the viewer is progressively obliged to put the scenes into the right order: but it is really difficult to follow the flow of events while simultaneously recalling the events already seen, and putting everything into a coherent sequence. These difficulties involve a more general question: is it possible to understand a narration in which time and causality are reversed?

In short, I will examine several features of the film, consider some basic elements of cinematic narration, and propose a model of the main strategies the director adopts to give the film on the one hand an effect of missing past (or of anterograde amnesia for viewers), and on the other hand a coherence despite the lack of chronological order and of causal relationships. We will begin by considering a key concept in narrative theory and its relationship with the viewer's activity.

The Concept of *Fabula* Construction

The *fabula* "embodies the action as a chronological, cause-and-effect chain of events occurring within a given duration and a spatial field"; it is "a pattern which perceivers of narratives create through assumptions and inferences" (David Bordwell 1985, p. 49). The process of *fabula* construction is of central importance: it is the result of the interplay between viewers and films, and it shows how deeply viewers' memory is involved in cinematic narrations. In *Memento*, as in a true detective tale, viewers can witness that almost everything in the main narrative line has already happened, and that it is necessary to go up along the temporal line, or to go back along the causal chain, to find significant elements which can help them interpret what happened. In progressive narrations the flow of events follows the temporal direction, the same flowing of time which view-ers experience in their ordinary life. While witnessing events and actions along this temporal flow, it is possible to keep track of the progression in characters' actions, states of mind, goals, and achievements. Even if film events are not in chronological order it is possible to arrange them into a loose scheme, which can be revised and corrected if necessary. This happens because, as Endel Tulving puts it, "[i]nformation in episodic memory of necessity must be recorded into the store directly" (Tulving 1972, p. 389). This can help to explain why it is difficult to remember *Memento* in chronological order: "For instance, for a person to remember that he experienced an event E2 after another event E1, he must have originally experienced those two events in this temporal order" (ibid.). The episodic memory system of encoding strictly keeps the temporal connections between events, and only a willing mental operation can dispose them in a different order. Using this memory function, we are able to manage a mental representation of the *fabula*.

We can go further by saying that the process of *fabula* construction involves many mental aspects, which allow us to form a mental representation of the state of affairs. It is not only a summarizing task: it involves our knowledge of the diegetic world as it progresses during the screening. When we are watching a movie we do not deal with abstracts; instead, we face audiovisual streams of data: images and sounds which refer to narrative worlds. During the screening we process these data: we actively review the important aspects and we put them into mental schemes, which are com-mitted to memory, revised and updated if necessary. We are able to pro-cess and store information concerning time, space, characters, state of affairs, following the actions depicted in films. A sudden revelation, a plot twist, may force us to change our mental representation of the state of affairs, sometimes they may oblige us to reconsider the whole mental construc-tion. This happens for instance in the final part of *The Sixth Sense* (M. Night Shyamalan 1999) when Crowe (played by Bruce Willis) realizes he is no longer a living man, but only a ghost. This revelation obliges us to revise the whole story, recalling the entire film or seeing it a second time, to find where the story bifurcation was located. (See Daniel Barrett's "'Twist Blindness': The Role of Primacy, Priming, Schemas, and Reconstructive Memory in a First-Time Viewing of *The Sixth Sense*" in this volume.)

We can watch films because we possess the capacity of sensing time, and memory is the mental faculty directly involved. This aspect is stated in *Memento*: at a certain point Leonard Shelby (Guy Pearce), whom Natalie

(Carrie-Anne Moss) asked to remember his wife, says: "How can I heal if I don't feel time?" No memory, no time: the unusual composition of *Memento* is intended to put the viewer in the same condition as the main character, sharing his anterograde amnesia, the impossibility of making new memories. As an effect of the backward narration it is very difficult for the viewer to have a clear idea of what actually happens. We'll try to understand how this effect is obtained by comparing two versions of *Memento*: the original release, screened in movie theaters, and the chronological version, provided as bonus material in the DVD edition. We have to deal firstly with the chronological version, the film that many viewers were probably expecting during the screening of the actual version of *Memento*. A quick analysis will help us to find out the basic story events.

The Chronological Version of *Memento*

The second disk in the DVD special edition of *Memento* arranges the film's scenes in chronological order. To mark the difference existing with the theatrical version, the end credits are shown at the beginning, scrolling down from the top of the screen to the bottom: a clear cue, referring to the fact that the narration of the original edition has been reversed. In the same fashion the opening credit sequence is shown at the end of the film moving backward, from the director's name to the cast members.

The film has not, in fact, been completely reversed: we should say that its structure of events has been linearized, and from this respect the film is similar to other "ordinary" films. Black and white and color scenes do not interpolate: all the scenes are arranged in their temporal succession, and the color scenes, with respect to the original version, are shown in reverse order, following diegetic time. In so doing two important plot tricks are lost: the alternation between black and white and color scenes, and the question concerning the relationships between them.

With the story events ordered in their normal succession, it is interesting to notice that the story line is very simple to follow. After the end credits a long black and white scene assembles the original 22 black and white segments. Fade-ins and fade-outs are kept in their original positions: this feature allows us to control where the segments were inter-cut with the color scenes. The action is continuous from segment 1 to segment 21, beginning from the awakening, and ending with the last phone call. No significant ellipsis is present. This action lasts for 17 minutes. It shows Leonard

Shelby who wakes up, shaves his left thigh, talks on the phone four times, watches himself in the mirror, discovers tattoos over his hand, chest, legs, arms, and makes a new tattoo on the shaved thigh. A climatic moment is when he uncovers a new tattoo on his bandaged right arm. It says: "Never answer the phone," and Leonard reads it while he is talking on the phone with an unknown person.

Two elements are worth noting: 1) Leonard's voiceover, expressing his stream of thought at the beginning of the scene; and 2) the long phone monologues, which narrate the story of Sammy Jankis. This story is shown in six flashbacks, and it is important because Leonard, as *Memento* viewers know, is unable to make new memories. He tells the Sammy Jankis story to other persons when he wants to explain his own condition. For him the story is an exhortation: making a comparison with Sammy, who was unable to overcome his impairment, Leonard tries to convince himself that he is facing his condition in the best possible way. He says: "I've got a more graceful solution to the memory problem. I'm disciplined and organized. I use habit and routine to make my life possible."

The long hotel scene, which opened with Leonard's awakening, ends when he exits room 21. He is going to kill a man, believing he is John G., the man who raped and murdered his wife. He meets Teddy (Joe Pantoliano) at the front office and they go together to the motel's car park. Teddy gives Leonard a lead to find the man.

The passage between black and white and color scenes is provided by scene 22, which begins, in black and white, in the motel room and ends, in color, when Leonard leaves the derelict building. It is clear at this point that in the chronological version black and white cinematography is not necessary, while in the original version it provides viewers a cue permitting them to easily distinguish two different temporal lines. In the chronological version the two lines are simply put one before the other. In the linearized plot it is also clear that Leonard gets his revenge, he forgets it, and he is ready for a new John G. The climatic moment of the original version is placed at the end, while in the chronological version it is simply a passing moment, which shows Leonard beginning a new search. There is no mystery: every action matches subsequent actions. The story outline is easy to draw, and it corresponds to a limited list of locations and actions, as shown in Figure 4.1.

The process of *fabula* construction is not particularly arduous, because as we can see, the basic events of the narrative are put in a linearized structure, and the connections are easy to understand. Hence what is at stake

BW1–BW22	Motel room (Leonard alone, phone calls, Teddy)
BW22–C1	Derelict building (Jimmy, Teddy)
C2	Tattoo shop (Teddy)
C3–C4	Ferdy's bar (Natalie -1-; 2 segments)
C5–C6–C7	Natalie's (1) (3 segments)
C8	Jaguar (Teddy)
C9–C10	Discount Inn (hooker; 2 segments) [1st night]
C11	Industrial area. Fire, Leonard alone
C12–C13	City street (Dodd; 2 segments)
C13–C14–C15	Dodd's (Dodd, Teddy; 3 segments)
C16–C17	Natalie's (2) (2 segments) [2nd night]
C18	Diner (Teddy)
C19	Discount Inn (Burt)
C19–C20	City Grill (Natalie -2-; 2 segments, one with L. alone)
C21–C22	Discount Inn (L. alone, Burt, Teddy; 2 segments)
C22–C23	Derelict building (Teddy; 2 segments)

BW = black & white; C = color, with corresponding scene number

Figure 4.1   Chronology of the movie *Memento*

with *Memento* is another element: the particularity of film form. We will consider it by examining the original version of the film.

Guess the Story

Memento's composition is arresting because of its elaborate structure, which presents a clever mix of chronological narration and reversed temporality. As an effect of this kind of composition, the main character's memory disease is directly perceptible to the viewers, who share with him the difficulty of providing a coherent account of the story. While watching the original version of *Memento*, we do not find it difficult to place the narrative elements into a coherent structure, but we feel a sense of difficulty in using our own memory. When recalling a part of the film, we are not able to place a fact after another, because we cannot remember whether it was before or after, whether we should place it in the structure of the film or in the film's *fabula*. For this reason the mental work we do while watching the film is a very interesting subject. The initial parts of *Memento* require the viewer to construct a specific schema, to comprehend the way in which the film proceeds: what is hard to determine is the narration itself. Knowing the narrative form of a film constitutes a heuristic schema: the viewer understands the narration when able to put the narrative information into connected cognitive modules, which are constantly revised as the film proceeds.

At the very beginning of *Memento*, we have to make an hypothesis concerning the film's form. Because of the characteristics of the film's composition, we need to see at least the first five scenes, before we can draw an acceptable model of the film's narration.

(C1)   Credit sequence (Teddy's killing)
(BW1) Black and white sequence
(C2)   Color sequence (motel, derelict building)
(BW2) Black and white sequence
(C3)   Color sequence (motel room, photograph of Teddy)

The credits sequence (C1) shows in reverse motion a Polaroid photograph, where the image gradually fades to white: this aspect is noticeable because it is contrary to our normal perception. The viewer directly witnesses the retrogression of time: the sequence is accurately prepared to show events moving in the backward direction. Time "turns back": the photograph returns into the camera, the killer throws away the gun, the cartridge comes back into the gun, the killer shoots, the victim shouts a last, ineffective invocation. The question asked by the viewer at this point is obviously why this form of presentation has been adopted. A possible hypothesis concerns artistic motivation; another, more detailed, is about the possibility of showing an event as inevitable, since the reverse motion documents a fact which has already happened, and it goes back to the moment in which a different choice was still possible.

The following sequence (BW1) does not offer a way to solve the perplexity. While the sound of the shooting is still echoing in the black of the fade out, an extreme close-up shows the eyes of the main character. The voiceover presents his thought: Leonard is asking himself where he is. Also the viewer is wondering whether a relationship between this black and white sequence and the preceding colored one exists. The use of the fading, and the black and white cinematography, create a neat separation between sequences. The identity of the character is the only shared element. No convincing hypothesis is possible at the moment, except for considering that the color sequence is a dream that abruptly woke Leonard up.

The following sequence (C2), in color, shows Leonard at the motel front office. From a photograph, the reception clerk recognizes Teddy, who is arriving. Leonard goes out with him, and they drive to a derelict building. Leonard finds some bullets on the seat of a pickup truck parked in front of the building. Then Leonard enters the house and finds a photograph of Teddy in his pocket. On the back, he sees handwriting reading: "He is the one. Kill him." Leonard draws a handgun, he leaps on Teddy who has entered the house, and after an impressive dialogue with him, he shoots.

Teddy's last scream and the noise of the gun going off enable the viewer to find a relationship between the second color sequence and the first one. A pattern of construction is recognizable. We have two connected color sequences, and a black and white scene embedded between them. The order of the events portrayed in the two color sequences is reversed: C2 is after C1, the event (e-1) in sequence C2 is anterior to the event (e) portrayed in C1.

$$[C1(e) + BW1 + C2(e-1) \ldots$$

When viewers recognize this pattern, they can generate the following primary hypothesis concerning the film's form: color sequences and black and white scenes are systematically alternated. This hypothesis is confirmed by the next scene (BW2), a black and white one. The action continues from the break caused by the change of sequence: Leonard is still sitting on a large bed and goes on asking himself the same questions, while surveying the room. He also says something about his disease, concluding that he has to adopt a rigorous method to cure it.

A new color sequence (C3) appears after a fade to black. Leonard is in a motel room: he is writing "Kill him" on the back of a Polaroid photograph. It is the same sentence he read before killing Teddy. Recognizing the sentence is a way for the viewer to find a relationship with the event depicted in sequence C2: the sequence shown before, and presenting subsequent events. At this point, a more comprehensive hypothesis about the film's form is possible: we find a reverse concatenation of events. What we are seeing (e-2) temporally precedes what we have seen (e-1) in the last color sequence, and what happens in the credits sequence is the most advanced event along the temporal line. The composition pattern of the film is now understandable, and it will be confirmed in the ensuing sequences. The film structure alternates color sequences with black and white scenes. The black and white scenes present a continuous event, interrupted by the changes of sequence. The color sequences show a flow of events (e) that moves backward (e-1, e-2, etc.):

$$[C1(e) + BW1 + C2(e\text{-}1) + BW2 + C3(e\text{-}2) + \ldots \rightarrow$$

Two strings of events, in black and white and in color, are linked together by the crosscutting editing, but they are not meant to be simultaneous. They have two different time directions: chronological in black and white scenes, reversed in color sequences. The fact that black and white scenes interrupt the color sequences creates an effect of interference: while we have to keep in mind the actions of the color sequence, a black and white scene wipes out our working memory and attracts our focus of attention. As the subsequent color sequence appears, it is difficult to remember the previous one. In other films that adopt a backward narration, such as *Betrayal* (by David Hugh Jones, 1983; based on Harold Pinter's play) or *Irréversible* (by Gaspar Noé, 2002), this effect is not present, because the sequences are connected to one another, and one can reflect on the causal relationship existing between them. In *Memento* the script is designed to create confusion in the viewer: beyond the crosscutting of two opposite time streams, we can notice that the average length of black and white scenes (except for the last two) is less than a minute, while color sequences (except for the last one) are from one to six minutes long. Such a fragmentation produces 22 black and white scenes and 23 color sequences which are systematically alternated. In addition, in the black and white part we find abrupt interruptions of action, which prevent the possibility of a plain reconstruction, and in the color part continuous actions are cut into two or three parts: it happens with Dodd's chase, Ferdy's bar, City Grill, the hooker and the derelict building scenes (two parts), and with Natalie's home and Dodd's room (three parts). This partition creates confusion because in order to reorder the color line of actions we have to recollect similar segments which can muddle, overlap, or be exchanged, and which appear as bewildering elements.

The Matching Shots

Such unusual and elaborate construction demands several points of control, to confirm the temporal or causal relationships. For this reason, each color sequence presents matching shots (MS) – both at the beginning and at the end – using a precise disposition. We can see it in the following scheme:

MS following sequence + SEQUENCE + MS previous sequence

In these shots, the repetition of already seen details helps to create a connection between the related color sequences that flow backwards and are interrupted by black and white scenes. In this perspective, the matching shots are mnemonic devices. They encourage the viewer to make the operation of mental rotation, which consists in putting the events of the two sequences in the right chronological order, to verify the temporal and the causal relationships. The scheme for the film's beginning is shown below:

$$[C1.ms1 + BW1 + ms2.C2.ms1 + BW2 + ms3.C3.ms2 + \ldots \rightarrow$$

The relationship between the sequences is found only at the end of each color sequence. As an example, we can take ms2, at the end of sequence C3: it is a matching shot because we recognize the beginning of sequence C2, already seen. Thus, at the beginning of each new color sequence a tension is created: the viewer tries to anticipate the relationship existing between the new events and the events already seen. It is important to consider the complexity of this construction, that is both chronological, as the film goes on, and retrograde, as the events move backward. The de-familiarizing effect is provoked by the necessity of this mental work: we have to arrange the events without the possibility of anticipating actions that have already happened. We can only investigate the causes at the origin of the effects we have witnessed.

Mental Rotation

The construction pattern we have found is bound to the temporality of the film's presentation. From a diegetic point of view, things are different. We have two main narrative lines. Black and white scenes show a single flow of events that is continuous from scene B1 to scene B21. Only sequence B22 introduces some ellipses. Color sequences, on the other hand, show the story going backward, ascending time from the end to the beginning. In order to obtain the sequence of events, temporally and logically ordered, we have to perform a continuous mental rotation by putting the

C1.ms1

ms2.C2.ms1

ms3.C3.ms2

ms4.C4.ms3

ms5.C5.ms4

Figure 4.2   Chronological structure of *Memento*

first sequence into the final position of the story, and adding each new sequence as a premise for the subsequent events:

$$(\ldots C3 + C2 + C1)$$

The effect of "a missing past" is due to the fact that we are going back and each time we need a new premise for the events we are seeing. The operation of mental rotation is not simple. We can do it at a point in time, but not for the whole range of the story. Each time we need a mental representation of the *fabula*, beginning from the end, and we have to consider a great number of elements. A sketch of the required structure is shown in Figure 4.2.

It is impossible to keep more than a few elements in our short-term memory. While the film continues to present new elements to be processed, we cannot keep the complete ordered *fabula* structure in mind. So, we tend to keep a local map of the events, mainly those that are under the focus of attention, and we need mnemonic devices that remind us of former or subsequent stages of the action. Another difficulty in the mnemonic reconstruction of the events comes from the backward direction. Except for the first sequence, which is in reverse motion, the color sequences are to be placed in the opposite direction of the film screening. Yet, the flowing of the film invites us to make progressive mental representations, and it is difficult, especially the first time we see the film, to make a clear distinction between the two different mental representations. We have a regressive concatenation, presented by the film, that flows in a "natural" way along time and that is processed by our episodic memory.

$$[C1 + C2 + C3 + \ldots \rightarrow$$

And we have a chronological concatenation of events, obtained by mental rotation.

$$\leftarrow \ldots + C3(e\text{-}2) + C2(e\text{-}1) + C1(e)]$$

While watching the film, it is very difficult to keep its stimuli distinct from our mental construction because our normal way of making memories follows the temporal arrow of the film's screening. So we experience, even after repeated visions, confusion between the two temporal dimensions. They interfere with each other, and we are not able to see them at the same time.

To complete the mental representation of the film structure, we have to wait for the final sequence, BW22, which begins in black and white, but switches to color. It is the solution of the puzzle that we have been expecting since the third sequence, for it explicitly signifies the temporal relationship that exists between the black and white and color sequences. At this point, the viewer can take a look at the whole *fabula* of the film. The transition between the first and the second story line is made using the Polaroid photograph taken after Jimmy's murder. As the image appears, the colors become progressively more definite, turning the entire scene to color.

Two photographs, two mementos of past events, are at the beginning and at the end of the film. It's indeed a stylish choice, but it's also the use of mnemonic devices, such as photographs, that appears to be a characteristic of the film.

The Film's Overall Structure

In order to understand and schematize the film's complete structure, it is worth using a more subtle notation, following the suggestion made by Andy Klein in a review of the film (Klein 2001). We shall number the black and white sequences from 1 to 22, and use alphabet letters for the color sequences, "A" being the color part of sequence 22, "B" the following color sequence in chronological order, and so on. We obtain not only a list of sequences, but also a mental diagram of the film. Such a diagram recalls mnemotechnical schemes of oratory teachers: when the memorizing task was difficult, their advice was to associate the things to be remembered to a well-known ordered list, like numbers and alphabet letters (Carruthers 1990). Two different dispositions of the ordered lists help us to recall the *fabula* structure or the film's structure. The latter starts from the last event (shown in the first sequence, W) and alternates color sequences with black and white scenes.

W-1-V-2-U-3-T-4-S-5-R-6-Q-7-P-8-O-9-N-10-M-11-L-12-K-13-J-14-
I-15-H-16-G-17-F-18-E-19-D-20-C-21-B-22+A

The *fabula* structure, as we already remarked for the chronological version, is obtained by postponing and inverting all the color sequences.

1-2-3-4-5-6-7-8-9-10-11-12-13-14-15-16-17-18-19-20-21-22+A-B-C-D-
E-F-G-H-I-J-K-L-M-N-O-P-Q-R-S-T-U-V-W

The two mental diagrams are simple and one can easily master them.
They are external memory aids: simple strings of ordered elements, easy
to recall, and useful as notation tools. They help us to remember *Memento*
without the uncertainties which come out when we are watching the
film. Unfortunately, we cannot use them during the screening, as they were
obtained only after a close analysis. Yet, they remind us that a film like
Memento must possess particular orientating elements, allowing the
viewer to understand what he or she is watching. These elements are progressive, as they appear following the screening time, also in the backward
narration, and mnemonic, as they are present in both story lines, and relate
to one another.

A Bidirectional Film

The chronological and the backward story lines of *Memento* meet at the
end, and as we see Leonard going to the tattoo shop, we can imagine what
happens next: all the events we have already seen can find a place in the
diegesis, which is now complete. But as we are at the end of the film we
are not able to recall all the episodes which compose the story, and we may
feel as amnesiac as the main character. Yet, we know many things about
the narrative, as we have been given a lot of information, a flow of data
arranged following the temporal line of the film screening. In the color segments of *Memento* several streams of data develop along time, organizing
relevant information about the characters and the action, and progressively
engaging the viewer's attention, even if the narrative time moves backward.
It is worth noting that from the beginning, while viewers are still wondering about the film's structure, new schemata are proposed for their attention:
for example, different aspects concerning the identity of the main character, which is a distinctive feature of the initial stage of any narration. Moreover,

Film form
   Main character's identity
      Why did Leonard kill Teddy?
         Sammy Jankis story
            Who is Natalie?
               What happened to Leonard's wife?
                  What's Natalie's game?
                     Why does Leonard kill Jimmy?
                        Film form (seq. 22+A)
                           Are Leonard's memories true?

Figure 4.3   Main aspects/questions presented in *Memento*

the flowing of the film will propose an entire set of schemata, concerning the other characters, the film form, and the outcome of the story. A list of the principal aspects is provided in Figure 4.3.

We shall now consider the main character's identity schemata, which is proposed at the beginning of the film. If we examine the first scenes we can notice that the tattoos which help to define the character's identity are shown repeatedly, and are present in both black and white and color scenes. We hear about Sammy Jankis or we see the tattoo on Leonard's left hand in three scenes (2, T, S), and after a few minutes the same happens in three other scenes (S, 5, R). We see other tattoos on Leonard's body in two contiguous scenes (T, 4): these scenes belong to different temporal lines, but they both show Leonard in front of the mirror, looking at his tattoos, and we can see how they read. In the subsequent scene (S) Natalie speaks about Leonard's "freaky tattoos." All these elements are present in contiguous segments, and while the narrative follows two opposite time directions, they form a robust cluster of references to the identity and to the mental state of the character. Despite the backward structure, after the occurrence of this set of elements, viewers can determine Leonard's goals and motivations. The primacy effect (see Bordwell 1985, p. 36), the initial frame of reference concerning Leonard's condition, is about the loss of his wife, and the search for revenge, and it is set in the first part of the film, even if most color scenes showing essential details are to be referred to the last part of the story.

The Problem with Lenny

Another very important cluster of elements is presented in a similar way: Leonard's memories and mental images, systematically distributed throughout the film via flashbacks. These images give glimpses of Leonard's earlier life, and lead the viewer to make uncertain or at least doubtful conclusions by the end of the film. The information conveyed by this set of images shows a development along the temporal line of the screening, leading from the curiosity about his wife's murder, to the discovery of what happened – as Leonard remembers it – and to two antithetical versions, evoked by Teddy's revelations. Most of these images belong to color segments of the film, but they follow the forward direction.

As we can see in Table 4.1 and Figure 4.4, several mental images are presented, associated with different characters or situations. We have also marked the black and white flashbacks concerning Sammy Jankis, and one can see how closely they are embedded in the other images' arrangement: they appear after the first memories of Leonard's wife (S), and their conclusion, showing the death of Sammy's wife (21), is not far from the scene of Teddy's revelations (A).

In the cluster of color mental images, depending on what they depict, we can recognize three main groups. The first group (S, K, A [Jimmy]) shows memories of Leonard's wife as she was alive. A stream of affection and a sense of loss are conveyed by these images, which have the intensity of Leonard's point-of-view shots. The second group (O, J, E [flashback]) increases curiosity and climaxes with a classical flashback of the night of the accident. The third group (E [syringe], A [Teddy], A [Leonard in the Jaguar]) collects startling mental images and uncertain memories. First of all is the mental image of Leonard handling an insulin syringe: there is an ominous association with Sammy Jankis' story, whose ending will arrive few minutes later, reverberating over Leonard's past. The same association is overtly reiterated during Teddy's revelations dialogue. In this case two groups of three images set an opposition between two conflicting interpretations of Leonard's story. In the first one, already seen in segment K, Leonard pinches his wife's thigh while she is brushing her hair, provoking her reaction; in the second one Leonard injects insulin into his wife's thigh, as Sammy Jankis did with the last injection, which provoked his wife's death. The ominous association with Sammy Jankis becomes, in Teddy's words, a complete identification: Leonard's wife

Table 4.1 Mental images, memories and flashbacks in *Memento*

Seq.	Location	Contents	Number	Time
S	City Grill	"Close your eyes, remember her"	1–13	19'28
5	Room 21	L. in his office watches people	1–8	21'55
6	Room 21	Sammy Jankis (1) exposition	1–29	26'05
7	Room 21	Sammy Jankis (2) conditioning tests	1–15	30'58
8	Room 21	Sammy Jankis (3) conditioning tests	1–18	38'07
O	Dodd's room	The night of the accident (dream)	1–13	38'50
9	Room 21	Sammy Jankis (4) Mrs Jankis tests	1–6	43'36
K	Industrial area	L. remembers his wife (objects)	1–14	51'50
J	Discount Inn – 304	The night of the accident (memories)	1–4	56'25
15	Room 21	Sammy Jankis (5) Mrs Jankis	1+1–20	60'38
E	Natalie's home	The night of the accident (flashback)	1–29	75'45
	Natalie's home	A syringe for insulin in L.'s hands	1	78'24
D	Ferdy's bar	The night of the accident (L.'s wife)	1	80'00
21	Room 21	Sammy Jankis (6) ending	1–49+4	83'48
A	Derelict building	L.'s wife alive, as Jimmy comes	1–5	93'16
	Derelict building	Teddy's revelations	1–14	98'32
	Jaguar – Strip mall	"I've done it"	1–4	105'11

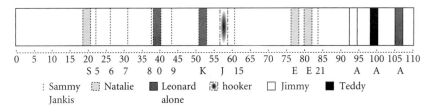

Figure 4.4   Chronology of memories in *Memento*

survived the rape, she was diabetic, Leonard injected too much insulin provoking her death.

The last four images show a false memory, a typical mental image depicting hopes or aspirations. We see Leonard on a bed with his wife. On his chest a new tattoo reads "I've done it." It is the fulfillment of the initial commitment, because by killing John G., Leonard had his revenge, but it is an imaginary situation. The fact that it appears in Leonard's mind after the killing of the wrong person puts the entire story under a different light, and we touch on the unreliability of the main character.

The cluster of mental images and memories is another example of how complex a narration can become: the list of mental images shows that they are disposed in order to obtain an increase of dramatic involvement, a feature which is missing in the chronological version of the film, where there is neither a significant improvement of knowledge nor a dramatic progression. This cluster is designed to fit the backward narration. The last four images are clear evidence in this respect: put at the beginning of the film in the chronological version they would quickly reveal Leonard's mental instability, creating a different primacy effect, based on Teddy's revelations and on Leonard's unreliability. We would simply see an impaired man manipulated by Teddy, then by Natalie, and we would quickly understand the cyclic time in which Leonard lives. The different position of these groups of images in the film contributes to a different signification, and in the chronological version the sense of a progressive discovery of clues is missing, as it is the mystery about the murder of Leonard's wife.

This difference existing between the two versions is a demonstration of the fact that Leonard's mental images and memories are not a simple catalogue: they are ordered in multiple series, explicitly designed to engage the viewers' interest. In this sense we say that they are mnemonic devices, and that they are parts of a mnemonic network of associations: they relate to one another even if they are not contiguous, and they can suggest a different signification by their repetition in new contexts, as is the case for the two groups of three images we evoked.

Owing to its particular form, *Memento* presents in fact a mnemonic system: a structured set of memory aids which parallels the two main story lines. We have already considered the matching shots, which help to create mnemonic connections between two sequences, and which help with putting in order the events depicted. When an element of the film becomes a memory device, its main function is to shift the focus of the viewer's attention to some significant detail: a comparison is made and a working hypothesis is outlined. Mnemonic connections are different from temporal or causal connections: they are free from a rigid direction as well as from strict chronological binds. They can be used as a differentiated set of memory functions, such as recognizing, comparing, anticipating, recalling, suggesting relationships, finding gaps, waiting for more details, and so forth.

Memory Moving Images

Perhaps a conclusive argument concerning the specific arrangement of elements in the original version, and their relevance as mnemonic devices, is the position of five key shots, which in their actual ordering can serve the function of recalling and summing up the whole film. They are repeated shots of the oil reservoirs, which Leonard passes when going to and coming from the derelict building.

1 (V, color)	The Jaguar passes by the oil reservoirs (going to the building).
2 (V, color)	The Jaguar enters the area in front of the derelict building; a pickup truck is parked near the building.
3 (22, black and white)	The pickup truck passes by the oil reservoirs (going to the building).
4 (22, black and white)	The pickup truck enters the area in front of the derelict building and stops.
5 (A, color)	The Jaguar passes by the oil reservoirs (coming from the building).

These shots, placed at the beginning and at the end of the film, are recognizable for their similarities, even if they change from color to black and white, and again to color. They are filmed in the same way and this quality gives rise to a comparison between the different moments of the story. The final shot, which is close to the end of the film, shows Leonard leaving Teddy, going in a direction that we know is senseless. We dare say the entire film can be understood in this shot. What lasts in the original version is a sense of uncertainty, conveyed by the open-ended conclusion of this sequence. The difference with the chronological version is striking, because as the arrangement follows the chronological order, the sequence is different: 3, 4, 5, 1, 2. We only see the characters' movements from and to the derelict building: the first time Leonard enters the area, then he goes out driving Jimmy's Jaguar, and finally he drives Teddy to the building before killing him. With this arrangement, the effect created in the original version is lost: the significance of the directions of movement is missing, the sense of the actions is misplaced.

Final Considerations

Memento is a complex film about memory and oblivion, about time elapsed, and about remembering. It tells the story of a "ten minute guy," who would be unable, as Sammy Jankis was, to remember an entire film. The viewer is invited to use his or her cognitive and memorial skills to comprehend what the main character is unable to master. If Leonard lacks the possibility of seeing the situation of his current life in its totality, the viewer can take this wide-range look.

The whole film is immersed in the past, and we can say that it is entirely based upon a memorial dimension, structured and reconstructed on the basis of the viewer's memory of selected images. In fact the most advanced point in time is not an action, but an image: the Polaroid photograph taken to document the past, after Teddy's death. We can see no future events, no successive actions from this point. If we want to know something more about the causes of the killing, we have to turn back in time. So memory is at stake, as well as the lack of memory. While watching the film, we can "feel" our own capabilities, because the main character lacks his own. *Memento*, like other contemporary films, offers the opportunity of considering this particular form of aesthetic response: we can study the viewer's experience of his or her mental absorption in a complex film, and the ensuing effects.

Bibliography

Bordwell, D. 1985. *Narration in the Fiction Film*. London: Routledge.

Carruthers, M. 1990. *The Book of Memory*. Cambridge: Cambridge University Press.

Klein, A. 2001. "Everything you wanted to know about *Memento*." http://archive.salon.com/ent/movies/feature/2001/06/28/memento_analysis/index.html (accessed December 30, 2006).

Tulving, E. 1972. "Episodic and semantic memory," in E. Tulving and W. Donaldson (eds.), *Organization of Memory*. New York: Academic Press, pp. 381–403.

5

"Frustrated Time" Narration: The Screenplays of Charlie Kaufman

Chris Dzialo

Charlie Kaufman's scripts exist as a contemporary configuration of complex storytelling – a historical phenomenon with a long genealogy in both literature and film. Proust's *À la recherche du temps perdu*, or films inspired by this exemplar of complex narration, such as *Time Regained* (dir. Raul Ruiz, 2000), have obvious correspondences to the insistent yet stubbornly hazy time frames of Kaufman. His films, such as *Being John Malkovich* (dir. Spike Jonze, 1999) and *Confessions of a Dangerous Mind* (dir. George Clooney, 2002), sometimes embody what Edward Branigan (2002) terms the "nearly true" or, borrowing and modifying David Bordwell's (2002) useful appropriation of Daniel Dennett's term, a "multiple drafts" style of filmic narration (see Branigan 2002, p. 108).

Notably, however, Kaufman's films always have one foot comfortably within the Hollywood studio system, ensuring that major plot elements are always comprehensible. Thus, Kaufman's films are not arguably *as* complex as Proust's novel or Ruiz's adaptation, for example, and "multiple drafts" may not be the most accurate heuristic to describe his work. Unlike classical narration, which does all it can to hide parallels and alternatives to preserve the illusion of unity, or "forking-path" narratives, such as *Sliding Doors* (dir. Peter Howitt, 1998), which "flaunt their parallels," the "multiple drafts" version of narration for Branigan embodies "a relationship among parallels and alternatives [that] is neither flaunted nor buried, but is ambiguous or indeterminate" (2002, p. 107). Although Kaufman follows many classical conventions, and can't resist underscoring many parallels, his films also traffic in the ambiguous and indeterminate. Certain elements, especially his use of time, remain indecipherable even after repeated viewings. In this way, they seem to occupy a more central place between "simple" and "complex" narration than many of the films Branigan uses to illustrate his claims.

Moreover, it is tempting to see Kaufman's work as seeding an intertextual matrix for a particular cycle of *relatively* complex contemporary cinema, in which the hero (usually a writer or artist) must write him or herself out of temporal indeterminacy. There is always a battle against time – but not usually in terms of beating deadlines. In Kaufman's narratives, there is dissatisfaction with the very concept of time (and time's arrow) in general, even as the necessity of the irreversibility of the arrow is signposted through stylistic elements. *Adaptation* (dir. Spike Jonze, 2002) and *Human Nature* (dir. Michel Gondry, 2001) illustrate the futility of writers struggling against adapting and evolving. *Being John Malkovich* is about an artist failing to conquer his own mortality, literally and creatively. *Eternal Sunshine of the Spotless Mind*'s (dir. Michel Gondry, 2004) antagonist constructs a time machine of sorts that only operates in the present, on the protagonist's memory.

Such frustration is also evident in other contemporary films such as *Science of Sleep* (dir. Michel Gondry, 2006), in which the artist hero constructs a campy time machine capable of going back only one second into the past; *Memento* (dir. Christopher Nolan, 2000), in which the protagonist struggles to write himself out of time's grip, or perhaps back into it, with tattoos and Polaroid pictures; *Stranger Than Fiction* (dir. Marc Forster, 2006), in which a wristwatch seems to be narrating the main character's destiny; *Irreversible* (dir. Gaspar Noé, 2002), which is told backward in time, perhaps in ironic attempts to erase the trauma of rape and revenge; and also in big-budget tent-pole pictures, such as *Click* (dir. Frank Coraci, 2006) and *Déjà Vu* (dir. Tony Scott, 2006). In all of these films, and with the majority of Kaufman's work, there is simultaneously a desire to beat, manipulate, or even destroy/obviate time as a variable, countered by the demands of narrative clarity and the irreversible nature of projection time. I shall refer to this push-and-pull mode of storytelling – between reversibility vs. irreversibility, formal complexity vs. narrative simplicity, space vs. time – as "frustrated time" narration.

The battle "against" time as a concept or variable that we have to "deal with" is nothing new, and throughout history has cropped up in philosophy, art, and the natural sciences. I intend for "frustrated time" narration, however, to stand as a symptom in this cycle of recent films – to crystallize our continuing bafflement with time and the intensified contemporary, popular desire (and inability) to contain it or eliminate it completely as a problem technologically (e.g., via the internet, cell phones, etc.). In most of these narratives, the desire to "frustrate" time (to dam up the river or twist the arrow) fails or even backfires, in many cases leading to the psychological frustration of the characters and spectators. Thus there is potentially a double or triple frustration or deferment, which serves ironically to delay and therefore amplify our pleasure. But we only want to *play* with the arrow, not destroy it; after all, if there is no arrow, there is no future, and therefore no chance for pleasure.

Nonetheless, with Kaufman I see a particularly strong yearning to break free from projector time, which is irreversible, linear, and simple. Instead, for him as "author" there seems to be a frustrating and ultimately unrealized desire to live in the reversible, mutable, contingent, and complex time of consciousness. His characters, on the other hand, generally crave linearity and chronology, though are always frustrated by Kaufman's temporal manipulations. The resultant tug-of-war leaves the spectator in the lurch. We, therefore, are the ones who are most "frustrated" by the fissure created by the simultaneous surfeit and lack of complex time.

My analysis of his script for *Adaptation* centers on how this work is both simultaneously simple and complex as it revels in "the impossibility of establishing a precise chronology" or "achronicity," as Mieke Bal terms this phenomenon (1997, p. 213). This is not an immediate impediment for the narrative meaning, however, as this temporal complexity is only fully realized after experiencing the work as a whole, and upon detailed reflection. *Adaptation*, therefore, works in the opposite manner than "more complex" films (such as *Time Regained* or *Last Year at Marienbad* [Alain Resnais, 1961], etc.), in which confusion produced by the work's temporal complexity is the primary experience, and narrative comprehension comes only at the end, if at all.

Eternal Sunshine might be viewed as "simpler" than *Adaptation*, given that virtually all temporal manipulations occur in the filmic present, inside the protagonist's head. However, I will argue that the script – and its attempts at spatializing multiple simultaneous time-frames graphically on the page – can be read as a treatise against projector time.

Crucial to my arguments about both *Adaptation* and *Eternal Sunshine* is the supposition that screenplays should be experienced not as a literary text (cf. Sternberg 1997; Mota 2005; Kohn 2000), as a form in between film and literature (cf. Pasolini 1999), or as a mere blueprint for a final celluloid (or digital) film, but as a form of cinema itself. I make this claim because of the ontological properties screenplays share with film: both, although via opposite polarities, are audio-visual (the screenplay cueing the images and sounds in our mind) and both have an *approximately* standardized running time (24 frames per second for film in the US, 25 frames per second elsewhere, and 1 page per minute for screenplays when "adapted" to celluloid).[1] It is impossible to do this sort of time-to-distance (i.e., speed) "clocking" with literary forms such as poetry and novels, which have no idealized reading time. A page of screenplay text, on the other hand – always rigorously formatted and standardized, down to the size and type of the font – takes about 25 seconds to read according to one estimate (Boyle, in Sternberg 1997, p. 78). Surely this varies, especially from one reader to another, but the idealized times of both projection and reading nonetheless quietly lurk in the ink and wood pulp.

It is for these reasons that I am choosing to examine the screenplays of Charlie Kaufman, with only passing, comparative reference to the celluloid films. Also crucial to my argument, however, is to recognize the ontological properties screenplays do *not* necessarily share with celluloid. In 1985 David Bordwell wrote, before the era of DVDs or DVRs:

> Under normal viewing circumstances, the film absolutely controls the order, frequency, and duration of the presentation of events. You cannot skip a dull spot or linger over a rich one, jump back to an earlier passage or start at the end of the film and work your way forward. (p. 74)

Since then, many filmmakers have seemingly embraced the chance to tell complex stories perhaps best suited for DVDs and other digital formats, which allow for a high degree of temporal manipulation by the viewer (cf. Bordwell 2006, p. 74). The statement above, however, has always been completely untrue of the screenplay and scenario, and their "viewing" contexts. If Charlie Kaufman's films are frustrated with losing the battle to time's arrow and the irreversible time of projection, then his screenplays (and our relationships with them) provide a glimpse of what total control and dominance over time – to the point of its annihilation – would allow us to experience. Thus, I am reading (and imagining) Charlie Kaufman's screenplays as the untenable ideal that "frustrated time" narration self-consciously seeks but always defers.

Complex Times and *Adaptation*

Most striking about reading the script *Adaptation* (a semi-fictionalized account of Charlie Kaufman and his imaginary brother, Donald [both played by Nicholas Cage in the film], adapting Susan Orlean's book *The Orchid Thief* into a screenplay) is the sheer audacity of the 10 temporal titles.[2] The second title, for example, is to "four billion and forty years earlier" and occurs only on page 3 of the script. Kaufman quite playfully, however, refuses to inform us through a title or other obvious marker in the script when we flash forward or back to the "present," instead letting us rely on sometimes subtle contextual clues. These clues are left especially hazy in the screenplay. While jarring at times, this complexity is usually not an impediment for the meaning – even if we're not completely sure of the *exact* present we inhabit at a particular moment.

The resultant temporal and spatial hi-jinks do not upend our experience of the story (or potential *stories*) perhaps because such entanglements mirror the fragmented potential stories of each day in ordinary life. After all, time itself is arguably complex. In fact, one should speak of different time*s* as opposed to one universal time. Each "time" is relative from one person to the next: a person traveling in a spaceship near the speed of light might only experience the passing of one year, whereas back on Earth decades will elapse. Such temporal relativity occurs in daily life, too – there is a time dilation, however slight, when objects move at any speed (e.g., walking up stairs). Passengers onboard a flight from Los Angeles to New York will have aged a few nanoseconds less than those on the ground. Time travel in a film, effected through moving at very fast speeds (e.g., *Flight of the Navigator* [1986], *Star Trek IV: The Voyage Home* [1986], *Event Horizon* [1997]) is not, therefore, all that far from the reality of things. Reading a screenplay also makes time relative, in the sense that two people will experience nearly the same amount of story/plot (fabula/syuzhet)[3] time but likely will live wholly different reading (projection) times.

A reader curled up with a script arguably embodies a complex system, which Paul Cilliers (1998) defines as that which "as a whole cannot be fully understood simply by analyzing its components. Moreover, these relationships are not fixed, but shift and change, often as a result of self-organization" (pp. viii–ix). While the reader might do most of the "self-organizing," we may think about how the physical nature of the script also puts constraints on the "reader/script" system (we listen to iPods and don't read scripts while jogging, for instance). Also, the relationships shift and change, differently than while sitting in a movie theater. Script pages might be flipped faster, for example, if the reader is in suspense and free from distractions. *Adaptation*, with its focus on both evolutionary and literary adaptation, combats the seemingly ineluctable march toward disorder with a complex, shifting network of temporalities – a "fight" made easier, perhaps, on the page.

Kaufman indeed exploits the ambiguities inherent in written language to further complicate these temporalities. For example, two title-cards on page 6 of the script situate us in Florida, in roughly the year 1993. Once the story about Laroche's (the orchid poacher's) apprehension by Ranger Tony in the Everglades finishes on page 9, we don't return to Susan Orlean (Meryl Streep on celluloid) in New York in 1995 or receive any other framing information. Instead, without any temporal or spatial "correction," or even a CUT TO title,[4] we jump to Charlie Kaufman in Los Angeles, in what we believe is the year 1998:

> RANGER TONY
> Yeah, but I don't . . . Uhh, I can't let
> you fellas leave yet. Just hold on there
> a minute. Okay?

INT. EMPTY HOUSE – DAY

Kaufman enters the house dejectedly. He climbs the stairs.

Such transitions abound in the script: a title will conspicuously announce a time shift, but then allow the subtle "shift back" to be to a different place or time entirely. While this occurs in many films, what is remarkable is its frequency and cumulative effect in *Adaptation*, especially in the shooting script – which is, after all, generally supposed to avoid ambiguity.

Kaufman-as-writer, however, exploits the slippage made possible by screenplays' reliance on both first (morphemes) and second articulation (graphemes) to his advantage. In the celluloid film, which has no double articulation, Kaufman-as-character must wear a particular, specific, and indexical costume. Thus, director Spike Jonze must make a choice: Is Kaufman coming home from his lunch meeting, from two scenes earlier the same day? Or is this a different day entirely? The screenwriter, not trapped by Metz's (1999) doggedly persistent filmic image,[5] is free to let this remain murky.

Jonze – perhaps in attempts to get around this pesky visual specificity – dresses Kaufman's character in the same costume for the vast majority of the film: an open plaid flannel shirt over a gray t-shirt. Orlean wears similar but recognizably different clothes for most disparate scenes – but interestingly wears the same beige nightgown to bed in New York and in

Florida at (supposedly different) time periods near the conclusion of the narrative (including a hallucinatory sequence brought about by ingesting the drug made from the ghost orchid). By failing to "take advantage" of the specificity the film image affords, Jonze exploits an intrinsic property of the screenplay and thus further complicates the celluloid film's time-frames.

Charlie Kaufman must make choices as well, but the screenplay format is more slippery than film in terms of *mise-en-scène*, figure movement, editing, costuming, etc. Moreover, screenwriters are taught to be economical with dialogue and description (cf. Hunter 1993). Kaufman, in a way, follows the letter, but not the spirit, of this rule by refusing to clarify important visual details. There are hardly, if any, references to costumes, for example. When reading the script, therefore, we are relatively certain of the general temporal era (i.e., the late 1990s as opposed to the Late Cretaceous) but increasingly grow confused as to the exact year or date. Such a move might not be exceptional, except for the clear attempts to (ironically) suggest a definite time frame or logic, vis-à-vis the temporal title-cards.

Indeed, it is impossible to assign only one coherent temporal progression to the screenplay, owing to various inconsistencies between the title-cards and diegesis. The reading below illustrates one reasonable time-frame for the script, in which events unfold slowly over a series of years between approximately 1993 and as late as 2000. Owing to the number of scenes occurring between and unannounced by these title-cards – in Florida, New York, and Los Angeles, in different time periods – the date ranges become gradually less certain. Each range indicates the possible years in which the events between the title-cards could occur:

1998	TITLE: ON THE SET OF "BEING JOHN MALKOVICH" SUMMER 1998 (p. 1)
	TITLE: FOUR BILLION AND FORTY YEARS EARLIER (p. 3)
1995	TITLE: NEW YORKER MAGAZINE, THREE YEARS EARLIER (p. 6)
1993	TITLE: STATE ROAD 29, FLORIDA, TWO YEARS EARLIER (p. 6)[6]
1895–1898	TITLE: ORINCO RIVER, ONE HUNDRED YEARS EARLIER (p. 14)
1995–1998	TITLE: FLORIDA, THREE YEARS EARLIER (p. 19)
1859	TITLE: ENGLAND, ONE HUNDRED AND THIRTY NINE YEARS EARLIER (p. 40)
1986–1989	TITLE: NORTH MIAMI NINE YEARS EARLIER (p. 44)
1998–2000	TITLE: THREE YEARS LATER (p. 63)
1995–1998	TITLE: FAKAHATCHEE THREE YEARS EARLIER (p. 79)

In this version, the reader assumes that the complicated plot regarding Orlean
and Laroche takes a number of years to unfold, and includes times from
1993, 1995, 1996, 1997, 1998, and even 1999 and perhaps 2000 – if we assume
that we move past the "now" of 1998 by the end of the film.

Further sources of confusion (besides Hurricane Andrew occurring
during the "wrong" year)[7] are the flashbacks of Orlean in New York. Is she
writing her *New Yorker* articles, in approximately 1995? Or is she working
on her book, a year or two or three later? Do we always come back to the
same scene, or do we see her writing at different points in time? This becomes
a question of temporal "frequency" for Gérard Genette (1980). Perhaps
we are seeing several singulative actions one time each ("narrating *n* times
what happened *n* times" [Genette 1980, p. 114]), or seeing one singulative
action repeated several times over ("narrating *n* times what happened once"
[p. 115]). Alternately, is each scene of Orlean typing actually a case of the
iterative ("narrating one time [or rather: at one time] what happened *n*
times" [p. 116]), in effect "standing in" for all such typical instances? Various
combinations of all three, at different times (i.e., narrating three times what
happened twice? Narrating three times what happened ten times?) We're
never quite sure, in the script at least.

Brian Henderson (1999), examining a sequence from *How Green Was
My Valley* (1941), marvels at how the voiceover narration and onscreen
action "almost imperceptibly" shift, when Huw meets Bronwen, from the
iterative to the singulative. Henderson remarks that "most interesting,
theoretically, is how and why such a slippage is possible in cinematic
iterative" (Henderson 1999, p. 66). He concludes that although it might
appear cinema only traffics in the singulative (owing to its indexicality),
the complexity of cinema as a system helps fulfill Metz's dictum that "the
fact to be understood is that films are understood, including the cinematic
iterative" (Henderson 1999, p. 67). He adds, however, that:

> Nevertheless, the singulative tendency of recorded sounds and images can
> have a backlash effect on iterative constructions. *How Green Was My Valley*
> goes from the iterative to the singulative by virtue of a tense change in the
> voiceover. A much more frequent figure is a scene that begins in the itera-
> tive, by virtue of a title or a voiceover, then becomes singulative, as though
> reverting to the singulative in the absence of continued linguistic definition
> to the contrary. (p. 67)

Thus, Henderson locates in the voiceover and title-cards a certain power,
an ability to confer a sense of the iterative on what might seem to be singulative in nature. Screenplays, based on written language, do not suffer

from this "problem." Kaufman, notably, over-uses both temporal titles as well as voiceover narration in his script. Screenwriting guru Robert McKee pointedly chastises his character at one point to avoid voiceover narration in screenplays, calling it "flaccid, sloppy writing" (p. 68). Is this an attempt to force the ambiguity of the iterative, from one form to another – and to where it might not belong?

Furthermore, the interpretation of the list of title-cards above satisfies one temporal logic; the notion that in life events *take time* to fully develop. Thus the beginning of the story is 1993, and the end of the story is "now." We might assume that the middle of the story, or its "core," will be the intervening years, with perhaps a few flashbacks or flashforwards out of and back into this territory. This recalls the "durative" tense – in which past events unfold somewhat slowly and continuously, matching roughly to the imperfect verb tense in the Romance languages (Bal 1997, p. 93).

Why, then, would title-cards be required? Indeed, the titles and their seemingly random deployment work against and compete with such an intuitive reading. Now, instead, we fear we have missed something. Our internal chronometers are jarred whenever we see one of the five inter-titles with the words "three years earlier/later" or "two years earlier" in them, in that we instantly want to assign specific years in order to have every-thing link together coherently. Furthermore, we reasonably assume, owing to the repeated invocation of such a specific quantity of time (two or three years), that the titles refer back to the *same* three years so that "three years earlier" cues us to 1995, "two years earlier" cues us to 1993, and "three years later" cues us back to 1998. Through this reading, we hypothesize that all the titles – except for the "two years earlier" title – are global, and refer to the "now" of 1998. If we use this logic, the temporal unfolding of the script reads as follows:

1998   <u>TITLE</u>: ON THE SET OF "BEING JOHN MALKOVICH" SUMMER 1998 (p. 1)
        <u>TITLE</u>: FOUR BILLION AND FORTY YEARS EARLIER (p. 3)
1995   <u>TITLE</u>: NEW YORKER MAGAZINE, THREE YEARS EARLIER (p. 6)
1993   <u>TITLE</u>: STATE ROAD 29, FLORIDA, TWO YEARS EARLIER (p. 6)
1895   <u>TITLE</u>: ORINCO RIVER, ONE HUNDRED YEARS EARLIER (p. 14)
1995   <u>TITLE</u>: FLORIDA, THREE YEARS EARLIER (p. 19)
1859   <u>TITLE</u>: ENGLAND, ONE HUNDRED AND THIRTY NINE YEARS EARLIER (p. 40)
1986   <u>TITLE</u>: NORTH MIAMI NINE YEARS EARLIER (p. 44)
1998   <u>TITLE</u>: THREE YEARS LATER (p. 63)
1995   <u>TITLE</u>: FAKAHATCHEE THREE YEARS EARLIER (p. 79)]

In this version, the logic of the inter-titles is explicit and consistent, but we scratch our heads and wonder what was so special about those three years of 1993, 1995, and 1998. Why does nothing occur during the gaps between these years?

This is the opposite of the "durative" tense, and more closely matches the "punctual" tense – aligning with the preterite/passé simple tense in the Romance languages (Bal 1997, p. 93). Here, specific actions occupy a brief, demarcated amount of time. Mieke Bal writes that the "punctual anachrony sometimes makes for a businesslike style" and, conversely, that "the reader quickly receives the impression that nothing particularly spectacular is happening" if the durative is relied upon. The "systematic combination" of *both* punctual and durative helps foment "the impression that the story is developing according to clear, causative laws: a certain event causes a situation to emerge which makes another event possible, and so on." She notes in *À la recherche du temps perdu* a productively confusing conflation of the two forms, remarking that "in this risky play with time, Proust announces the postmodernist experimental novel half a century beforehand" (p. 94).

Kaufman, in a sense, takes risks by *not* conflating these two tenses. Bal labels "a deviation of time which cannot be analyzed any further" as an "achrony" (p. 97). In the same vein, we may read the script as a series of punctual events taking place in specific, bounded years – or, we may choose to see the story in a more durative sense, over spans of years. We cannot comfortably do both, however. Such is the result of the clash between insistently punctual title-cards versus the durative nature of the events involved (it is a film putatively about orchids, after all), along with the anachronistic *Vent d'Est* of Hurricane Andrew that manages to disrupt both readings.

Returning to the iterative vs. the singulative, Marsha Kinder (1999) argues the iterative is "inherent in cinema" (p. 131) but that Hollywood classical cinema "uses iterative implications to naturalize the singulative and [render] the slippage between the two aspects invisible" (p. 129). She adds:

> [I]f the iterative implications and the slippage between the two aspects were ever foregrounded, then they would potentially call attention to the process of naturalizing ideology through the reading of singulative events of fiction as universal truth, a reading that reinforces the dominant cultural paradigms and genres. (p. 133)

Kinder then goes on to examine several avant-garde and Italian neorealist modes of foregrounding this slippage. Perhaps we might view Kaufman's work as not quite as explicitly calling attention to the apparent slippage between different forms of the singulative, or between the iterative and the singulative, or between the durative and punctual; rather, by conspicuously ignoring such slippages, they become thrown into relief at the conclusion of the film or script, perhaps subconsciously, while not disturbing comprehension of the narrative. Not just one time, but several times, they are frustrated and made mutually exclusive while reading *Adaptation*.

Eternal Sunshine of the Spotless Mind: Don't Break the Projector

With *Eternal Sunshine of the Spotless Mind*, Kaufman exploits not the textual and temporal slippage inherent in the screenplay's use of graphemes, but the conflation of time and space this form encourages. The story, in which the protagonist (named Joel, played by Jim Carrey in the film) attempts to stave off the Lacuna Corporation from erasing his bittersweet memories of girlfriend Clementine (Kate Winslet), by hiding out in different parts (cells, scenes, times) of his memory, provides a corollary to this conflation in the narrative. If *Adaptation* is ultimately about how time is relative and complex, then the script of *Eternal Sunshine* is about the dissatisfaction with time's arrow, and symptomatizes the struggle against the endless erasure of projector time. That is, *Eternal Sunshine* invites us to think about time in terms of space. However, space becomes not just a representation or signifier of time, but threatens to metastasize and replace time.

Such a move is not unique. Rudolf Arnheim writes about the apparent "priority of space" in visual perceptual studies and art hermeneutics (Arnheim 1986, p. 79). The concept of "block time," in which "past, present and future must be equally real" and "all of eternity is laid out [simultaneously] in a four-dimensional block composed of time and the three spatial dimensions" (Davies 2006, p. 9) is seemingly becoming a more popular paradigm with scientists. Prominent physicist Julian Barbour argues "against" time even more vociferously, as evidenced in the title of his book *The End of Time: The Next Revolution in Physics* (1999). For him, time does not exist at all – only a vast synchronic "land" he calls Platonia, which possesses an asymmetrical structure:

> [T]he great asymmetries of our existence – past and future, birth and death – arise from a deep asymmetry in being itself. The land of possible things has one absolute end, where it abuts onto mere nothing, but it is unbounded the other way, for there is no limit to the richness of being. (p. 55)

Might the shift in the scientific paradigm, in which time is forsaken for space, have something to do with our popular frustration with time?

The most apparent spatial-temporal conflation in the script for *Eternal Sunshine* takes place through the constant referencing of Joel's brain as a "map" of memories by Dr Mierzwiak, Patrick and Stan of the Lacuna Corporation, whom Joel has enlisted to erase his memories of Clementine. Stan, at the keyboard of his computer next to an unconscious Joel, exclaims such things as "He's off the screen" (p. 69) and "He's disappeared from the map. I can't find him anywhere" (p. 71). Implicit military and tactical spatial metaphors also abound in the description/action sections as well:

> Mierzwiak locates a light hidden very deep in the map of Joel's brain. He targets it. (p. 88)

The Lacuna Corporation views this map as an ideal *representation* of chronological time and memory, around which to pattern the *actual* chronology and memory. Responding to Joel's question about whether or not he is "in my head already," Dr Mierzwiak looks around and says "I suppose so, yes. [. . .] This is what it would look like" to which Stan replies "we're getting healthy read-outs" (p. 39). Such representations and read-outs start to stand in for the real thing, prompting the film's existential crisis. They also parallel the way in which Stephen Mamber (2003) argues narrative maps may operate:

> [Maps] can stand in for, even replace, that which they seek to model. Particularly with complex instances of narrative structure, they can do what all good maps do – offer a visually readable opportunity to see both grand contours and areas of specific interest. A narrative map, as it seeks to provide a visual theory of the work (or the event) subsequently vies with the original (and other possible mappings). (p. 146)

Dr Mierzwiak and the Lacuna Corporation are attempting to do something analogous to this; not only to map but to *replace* the actual, flawed, complex narrative of Joel's consciousness with a new, ideal, simpler one, in the form of an easy-to-read computerized map. Here, we have a bittersweet conception of time. Kaufman "maps" space and its representations as a powerful but potentially simplifying destructive force that may interfere with the "natural" chronology and complex interplay of time and memory. Such tensions and contradictions pop up frequently in "frustrated time" films. The popular imagination perhaps wants to have its cake and to eat it, too. We want to control and therefore vanquish the ravages of time (through laptop computers, the internet, computerized maps, etc.), but not at the expense of our humanity.

Attenuating this anxiety slightly is the representation of Clementine and Joel in Joel's memory. They exist not in a simplified representation of his memory but a phenomenal, complex, and dynamic spatiotemporal geography. Instead of a computer map to plot his memories in the "real" world, Joel uses a loose-leaf journal – though one in which all the pages are curiously blank. When Joel, inside his mind, decides he does not want to forget Clementine and tries instead to outrun the destruction of his memories of her, spatiotemporal metaphors still abound:

> Clementine
> (formulating)
> I mean, here. This is a memory of me.
> The way you wanted to fuck on the couch
> after you looked down at my crotch.

> Joel
> (embarrassed)
> Yeah.

> Clementine
> Well then they're coming here. So what
> if you take me somewhere else, somewhere
> where I don't belong?
> (proud)
> And we hid there till morning? (p. 67)

After this suggestion from Clementine (or, Joel's memory of Clementine), the real fun of the film begins. Joel takes Clementine where (really *when*) she doesn't belong, in attempts to avoid the memory-erasing computer. This results in their "traveling" to his infancy and adolescence.

However, soon the Lacuna team finds them in these parts of Joel's memory, and starts the destruction anew. The projector always claws inexorably forward, drawing in the future ("the past" from the point of view of the narrator), illuminating it in the present, and discarding it on the take-up reel (the past). According to Mary Ann Doane:

> In his essay on photography, Kracauer claims, 'A shudder runs through the viewer of old photographs. For they make visible not the knowledge of the original but the spatial configuration of a moment'. Similarly, film makes visible not a knowledge of the original but a certain passing temporal configuration. The grandchildren in Kracauer's essay shudder when confronted with the photograph of the grandmother because they see not the grand-mother but an image of time, and a time that is not necessary but contin-gent. This is the pathos of archival desire. (2002, p. 23)

Joel tries to hold on to the contingent, to a "certain passing temporal configuration," but is frustrated time and time again. This is particularly traumatic when, hiding with Clementine in a memory of being bathed as a child by his mother in the sink, the scene fades, and Joel is sucked down the sink. He finds himself watching a drive-in movie with Clementine – who impersonates the characters onscreen:

> CLEMENTINE
> Yes, but who could love a man named
> Wally?

She starts to fade. Joel looks confused. The scene starts to fade.

> JOEL
> (remembering)
> Oh!

> CLEMENTINE
> Shhh! I want to watch the movie!

> JOEL
> Clem, think! They'll find you here.

He looks over and she's gone. (p. 77)

After we see Mierzwiak deleting the blip of memory from the computer screen, Joel actually wills Clementine back into existence (making the blip on the screen, outside, reappear as well) by exclaiming "Tangerine" – his pet name for her, based on her fiery hair color. This recalls yet another form of writing/imagining. When Joel "first" meets Clementine, she day-dreams about a job in which she will write clever names for hair dyes: "My writing career! Your hair written by Clementine Kruczynski" (p. 7). In order to escape the cruel time of projection in the scenes above, Joel must travel beyond the passing temporality of the film at the drive-in. Only by "writing" Clementine through her hair color is he able to "read" her – causing the blip, the presence of the past, to reappear again.

Perhaps what is being sublimated here, in the desire to hang on to a "passing temporal configuration," is a yearning for what is in some senses "reversible" (writing, scripts) over what is irreversible (a projected film, dyed hair). Projector time lurks in the background of the script, but we are free or even encouraged to flip back and forth through the pages in order to aide our comprehension of the repeated flashbacks. Charlie Kaufman on this point says:

> . . . The big problem with the script is that cause and effect are reversed, and I didn't know how that played. I mean, it plays okay on paper because you can kind of flip back and go, Oh, okay, I understand why that happened. . . . (in Feld 2004, p. 136)

Besides the spatial-temporal conflation inherent in the narrative and diegesis, the graphical way Kaufman chooses to lay out his words on the page also speaks to a desire to overcome the time of projection:

JOEL
You said —

She picks a drumstick off of Joel's plate.

CLEMENTINE	JOEL
I'm Clementine. Can I Borrow a piece of your Chicken?	And you picked it out of my plate before I could answer And it felt so intimate like We were already lovers.
JOEL (CONT'D)	VOICEOVER
I remember —	The grease on your chin in the bonfire light.

Shot of a smudge of chicken grease on Clementine's chin.

CLEMENTINE
Oh God, how horrid.

JOEL	VOICEOVER
I'm Joel.	No, it was lovely. (p. 100)

Here, Kaufman presents dialogue simultaneously, which is not an uncommon script convention. Certainly less common is how he presents dialogue from the same character (Joel) at the same *time*, especially when this character seems to be existing in several different *times*. It is unclear, interestingly enough, to which time frame Clementine belongs, when she says "How horrid." Anchored in the middle of the page, she seems to exist ironically (or perhaps fittingly, for Hollywood classical cinema) outside time.

   Also unclear is how Kaufman intends this all to translate into celluloid. Indeed, he remarks:

> [There's] dual dialogue. Voiceover and dialogue happening at the same time. Which didn't end up in the movie, really. It's in the script. I was really interested in seeing how that would work and how that would feel. And that's the issue of having the two Joels: having a Joel in the scene and having the Joel watching and commenting on it. Because he's trying to stop it, you know. And to me that's the real experience of memory. (in Feld, p. 138)

While possible in celluloid, overlapping dialogue can be extremely difficult to comprehend. Even with multiple rewinding and reviewing, sometimes the dialogue track is just too muddied.[8] The screenplay format allows dialogue snippets to be read individually, and then to be imagined (later) as spoken simultaneously. Or, one may even put the script on the floor, stand up and read both sides of the dialogue all at once (an exhausting exercise, though, for more than a few words). Celluloid can display multiple elements on the screen simultaneously, and cross-cutting is a way to approximate simultaneity of different narrative strands. However, each of these elements is still in some ways beholden to projector time. For Doane:

> Film narrative can and does depend upon the temporal aberrations of memories and projections, incarnated in flashbacks, flashforwards, and radical ellipse. Each of these, however, depends upon the cut. [. . .] Within the unit of time covered by the flashback, time is irreversible; the linear 'forward' nature of movement is acknowledged and honored. (p. 131)

Of course, the screenplay is in some senses irreversible. We can't read letters, words, or sentences backward. But in a relative sense, it is *more* reversible than celluloid or video. The phrase or sentence becomes the primary unit, not the shot as it is for Metz (which, interestingly, he equates to the sentence). A shot may be composed of several, or even many, sentences in a screenplay. Or one sentence might equal several, or even many, shots. Thus, although the cut might seemingly function as a guarantee of irreversibility (although this discounts multiple, competing temporal durations and directions that might occur within the *same* shot via split-screen), in the screenplay such "guarantees" are more difficult, if not impossible, to pin down.

Kaufman's most overt assault on linear projector time occurs near the end of the script. In this scene, Clementine plays the tape of her memory-erasing consultation at Lacuna Corporation, while she and Joel sit in his car. The strip of audio-tape dialogue is drawn graphically with single, non-overlapping dialogue, which never "splits" across the page. On the other hand Clementine and Joel's comments on this linear, mechanical, and irreversible progression (which, indeed, threatens irreversibly to break them up) often sit astride this line, simultaneously, challenging its very linearity:

> CLEMENTINE'S VOICE [on tape]
> Well, he's a giant asshole. Is that
> enough?

> MIERZWIAK'S VOICE [on tape]
> No, I'm afraid we really do need to
> delve.

> JOEL
> What is this?

> CLEMENTINE
> I don't know.

> CLEMENTINE'S VOICE
> I can't stand to even look at him.
> [. . .] Is it so much to ask for an
> actual man to have sex with?

JOEL	CLEMENTINE
What are you doing?	I'm not doing anything.

CLEMENTINE'S VOICE (CONT'D)
... I might as well be a lesbian. At
least I could have someone to look
at while I'm fucking. [. . .]

JOEL	CLEMENTINE
Why did you make this tape?	I didn't do this!
I completely don't understand	
what you're doing.	

JOEL	CLEMENTINE
It's your voice!	I know!

CLEMENTINE'S VOICE (CONT'D)
... Now the only fuel keeping it going is
my feeling sorry for him. [. . .]

CLEMENTINE
Joel, I don't understand. I swear.

CLEMENTINE'S VOICE
... I remember this time I made him come
out onto this frozen river with me. He
was terrified. Like a goddamn girl ...

Joel turns the car around.

JOEL
So someone just recorded you saying this
without you knowing you were saying it.

CLEMENTINE	JOEL
I don't know! Maybe it's	This is fucked up! That's
Some kind of Future thing,	rididculous [sic]. This is fucked
Like a look into the future.	Up! It's called A Christmas
Like that thing in Scrooge!	Carol, not Scrooge.
Maybe some force is trying to	
help us. I think I've read	
about that happening. I'm	
sure I have.	

> CLEMENTINE'S VOICE
> . . . Ugh. I don't want to think about all
> The time I've wasted in this quote–
> unquote relationship. Isn't it about
> fun? (pp. 121–2)

Here, the cold, mechanical hissing time of projection is represented by the two-dimensional, chronological linearity of the audio-tape strip. When Clementine and Joel begin to finally deal with the trauma this memory erasing has caused, and to confront one another, the dialogue splits across the page and becomes simultaneous and reversible. At the very end of the script, however, and before they resume their relationship, Clementine reminds Joel that their future may be difficult – thus reinscribing time's arrow, and with it the possibility for more pain as well as pleasure.

Change is not a Choice

To discount the arrow's existence, or to stymie it into retreat via technology, is to tread into territory previously only open to metaphysics. As Susan Orlean says in *Adaptation*:

> ORLEAN (VOICE OVER)
> What I came to understand is that change
> is not a choice. Not for a species of
> plant, and not for me. It happens, and
> you are different. (p. 79)

In my reading, Kaufman wants to "change" classical Hollywood storytelling and the way it is experienced to make it more complex, like flipping back and forth through a screenplay. Thus he even plays with the idea of eviscerating the arrow altogether, to the great frustration of his characters. However, Kaufman realizes that "change" in a different sense (i.e., the change from frame to frame that creates movement; cause and effect; narrative progression) is also wholly unavoidable in the classical Hollywood cinema.

To obliterate the arrow is to throw oneself into a place where narrative does not exist (to the timeless close-up shots of orchids in *Adaptation*, to structural film, etc.). "Frustrated time" narratives use (relatively) complex narrational strategies to try to make time compliant, but ultimately the river always resists and breaks the dam, leaving the spectator frustratingly unmoored between a rock (reversibility, achronicity, complexity) and a hard place (irreversibility, chronology, and simplicity). Our popular ambiguity over both the positive and negative facets of an increasingly "time-shrinking," electronic, synchronic existence perhaps becomes increasingly symptomatized in such films and modes of storytelling.

Notes

1 This running time is a spatial quality of each medium: one minute of film at 24 frames per second is equal to about 90 feet or 27.4 meters of celluloid (93.8 feet or 28.6 meters at 25 frames per second), whereas one minute of screenplay (on celluloid) is equal to about 11 inches of paper (210mm for A4-sized paper).

2 In the film version there are two more temporal titles than in the script, for a total of 12. One of these titles moves us "forward" six months, from the time Laroche is arrested in the swamp to the date of his trial. The other title occurs near the end, and serves once more to flash us "forward" three years (from FAKAHATCHEE THREE YEARS EARLIER [in the script and film] to FLORIDA THREE YEARS LATER [only in the film]), presumably to the "present." These additional titles remove some "confusion" in one regard, but also further amplify the numbing effect of the many relative (i.e., "*n* months/years earlier/later" as opposed to absolute, i.e., "2001") temporal titles.

3 Cf. Bordwell (1985) for a description of terms adapted from the Russian formalists.

4 The "cut to:" is frequently used to announce jarring cuts in screenplay format, in order to mark a formal separation between scenes – and is used in other places in this script by Kaufman.

5 Metz (1999) writes "A film is difficult to explain because it is easy to understand. The image impresses itself on us, blocking everything that is not itself" (p. 69).

6 The trial actually occurred on Dec. 21, 1994, or less than 6 months "earlier," according to Orlean's (1998) book.

7 Hurricane Andrew is a major paradox. By the above scheme, it would have occurred in the script during 1987 or 1988 (9 years earlier than 1996/1997). This is an anachronism, as Hurricane Andrew actually made landfall in 1992. Unless, of course, the script ends in 2001, and/or the NINE YEARS EARLIER is a global title-card from the approximate year of the film's production – throwing another disparate element into the temporal mix.

8 With discrete multi-channel sound, and the possibility to choose between various dialogue tracks on DVDs, this is less true.

Bibliography

Arnheim, R. 1986. "A stricture on time and space." *New Essays on the Psychology of Art*. Berkeley: University of California Press, pp. 78–89. (Original work published 1978.)

Bal, M. 1997. *Narratology: Introduction to the Theory of Narrative*, 2nd edn. Toronto: University of Toronto Press.

Barbour, J. 1999. *The End of Time: The Next Revolution in Physics*. Oxford: Oxford University Press.

Bordwell, D. 2002. "Film futures." *Substance #97*, 31, 1: 88–104.

Bordwell, D. 1985. *Narration in the Fiction Film*. Madison: University of Wisconsin Press.

Bordwell, D. 2006. *The Way Hollywood Tells It: Story and Style in Modern Movies*. Berkeley: University of California Press.

Branigan, E. 2002. "Nearly true: Forking plots, forking interpretations. A response to David Bordwell's 'Film futures'." *SubStance #97*, 31, 1: 105–14.

Cilliers, P. 1998. *Complexity & Postmodernism: Understanding Complex Systems*. London: Routledge.

Davies, P. 2006. "That mysterious flow." *Scientific American*, 16, 1: 6–11.

Doane, M. A. 2002. *The Emergence of Cinematic Time: Modernity, Contingency, the Archive*. Cambridge, MA: Harvard University Press.

Feld, R. 2004. "Q & A with Charlie Kaufman," in C. Kaufman (ed.), *Eternal Sunshine of the Spotless Mind: The Shooting Script*. New York: Newmarket, pp. 131–45.

Genette, G. 1980. *Narrative Discourse: An Essay in Method* (trans. J. E. Lewin). Ithaca, NY: Cornell University Press. (Original work published 1972.)

Henderson, B. 1999. "Tense, mood, and voice in film: (notes after Genette)," in B. Henderson and A. Martin (eds), *Film Quarterly: Forty Years – A Selection*. Berkeley: University of California Press, pp. 55–75. (Original work published 1983.)

Hunter, L. 1993. *Lew Hunter's Screenwriting 434: The Industry's Premier Teacher Reveals the Secrets of the Successful Screenplay*. New York: Perigee Books.

Kaufman, C. 2004. *Eternal Sunshine of the Spotless Mind: The Shooting Script*. New York: Newmarket Press.

Kaufman, C., and Kaufman, D. 2002. *Adaptation: The Shooting Script*. New York: Newmarket Press.

Kinder, M. 1999. "The subversive potential of the pseudo iterative," in B. Henderson and A. Martin (eds), *Film Quarterly: Forty Years – A Selection*. Berkeley: University of California Press), pp. 127–48. (Original work published 1989–90.)

Kohn, N. 2000. "The screenplay as postmodern literary exemplar: Authorial distraction, disappearance, dissolution." *Qualitative Inquiry*, 6, 4: 489–510.

Mamber, S. 2003. "Narrative mapping," in J. T. Caldwell and A. Everett (eds.), *New Media: Theories and Practices of Digitextuality*. New York: Routledge, pp. 145–58.

Metz, C. 1999. *Film Language: A Semiotics of the Cinema* (trans. M. Taylor). Chicago: University of Chicago Press. (Original work published 1974.)

Mota, M. 2005. "Derek Jarman's Caravaggio: The screenplay as book." *Criticism*, 47, 2 (Spring): 215–31.

Orlean, S. 1998. *The Orchid Thief*. New York: Ballantine Books.

Pasolini, P. P. 1999. "Aspects of a semiology of cinema," in K. Cohen (ed.), *Writing in a Film Age: Essays by Contemporary Novelists*. Niwot: University Press of Colorado, pp. 191–226. (Original work published 1972.)

Sternberg, C. 1997. *Written for the Screen: The American Motion-Picture Screenplay as Text*. Tübingen, Germany: Stauffenburg Verlag.

6

Backbeat and Overlap:
Time, Place, and Character
Subjectivity in *Run Lola Run*

Michael Wedel

When *Run Lola Run* (*Lola rennt*) premiered in 1998, it became an instant box-office success in Germany and has subsequently enjoyed large-scale international distribution (Jaeckel 2003, pp. 121–3). Almost single-handedly, the film elevated its director, Tom Tykwer, to the top ranks of narrative avant-garde filmmaking in Europe and has since become the emblem of a substantial artistic renewal within contemporary German cinema (Töteberg 1999; Garwood 2002). A kinetic *tour de force* through Berlin driven by a heart-stopping techno beat, packed with unexpected twists and turns, combining still photography, video technology, and animation sequences, *Run Lola Run* is notable for its way of telling a very simple story – Lola must find 100,000 DM within 20 minutes in order to save her boyfriend Manni – in an extremely complex fashion.

In what follows, I want to consider the film's storytelling techniques as constituting a particular mode of narration that reconfigures temporal linearity and circularity, action and causality, movement and stasis around the central problems of embodied subjectivity, spatio-temporal intervals, and hetero-topic experience. Taking a Bordwellian theory of cinematic narration as its starting point, this chapter sets out to remodel the film's audiovisual organization and spectatorial address across the double matrix of, one the one hand, Foucault's notions of the "limit-experience" and hetero-topic and hetero-chronic subjectivity; and, on the other, Henri Lefebvre's methodological tool of "Rhythmanalysis." On the basis of rereading *Run Lola Run* along these concepts, I argue that an analysis of the film's sequential ordering of the story events, as provided by Bordwell, needs to be complemented and counterbalanced with an understanding of its overarching narrative rhythms and frequencies as equally significant levels of narration.

The Opening Sequence

From a narratological perspective, the category of rhythm is as "striking" and "effective" as it is "elusive," since the central problem in the analysis of narrative rhythm is "the question of what to take as a measure of the speed of presentation" (Bal 1997, pp. 99–100). It is exactly this question of temporal measuring which *Run Lola Run* takes as its point of departure: the film's first image shows a gigantic pendulum swinging across the screen, strung up to a gothic wall-clock and sporting the face of Chronos that, by the end of the shot when the movement of the pendulum has come to a rest, swallows its own image. Merging from the dark is then a meandering flow of human bodies and an acousmêtric voice[1] posing a number of unanswered (unanswerable?) onto-epistemological questions:

> "Who are we? Where do we come from? Where are we going? How do we know what we think we know? Why do we believe anything at all? Countless questions in search of an answer that will give rise to a new question and the next answer will give rise to the next question and so on. But in the end, isn't it always the same question? And always the same answer?"

The film's ultimate project to fold cause-and-effect patterns into a self-reflexive temporal knot is announced already in these first words spoken during the prologue. Further philosophical ammunition, if of a somewhat more pragmatic nature, is added when the character whom we will meet again in due time as the security guard Schuster, states: "The ball is round. The game lasts 90 minutes. That's a fact. Everything else is pure theory." Referring the spectator back to legendary football-coach Sepp Herberger's motto "After the game is before the game" which had set off the film (juxtaposed to T. S. Eliot's famous lines "And at the end of all our exploring / we will arrive where we started / and know the place for the first time"), the opening sequence not so much serves as an exposition to a fictional narrative in a traditional sense, but rather sets the rules of a game into which the audience is invited to enter.

The analogy to video game aesthetics is reinforced at several points in the first few minutes of the film, e.g., when Lola is encircled by a 360-degree camera movement and we get snapshots of her mental selection of an appropriate candidate for providing the necessary amount of money within the given time-frame, a shot strongly reminiscent in design and visual choreography of the intro level in a computer game where the gamer can make his choice from a menu of different avatars as fictional alter-egos.[2] In a similar vain, the animated title sequence is designed as if seen from a perspective familiar from first-person shooter games. Finally, "the most clearcut resemblance to the virtual world of computer games resides in the key narrative device of the film, namely Lola's three 'lives'" (Evans 2004, p. 109). Although there is no space here to fully explore the film's manifold references to the intertext of the computer game, we can assume it provides a key cultural model for the degree to which its overall conception of narrative structure, diegetic space, and character agency can be called innovative.[3]

Apart from the fluent transition from photographic film to animated sequences, and the internal montage or juxtaposition of in-focus/out-of-focus material as well as animated inserts, the first 10 minutes of *Run Lola Run* introduce a whole range of visual modalities of different material status and ontological provenance: with the transition from one temporal layer to the next, 35mm film changes into grainy video footage, color to monochrome black-and-white, normal speed into slow motion or artificially accelerated action. Whereas one is tempted to relate those different visual ontologies to different temporal layers (35mm, normal speed, color for the present tense; manipulation of speed and black-and-white for the past; snapshots for the future), or to different levels of reality (where black and white snapshots of still images would represent mental activity and subjective memory or fantasy), or, indeed, understand them as a particular mode of character focalization,[4] the film as a whole is consistent only in complicating and disorienting any such straightforward attempts at identifying one-to-one relationships between the materiality of the signifier and the time and reality status of the signified at a given moment.

Three Cycles

Maybe also due to these complexities on the micro-level of *Run Lola Run*'s mode of narration, commentators have largely focused on what also constituted the film's major audience appeal and cult value, namely its narrative construction on the macro-level, characterized by what appears to be a time-loop structure of Lola's three attempts to come up with the money and save her boyfriend, aptly called "Manni" (and here, as so often, *nomen est omen*), from certain death:

Lola runs in three experiments or 20-minute rounds – all in an attempt at continuity. In "theory" she must find 100,000 DM with which to save her boyfriend, Manni, who in his attempt to prove himself to several members of organised crime, acts as a courier for their cash and then proceeds to lose it on Berlin's U-Bahn. And Lola runs. She runs in three 20-minute cycles or rounds. In each the ends are changed even though she encounters the same bodies and forces along the way; however, in this game on the Butterfly Effect, each round reaches out to several virtual futures because of the slightest modulation of time from run to run. The game is rebooted but the game remembers. (Bianco 2004, p. 378)

Chance encounters, and the slightest delays they ensue, lead to chain reactions which determine a different outcome for each round: at the end of the first round, Lola is shot by a policeman after she and Manni rob a supermarket; at the end of the second round, Lola shows up with the money on time (from robbing her father's bank), but Manni is run over by the ambulance, which had crossed Lola's path several times earlier on; only by the end of the third round, after both Manni and Lola raised DM 100,000 each, can they walk away into a new life.

Points of Transition

The three episodes are bridged by two interludes, each featuring an intimate dialogue between Lola and Manni in bed together, shot from above and soaked in red monochrome. These points of transition from one cycle to the next are remarkable not only for their exceptional aesthetic status, which radically detaches them from the rest of the film's action, but also because it is difficult to define whether what these transitional scenes result in is really a backtracking of the action, or not rather the establishment of an uncanny continuity, folded across the deaths of the two main protagonists.

For David Bordwell, who has discussed *Run Lola Run* as one of his examples among a number of what-if plots to be found in recent "forking-path films" (2002), the top-shot scenes with Lola and Manni meditating over their love serve as central "branching-points" which need to be clearly indicated and therefore in one way or another strongly accentuated and removed from the rest of the film. According to Bordwell, both that "*Run Lola Run* replays the fall of Lola's bright red phone receiver and her racing through her mother's room, down the stairs, and out into the street," and that "before each new future, Tykwer provides a slow, red-tinted scene" work as "a kind of highlighted 'reset' button, usually emphasizing matters of timing" (Bordwell 2002, p. 94). As such, these shots correspond to what Bordwell has identified as a "viewer-friendly device in the context of what might seem to be ontologically or epistemically radical possibilities" of the forking-path film, namely that "the fork is signposted" (Bordwell 2002, pp. 91, 93).

Forking-Path Plot, Multi-Draft Narrative

Altogether, Bordwell defines seven key conventions on which this genre of the forking-path film is said to rely, in order to "trim back [their potential futures, MW] to cognitively manageable dimensions, by means of strategies characteristic of certain traditions of cinematic storytelling," thereby stretching and enriching extant narrative norms, without, however, "subverting or demolishing them" (Bordwell 2002, p. 91).

The first of these conventions is: "Forking paths are linear." Bordwell argues that in films with forking-path plots, "each path, after it diverges, adheres to a strict line of cause and effect." "Instead of each moment being equally pregnant with numerous futures," he writes, "one becomes far more consequential than the others, and those consequences will follow strictly from it. Such linearity helps make these plots intelligible, yielding two or three stories that illustrate, literally, alternative but integral courses of events" (Bordwell 2002, p. 92).

Following on to the second convention that the fork needs to be signposted, the third convention that forking paths tend to intersect includes recurrent characters and background conditions across the different lines of action (Bordwell 2002, pp. 94–5). Bordwell's fourth convention consists in the contention that "Forking-path tales are unified by traditional cohesion devices" (Bordwell 2002, p. 95), such as appointments and deadlines. The fifth convention, that forking paths "will often run parallel," refers to the observation that central components of the plot "emerge as vivid variants of one another" in each trajectory. One example given by Bordwell is Lola's power to restore life in each of the episodes: "to herself at the end of the first episode, to Manni at the end of the second, and to the security guard Schuster, whom she revives in the ambulance at the close of the third" (Bordwell 2002, pp. 96–7).

In the context of defining the sixth convention, "All paths are not equal; the last one taken presupposes the others," Bordwell argues that "forking-path narratives tend to treat what we learn about in one world as a background condition for what is shown later in another" (Bordwell 2002, p. 98). For Bordwell, the clearest instance for forking paths "contaminating" each other comes from *Run Lola Run*, where Lola from one episode to the next learns to control her immense screaming power, until in the third episode she "calculatedly emits another scream, and this one not only breaks glass but guides the ball into the winning slot" after she had bet on a spin of a roulette wheel in the casino. Bordwell concludes: "It's as if she has learned to tame what was initially a sheer expression of desperation, turning it to her purposes" (Bordwell 2002, p. 99).

The seventh, and final, key convention identified by Bordwell is summarized as: "All paths are not equal; the last one taken, or completed, is the least hypothetical one" (Bordwell 2002, p. 100). Apart from what Bordwell refers to as folk-psychology's "recency effect" which always tends to privilege "the final future we see," this convention is built upon the previous one insofar as the last future here appears as a consequence of the other two.

The contention that "the last future we encounter is privileged by its absorption of the lessons learned in an earlier one" leads Bordwell to suggest that these "forking-path" plots might be better described as "*multiple-draft narratives*, with the last version presenting itself as the fullest, most satisfying revision" (Bordwell 2002, p. 102).

Bordwell notes that he has to sidestep a number of important differences among his selection of films, for the sake of arriving at a coherent set of generic conventions. These dissimilarities include, as he admits, major differences between the individual films' rhythms and soundscapes, which would set *Run Lola Run's* "techno rush" miles apart from, for example, the "sober, philosophical pacing of *Blind chance*" (Bordwell 2002, p. 102).

There are a number of objections or, rather, refinements, to be made to Bordwell's application of his set of conventions to a film like *Run Lola Run*: for one, I would argue that the temporal structure of the film's individual episodes or trajectories is, in fact, not circular at all, if one thinks of the many more instances where we encounter moments of overlap and recognition across the episodes. Lola not only learns how to manipulate and use her screaming to good ends, but she also uses her knowledge on how to unlock a gun, a procedure Manni taught her in the first episode and whose intuitive knowledge enables her to rob the bank in the second. The moment she remembers how to use the mechanism constitutes a moment of recognition which is strongly emphasized in the film by an extended close-up of both her face and her gun, and thereby made explicit to, and thus doubled by, the viewer. Furthermore, the temporalities within each individual episode are in themselves far too complex and convoluted – perforated and punctuated as they are by jump cuts, discontinuities on various levels, internal repetitions, snapshot bits and pieces, slow and fast motion shots – for one to really speak, as Bordwell does in his first definition, of each forking path as being organized in a strictly "linear" fashion.[5] Bordwell contends that, in *Run Lola Run*, "each path, after it diverges, adheres to a strict line of cause and effect" (Bordwell 2002, p. 92). This has its cause, as I would claim, less in an internal linearization of narrative time than in a conception of cinematic time and space informed by movement and rhythmicality and, in the final analysis, radically diverging from linear or chronological temporal modes.

It is therefore exactly on the grounds of a reconsideration of cinematic rhythm and sound that I think Bordwell's set of conventions and his reading of *Run Lola Run* need to be complemented. This is what I want to devote the remainder of this chapter to, by drawing our attention to how music and sound effects establish another, more intricate and paradoxical temporal logic of extreme rhythmicality (characterized by the opposition between repetition and the linear forward drive), the orchestration of modulations and singular aural events (the acoustic *punctum*) and sonic intervals. The second half of this essay will then relate *Run Lola Run*'s acoustic dimension to a broader model of understanding and analyzing rhythm proposed by Henri Lefebvre, before finally turning to Foucault in order to further conceptualize not only the film's spatio-temporal organization, but also its particular mode of spectatorial address.

Run Lola Run's Musical and Temporal Spine

Run Lola Run begins with the ticking sound of a clock, before we even get to see the first image – of the clock itself, or is it another clock? At any rate, it is the regular rhythm of time, not necessarily chronological, however, which sets into motion the film's action, or rather: a visual illustration of the concept of rhythm, split between the pendulum and the gothic wall-clock. Already with those two emblems of time, a tension is created between the rhythmical measure of linear or chronological time, the repetitive rhythm of cyclical or looped temporality (the movement of the pendulum) and the event of the single beat (the temporal *punctum*).

This tension around the triple split of temporality is the film's central structural motif pervading both its acoustic and visual organization. Visually, it builds on the inherent dynamism of the film's seminal image of "a woman with flame-red hair running and running and running" (Tykwer, quoted in Töteberg 1998, p. 129) and it recurs frequently in the form of

- *the dot* (e.g., the circular-shaped clock faces, the ball kicked off in the beginning and during the roulette game, geographically also the place where Manni waits for Lola);
- *the grid* (e.g., the time scale through which the watch hand has to pass, the urban architectural patterns Lola passes by on her way to Manni);
- and *the spiral* (e.g., the signboard of the night club of the same name, the ornament on the pillows on which Lola and Manni's heads rest in the red-tinted top-shots, the staircase in the animated sequences, Lola's earring, the bun in the Vertigo-like painting in the casino).

On the figural level, therefore, the film's visual style translates and transposes the temporal dimensions of narrative linearity vs. circularity into a superordinate web of motifs, metaphors, and concepts which structurally entertain a close relationship to the abstract categories of musical time and the rhythmicality of acoustic events. As a result, the film establishes another structural layer of spatio-temporal ordering, which not only works parallel to the narrative level, but which enfolds and cuts across the internal logic of the whole film's – and each of its individual episodes' – temporal and narrative progression.

In this sense, *Run Lola Run*'s techno music with its backbeat rhythm can be seen as de-centering the experiential (as much as our analytical) focus on a temporality that is defined solely by the cause-and-effect narrative progression. And this in a similar, only much more radical, way as it has been claimed for pop music in general:

> The relationship between pop music and time has to be seen as one of direct effect: pop music harnesses and articulates time. It concretises time by converting real or experiential time into a regulated musical time. One of the central attractions, and indeed the primary uses of pop music – dancing –, attests to the musical articulation of time, largely through rhythm in its relation to the human body. The beat of pop music is formalised into what is customarily known as the "backbeat", characterised by the snare drum's provision of an emphatic accent on the second and forth beats of the bar. This is precisely a musical and temporal spine. (Donnelly 2005, p. 28)

As Caryl Flinn points out (2003), *Run Lola Run*'s musical backbeat is not only regulating time in the sense of a permanent forward drive. On the one hand, "techno is a perfect, if obvious, choice" because as dance music, "it immediately connotes high charged physical movement," with "[t]he film's techno tracks [being] closely knit to its activity" and the "musical beats dictating much of its rhythm, pace, editing, and energy." On the other hand, however, Flinn puts equal emphasis to the fact that "unlike traditional tonal music, techno has no clear beginning, patterns of development, or resolution; unchanging and energetic, it is repetitive without standing still." As a musical idiom and temporal marker which is both a linear forward driving force that vectorizes movement and unleashes a pulsating energy and, at the same time, constitutes a highly "repetitively structured form, organized around beats per minute," techno's "compressed, hypnotic beats, sequenced loops, and harmonic stability" indeed "seem the perfect accompaniment" for a filmic articulation of time whose ultimate goal consists in synthesizing linear and cyclical temporalities into the one common logic of rhythm. As Flinn detects, *Run Lola Run* "even modulates the sound of a heartbeat into one section" (Flinn 2003, p. 202).

Flinn has also observed, a few notable exceptions notwithstanding, that the music in *Run Lola Run* does not change significantly throughout the film. The music might move from minor to major keys, or gradually change into much more of an overall sense of formal stability in the third episode, but these shifts and modulations, significant as they are, remain subtle: "While the textures shift," she concludes, "the fundamental beat remains unchanged" (Flinn 2003, p. 202). In this fashion, also the musical structure itself resembles and mirrors the dialectical tension between linearity and circularity which is at the heart of the film: under the rule of rhythm, techno's internal forward drive – "music with a goal," as Flinn (2003 p. 204) puts it – is paired with the absence of a clear beginning or end: various modulations of the same beat, ever recurring, replace the ordered succession of the number principle in traditional background music, be it in the form of psychological leitmotifs or the MTV-style alternation of readily identifiable signature songs and melodies.

Unity in Opposition: Rhythm, Repetition, and Interval

What *Run Lola Run*'s techno soundtrack establishes, then, seems to relate closely to what Henri Lefebvre once called a "dialectical relation" or "unity in opposition" between different spatio-temporal logics.[6] Within this contradictory unity, "Time and space, the cyclical and the linear, exert a reciprocal action: they measure themselves against one another; each one makes itself and is made a measuring-measure; everything is cyclical repetition through linear repetitions" (Lefebvre 2004, p. 8).

It is Lefebvre's idea of "rhythmanalysis" that can provide a model for conceptualizing this intertwinement of different temporalities, where one temporal layer simultaneously brings forth and contests the other.[7] For Lefebvre, the concept of rhythm is the key to any understanding of time, especially non-linear temporalities such as repetition. The heuristic framework of his rhythmanalytical project is provided by the everyday work-ings of urban life and its orchestration of movements through space, the collision between natural biological and social timescales, the coordination of the rhythms of our bodies and the rhythms produced by society. Following on from his earlier analysis of spatial organization, and in par-ticular urban environments, in *The Production of Space* (1991) and his three-volume *Critique of Everyday Life* (1992, 2002, 2006), the question of the body under the conditions of capitalism has remained a central concern right through to his late undertaking of the rhythmanalytical project.[8] In this respect close to Foucault, the body here figures as the point of con-tact in a field where the social meets the biological, where the workings of natural, corporeal, and mechanistic machine rhythms coexist and inter-fere with each other: in the modern experience of the object world the body serves the subject as a metronome (Lefebvre 2004, p. 19).[9]

Already in the late 1920s, Lefebvre had challenged the then dominant philosophical theorization of time along Bergson's notion of *durée* (dura-tion), and set out to develop what he himself referred to as a "theory of moments," privileging the importance of the instant. In Lefebvre's under-standing the single instant as potentially non-calculable, as a critical moment of virtual openness, as a contingent unit of temporal resistance encapsulates both the difference between linear and cyclical time, and the contrast between clock time and "lived" time.

The main source of inspiration for Lefebvre's re-conception of time was music which he thought could be theorized in relation to three basic concepts:

- *melody* as a linear sequence of notes in temporal succession;
- *harmony* as the simultaneous sounding of notes;
- and, finally and most importantly, *rhythm* as the placement of notes and their relative length, that is: the instant of the single beat as the

concentric moment of musical measure which gives rise to issues of change and repetition, identity and difference, contrast and continuity.

According to Lefebvre's understanding of the term, rhythm is not to be confused with "movement [*mouvement*], speed, a sequence of movements [*gestes*] or objects (machines, for example)" (Lefebvre 2004, p. 5). Instead, he generally defines rhythm as emerging everywhere "where there is interaction between a place, a time and an expenditure of energy" (2004, p. 15). This definition allows Lefebvre to establish a number of subcategories which form integral parts of the analysis of rhythm: repetition (of movements, gestures, actions, situations, differences); interferences of linear processes and cyclical processes; birth, growth, peak, then decline and end.

In rhythm, the repetitive and the differential go hand in hand (Lefebvre 2004, p. 6), as Lefebvre asserts. And this is because "[r]*hythm* reunites *quantitative* aspects and elements, which mark time and distinguish moments in it – and *qualitative* aspects and elements, which link them together, found the unities and result from them. Rhythm appears as regulated time, governed by rational laws, but in contact with what is the least rational in human being: the lived, the carnal, the body" (2004, p. 9). In this sense, rhythms escape logic, but they also contain a logic, "a possible calculus of numbers and numerical relations," because "we know that a rhythm is slow or lively only in relation to other rhythms" (2004, pp. 10–11).

Bypassing a whole array of implications (as, e.g., the crucial distinction between "present" and "presence"[10]) that Lefebvre's rhythmanalytical project brings with it, in the context of our present narratological concerns it can help us to radically refigure the complex spatio-temporal organization that we find in *Run Lola Run*. Instead of foregrounding, as Bordwell does, the cognitive aspects of narrative comprehensibility, and the disguised persistence of linearity as the film's basic concern and organizing principle, Lefebvre's approach makes us attentive to those dimensions of space, time, and subjective experience opened up by rhythms, repetitions, and intervals. Lefebvre's analytical categories suggest to transcend the narrative level and to cut the structure of the three forking-path futures across the repetition of instantaneous moments in order to grasp *Run Lola Run*'s rhythmical structure as a complementary organizing principle of the filmic construction. Instead of dividing the film according to a sequence of plot points or a number of narrative branching points, we are now prepared to dissect it along the rhythmical recurrence of events, as prominent markers of the process of narration: Lola's screams, her various street encounters with the nuns, the tramp, the ambulance, the passing of the underground train, the dialogue between her father and his lover, and so on. On the film's macro-level, the action of each of the three branching plots is temporally encased in the interval of the phone receiver and long fall back on the cradle. Clocked and synchronized on numerous parallel and multiply overlapping levels, each new moment opens up a different interval, an in-between space of movements, gestures, actions, situations, differences. At the extremes of the alternative measures that divide and subdivide the film into events, rhythms, and intervals, emerge two temporal dimensions: on the one hand, the horizon of the macro-interval, which is the film itself or, at least, its fictional universe. For, after all, everything we see within the diegetic world – if one can speak of something like a diegesis in *Run Lola Run* – occurs within the never-closed interval opened up by the security guard shooting off the ball. At the other end of the spectrum there is the Polaroid snapshot and the still image as the smallest possible units of the cinematic representation of time. In between those two extremes the kinetic experience of *Run Lola Run* can be reconsidered to unfold by a per-manent modulation, alternation, and interference of different speeds and frequencies. For Tykwer himself it was "absolutely clear (. . .) that a film about the possibilities inherent in life had to be a film about the possib-ilities inherent in film as well. That's why the film contains colour and black and white, slow motion and time lapse, in other words, all the basic components which have been used throughout film history" (Tykwer in Töteberg 1998, p. 131). As Lutz Koepnick has pointed out, it is not least the radically heterogeneous materiality of the narrative discourse in Tykwer's "filmic ruminations" that defines its mode of spectatorial address as historically contingent, because "it opens a fragmented image space in the present in whose ruptures and discontinuities we can reinsert the possib-ility of meaningful narration, understood here as an open-ended activity that in establishing connections – connections between people, objects, sites, and different temporalities – allows us to recuperate a sense for the aleatory and transitional nature of historical time" (Koepnick 2004, p. 127).

A Drama of Emplacement

There are at least three thematic markers with which the film reflects the contingency of its historical time and place as aleatory and transitional. Apart from the struggle between capitalism and love, two central thematic concerns of *Run Lola Run*, the ultimate horizon into which the film inter-venes and inserts itself, both on a representational and on a broader social-cultural level, is the city of Berlin. It has often been noted that Tykwer's representation of Berlin is extremely contradictory: Although, as one commentator put it, "the film is replete with images and reminders of divi-sions and separations past and present that continue to exist in Germany and particularly in Berlin after the *Wende*," most of the identifiable sites, as, e.g., the *Gendarmenmarkt* or *Friedrichstraße*, largely have a de-contextualized, de-territorialized "symbolic function" (Hamm-Ehsani 2004, p. 53). While Berlin is thus still recognizable, the film consciously avoids drawing Lola's route across the signature tourist attractions, but rather creates an abstract or virtual urban space, in which Lola, simply by turn-ing around a corner, from one shot to the next, is transported from *Potsdamer Straße* in *Kreuzberg* to *Unter den Linden* in *Mitte*. Tykwer even goes so far as to intentionally, in only one reverse cut, have the road sign "Friedrichstraße" change into "Behrendtstraße."

But why "would Tykwer strive to make Berlin 'as unrecognizable as pos-sible?'" (Flinn 2003, p. 208), for example, by overtly employing Kuleshov effects like the one just mentioned. Flinn has answered this question in explaining the utter heterogeneity of the urban environment in which the action takes place as a challenge or just another invitation to the audience to "enter into a 'game' [. . .] of identifying locations" (2003, p. 208). Others have interpreted the fact that in *Run Lola Run* "Berlin becomes a somewhat nonessential, generic urban place" (Flinn 2003, p. 208) as a strat-egic concession to an international audience appeal, or they have argued that in the end it would not be of central importance that Lola's trajecto-ries through Eastern and Western neighborhoods are disjointed and the city locations jumbled, because the film's vitality and energy would have more to do with the promise of risk-taking and individual self-renewal than with the construction or de-construction of a historical and localiz-able urban space.[11]

Plausible as these explanations may be, they seem to underestimate the central role the construction or deconstruction of the urban environment plays in the overall aesthetic concept of the film, by neglecting how much the discontinuities and incongruities in the representation of Berlin are in tune with the highly fragmented, virtual and highly paradoxical aesthetic disposition of *Run Lola Run* as a whole. Rather, the film's paradoxical topo-graphy and discontinuous rhythmical orchestration of the city seem to create a representation of Berlin as a transitional point between the "'no longer' and the 'not yet'" (Schlipphacke 2006, p. 135).[12] Therefore, it could be argued instead that the film consciously transforms Berlin into a heterotopia in order to capture and make productive for its own aesthetic project the overwhelming richness of its rhythmical orchestration. Foucault has defined heterotopias as "real places, actual places, places that are designed into the very institution of society, which are sorts of actually realized utopias in which the real emplacements, all the other real emplacements that can be found within culture are, at the same time, represented, contested, and reversed, sorts of places that are outside all places, although they are actually localizable" (Foucault 1984/2000, p. 178).[13] In what he proposed as the inauguration of a systematic description of different heterotopias, an epistemological undertaking he called "heterotopology" (p. 179), Foucault identified "two major types" of heterotopias: "crisis heterotopias" and "heterotopias of deviation" (pp. 179–80). A "crisis heterotopia" is a heterotopia without precise geographical coordinates (but still localizable in society and culture), an "anywhere place," an "elsewhere" which is "reserved for individuals who are in a state of crisis with respect to society and the human milieu in which they live" (pp. 179–80). As such, Foucault's notion relates to the crisis Lola finds herself in and how her personal crisis is related to the society (capitalism) and the milieu she lives in (her family, her lover).

The second type of heterotopias identified by Foucault subsumes what he calls "heterotopias of deviation: those in which individuals are put whose behavior is deviant with respect to the mean or the required norm" (1984/2000, p. 180). This can be related to the degree to which Lola, both in her punk-like appearance and in her transgressive and radical behavior, deviates from the norms that not only her family, but also society at large, down to the safety regulations operating in an urban environment, are imposing upon her.[14]

Among the principles Foucault establishes for heterotopias in general, the three that are most relevant for our purposes are: that the heterotopia "has the ability to juxtapose in a single real place several emplacements that are incompatible in themselves" (1984/2000, p. 181), which corresponds to the many topographic jolts and discontinuous jumps between shots in *Run Lola Run*. Secondly, Foucault asserts that in most cases "heterotopias are connected with temporal discontinuities [*decoupages du temps*]; that is, they open onto what might be called, for the sake of symmetry, heterochronias. The heterotopia begins to function when men are in a kind of absolute break with their traditional time" (1984/2000, p. 182). This principle, brought into constellation with Tykwer's film, highlights the existential crisis, or in Foucauldian terms: the state of "limit-experience,"[15] that not only Lola, but almost each single protagonist of the film finds him-/herself exposed to, and how it affects and substantially alters their traditional time-frames and rhythms. Finally, the point that heterotopias "always presuppose a system of opening and closing that isolates them and makes them penetrable at the same time" (Foucault 1984/2000, p. 183) refers us back to the various rhythms and temporal intervals into which both *Run Lola Run* and the city which it represents/misrepresents are so neatly, but also paradoxically, organized.

As should become clear from this quick gloss on Foucault's idea of heterotopia, it not only provides a model for conceptualizing the fragmentary and discontinuous representation of Berlin in *Run Lola Run*, but it also closely corresponds to Lefebvre's dialectical sublation of linear and cyclical time in the concept of rhythm, and allows us to comprehend Lola's dilemma as a drama of emplacement – being at the right spot on the right time in a discontinuous and elusive virtual environment, full of surprises and chance encounters – a game she can only win if she manages to synchronize herself to all the other rhythms around her.

Return Effects and Tender Intervals

If the construction of the city – including all the other temporal and spatial intervals Lola has to traverse in her race to rescue – can be understood as quintessentially heterotopic and heterochronic, then the red-tinted moments (or intervals) of Lola and Manni in bed, when the lovers are frozen into "sculptural immobility" (Lefebvre 2004, p. 31), correlate to what Foucault qualifies as utopian: "Utopias are emplacements having no real place. They are emplacements that maintain a general relation of direct or inverse analogy with the real space of society. They are society perfected or the reverse of society, but in any case these utopias are spaces that are fundamentally and essentially unreal" (Foucault 2000, p. 178). In the film, these are also rare moments without any musical accompaniment, when the acoustical rhythm is solely provided by the dialogue between the two lovers. These scenes not only mark the launching pads for alternative forking futures (in a narrative sense) or form autonomous rhythmic intervals within the film's overall structure (from a rhythmanalytic point of view). They also constitute bridges or points of contact between life and death within the logic of the film, and insofar amount to that enigmatic "place-less place" of which Foucault speaks, which is a utopian place (Foucault calls it a "mirror utopia") but where there must be, as Foucault writes, "a kind of mixed, intermediate experience" (Foucault 2000, p. 179). And indeed, in these scenes both Manni and Lola seem to be "here" and "over there," in bed and on the street, at the same time, as if in a mirror where, to para-phrase Foucault, "I see myself where I am not, in an unreal space that opens up virtually behind the surface; I am over there where I am not, a kind of shadow that gives me my own visibility, that enables me to look at myself there where I am absent – a mirror utopia. But it is also a heterotopia in that the mirror really exists, in that it has a sort of return effect on the place that I occupy" (Foucault 2000, p. 179).

Not only from a strictly narrative perspective, then, it seems more than justified to ascribe to the utopian intervals in *Run Lola Run* a "return effect." More than "a kind of highlighted 'reset' button, usually emphasizing mat-ters of timing" (Bordwell 2002, p. 94), they carve out for Lola and Manni a utopian space of being in the world by transcending it. In their multiple doubling and self-reflexive dimensions they also serve to (once more) open up the story space of the diegetic action towards the space of cinematic perception itself: via their exceptional formal status in terms of framing, coloring, and acoustic texture, as well as in view of the fact that the dia-logue is directly addressed to the camera at the ceiling, the intervals between the cycles also mark strong moments of a cinematic discourse turned inside out, offering itself to revision and contemplation for the protagon-ists and the audience alike. Vladimir Nabokov once spoke of something like "true Time" that would emerge from such "tender intervals": "Maybe the only thing that hints at a sense of Time is rhythm; not the recurrent beats of the rhythm but the gap between two such beats, the grey gap between black beats: the Tender Interval. The regular throb itself merely brings back the miserable idea of measurement, but in between, something like true Time lurks" (Nabokov 1969, p. 572).

Conclusion: Spirals of Historicity

Throughout this essay it has been argued that the complexity of *Run Lola Run*'s mode of narration can fruitfully be located in the tension created between, on the one hand, a sequential ordering of events on the narrat-ive level and, on the other, the spatio-temporal suspension of linearity on the level of the cinematic discourse, including the acoustic dimension, recurrent visual motifs, and the loss of goal-oriented character agency in the workings of the urban environment. Other commentators have considered this suspension as indicative of the emergence of a mythical or "spatialized" temporality from within that would remove Tykwer's film from any identifiable historicity or present-day reality and mark it as either belonging to the genre of the modern fairy-tale (Rings 2005) or to the discourse of postmodernism (Bianco 2004; Evans 2004).[16] To the degree to which the effect of *Run Lola Run*'s mode of narration can be seen as a modular database narrative, making "the narrative, like the diegesis, spatial" and encouraging games with flashback and flashforward, time loops, and temporal dislocation, it seems to share some central characteristics with what Sean Cubitt has called the "Neobaroque film" of contemporary cinema. In this set of films, narrative serves to reveal "the coincidences, the flukes of chance that give us the specific version of the story, making play of the casuistry that allows the manipulation of narratemes to pretend to some sort of causality." Like Lola, their protagonists are deprived of all "causal chains of anything more than pure luck, good or bad", having "only to understand, as the audience must, their position in the web of events to realize their goal." This goal, however, "already exists as the resolution of the riddle of the world they inhabit. Personal destiny coincides with the destiny of a Hegelian world, whose task is to understand itself" (Cubitt 2004, p. 239).

As plausible as this characterization and repositioning of *Run Lola Run* within a larger trend and international body of films may be, it is again at the micro-level of the textual articulation that significant differences can be located. For, whereas in Cubitt's view, it is the "micro-ordering of time as space that emerges from this infinitesimal conversion of duration to extension" and that opens the films into a "fractal chaos" (2004, p. 361) at the basis of a self-enclosed diegetic universe cut off from any direct connection to the "real world," it is exactly at this micro-level that in Tykwer's film the diegetic world itself becomes fragile to the point of dissolution, opening up toward a radically dialogical and communicative form of interaction with its historical audience. Insofar as the incessant transformation of space into place and time into event – two of the central processes cinematic discourse performs in the process of narration (Heath 1986) – via narrative rhythm and character emplacement can be regarded as central organizing principles in *Run Lola Run*, they operate to bridge the gap between the filmic articulation and the social (media) reality to which the film seeks to connect and into which it aims to intervene. In this sense, the

spiral as one of the film's central visual tropes can be read less as a metaphor for an inward movement, turning only upon itself, but should be understood in a more Foucauldian sense as the emblem for the centrifugal forces
unleashed by the film's rhythmical deconstruction of a diegetic world that
would be dissociated from the social reality of its audience.[17]

That *Run Lola Run* presents its narrative on ever-shifting ontological
grounds and within an overall dynamic that points beyond the narrative
itself and sets up, in the words of Foucault, "not boundaries not to be crossed,
but *perpetual spirals* of power and pleasure" (quoted in Michon 2002,
p. 174), is once more reinforced by the film's ending. In a strictly narrative sense, the final shot with Lola and Manni walking away with a plastic
bag full of money may qualify for a happy ending, finally uniting the couple and resolving the narrative conflict.[18] On the level of the concrete filmic
presentation of this apparently successful "escape," however, the sense of
a neat narrative closure is ironically undermined by the fact that the protagonists' movement is frozen into another still image in the middle of
the action: abstracting the liberating dynamic and violently interrupting
the dialogue over Lola's knowing smile after Manni had asked "What's
in the bag?" What makes this final still image so ambiguous is that it refers
the viewer back to the series of Polaroid snapshots with which Tykwer,
throughout the film, summarized the alternative futures of a number of
people met by Lola on her race through Berlin. In the final analysis, then,
we are to understand that the film's threefold narrative trajectory, when
finally arriving at the point of harmonic equilibrium, constitutes nothing
more than one single modular interval encapsulated in a single snapshot,
as other slices of future life had been summarized in an elliptical fashion
before. What makes this ending so ambivalent is its radical openness
toward both the futures of the protagonists – and the cinematic experience of the film itself. For, just as the still image – into which the very movement of the film is discharged – stands in for the smallest possible unit of
temporal representation in the cinema, it paradoxically also encapsulates
the temporal interval of the film as a whole and opens it toward the time
of its reception. At the closing beat of *Run Lola Run*'s narrative rhythm,
narrative time and the time of narration, story time and viewing time are
integrated into a single interval mediating between the different levels and
timescales of narrative, narration, and reception within and beyond the film.
Its historical dimension can be located exactly at this contingent point of
intersection between the different temporalities involved. Not every time,
Chronos swallows his own image, this also means the end of history.

Notes

1   The acousmêtric voice is an unsettling, floating voice "that speaks over the image but is also forever on the verge of appearing in it" (Chion 1994, p. 129).

2   For a close reading of the circular camera trajectories in *Run Lola Run*, see Mergenthaler (2006, pp. 278–83).

3   See Grieb (2002). In relation to *Run Lola Run*'s opening "shot," Schuster kicking off a ball, one is immediately reminded of ludologist Markku Eskelinen's polemical remark: "Luckily, outside theory, people are usually excellent in distinguishing between narrative situations and gaming situations: if I throw a ball at you, I don't expect you to drop it and wait until it starts telling stories" (Eskelinen 2004, p. 36). For a general introduction into the narrative principles of computer games, see Atkins (2003) and Jenkins (2004).

4   "Despite the protagonists' criminal activities, Tykwer reinforces our identification with them by using 35mm film to shoot those scenes in which they appear. The crispness of these moments contrasts with the less sharp, more grainy texture of those scenes where Lola and Manni are absent and Tykwer uses video" (Evans 2004, pp. 107–8).

5   The linearity that Bordwell refers to here seems to be limited to the series of events as they are presented in the fabula and exclude the level of the actual textual articulation. For an account of how these two levels interact in establishing or undercutting a "double linearity," see Bal (1997 pp. 81–99).

6   "The linear, which is to say [. . .], succession, consists of journeys to and fro: it combines with the cyclical, the movements of long intervals. The cyclical is social organization manifesting itself. The linear is the daily grind, the routine, therefore the perpetual, made up of chance and encounters" (Lefebvre 2004, p. 30).

7   Lefebvre himself generally envisaged "rhythmanalysis" as "a new field of knowledge" (2004, p. 3). More moderately framed, it offers a different analytical terminology and alternative methodology of understanding and describing the spatio-temporal organization of complex cultural systems: As a methodological tool with practical ambitions, rhythmanalysis "does not isolate an object, or a subject, or a relation. It seeks to grasp a moving but determinate complexity" (2004, p. 12).

8   "At no moment have the analysis of rhythms and the rhythmanalytical project lost sight of the *body*" (Lefebvre 2004, p. 67).

9   In a reflexive methodological move, again reminiscent of Foucault's revision of the subject/object relationship, e.g. in *Discipline and Punish* (Foucault 1979), Lefebvre considers the body not only as the first object of analysis, but also as that which defines, to a certain extent, the mode of analysis itself. This is at least what is implied by the neologism of "rhythmanalysis" which wants to be more than just an analysis of rhythms (Lefebvre 2004, pp. 19–26).

10   For Lefebvre's distinction between presence and the present, see Lefebvre (2004, p. 47).
11   For example, Margit Sinka, quoted in Flinn (2003, p. 208).
12   As Lefebvre points out, the rhythmical orchestration of the city is the most complex phenomenon imaginable: "the music of the City, a scene that listens to itself, an image of the present of a discontinuous sum. [. . .] No camera, no image or series of images can show these rhythms" (2004, p. 36).
13   Foucault sketched contemporary space (in the age of structuralism) as a space of "Emplacement [. . .] defined by the relations of proximity between points or elements" (2000, p. 176): "We do not live in a void that would be tinged with shimmering colors, we live inside an ensemble of relations that define emplacements that are reducible to each other and absolutely nonsuperposable" (2000, p. 178). Instead of an attempt at describing in a comprehensive fashion "the set of relations that define emplacements of transit, streets, trains," Foucault was especially interested in utopias and heterotopias as two types of spaces "which are linked with all the others, and yet at variance somehow with all the other emplacements" (2000, p. 178).
14   In this respect, the narrative logic of *Run Lola Run* can be seen as being caught in the dialectic of entrapment and escape that one can also find in Tykwer's other films. See Schlipphacke (2006, p. 109).
15   In his characterization of the limit-experience, Foucault stressed its transgressive quality, and he chose precisely the metaphors of the "spiral" and the "flash of lightning," motifs which figures prominently in *Run Lola Run*'s visual logic, to describe the transgressive act at the core of the limit-experience. See Foucault (2000, p. 74). For a detailed discussion of Foucault's notion of the limit-experience and its relation to aesthetic experience, see Jay (2005, pp. 390–400).
16   For a recent discussion of the idea of the "spatialization" of time in postmodernist art, see Jameson (2003).
17   According to a Foucauldian conception of different temporal regimes coexisting in social reality, "time can be seen as a stratified flow composed of temporalities proceeding at various speeds, as a string of immobile blocks separated by swift breaks, as a succession of exploding events, as a series of sequences progressing in spirals, as an oriented length of time following another length of time subjected to a slow systemic drift, or as a present which raises vertically its practices of liberty. Time has changing faces according to the objects whose transformation it measures (dividing practices of reason, rules of knowledge generation, apparatus of power-knowledge disciplining the bodies, productions of moral subjects), but these objects are themselves chosen accordingly to moral and political projects" (Michon 2002, p. 185).
18   Both Evans (2004) and Schlipphacke (2006) read the film's ending as a happy ending without any sense of ambivalence.

Bibliography

Atkins, B. 2003. *More Than a Game: The Computer Game as Fictional Form.* Manchester: Manchester University Press.

Bal, M. 1997. *Narratology: Introduction to the Theory of Narrative,* 2nd edn. Toronto: University of Toronto Press.

Bianco, J. S. 2004. "Techno-cinema." *Comparative Literature Studies,* 41, 3: 377–403.

Bordwell, D. 2002. "Film futures." *SubStance,* 31, 1: 88–104.

Chion, M. 1994. *Audio-Vision: Sound on Screen* (ed. and trans. C. Gorbman). New York: Columbia University Press.

Cubitt, S. 2004. *The Cinema Effect.* Cambridge, MA: The MIT Press.

Donnelly, K. J. 2005. *The Spectre of Sound: Music in Film and Television.* London: BFI Publishing.

Eskelinen, M. 2004. "Towards computer game studies," in N. Wardrip-Fruin and P. Harrigan (eds.), *First Person: New Media as Story, Performance, and Game.* Cambridge, MA: The MIT Press, pp. 36–44.

Evans, O. 2004. "Tom Tykwer's *Run Lola Run*: Postmodern, posthuman or 'post-theory'?" *Studies in European Cinema,* 1:2, 105–15.

Flinn, C. 2003. "The music that Lola ran to," in N. M. Alter and L. Koepnick (eds.), *Sound Matters: Essays on the Acoustics of Modern German Culture.* New York: Berghahn, pp. 197–213.

Foucault, M. 1979. *Discipline and Punish: The Birth of the Prison* (trans. A. Sheridan). New York: Vintage.

Foucault, M. 2000. "Different spaces," in *Aesthetics, Method, and Epistemology* (Essential Works of Foucault, 1954–84, vol. 2, ed. J. Faubion, trans. R. Hurley and others). London: Penguin Books, pp. 175–85.

Garwood, I. 2002. "The autorenfilm in contemporary German cinema," in T. Bergfelder, E. Carter and D. Göktürk (eds.), *The German Cinema Book.* London: BFI Publishing, pp. 202–10.

Grieb, M. 2002. "Run Lara run," in G. King and T. Krzywinska (eds.), *Screenplay: Cinema / Videogames / Interfaces.* London: Wallflower Press, pp. 171–84.

Hamm-Ehsani, K. 2004. "Screening modern Berlin: Lola runs to the beat of a new urban symphony." *Seminar,* 10, 1 (February): 50–65.

Heath, S. 1986. "Narrative space," in P. Rosen (ed.), *Narrative, Apparatus, Ideology: A Film Theory Reader.* New York: Columbia University Press, pp. 379–420.

Jaeckel, A. 2003. *European Film Industries.* London: BFI Publishing.

Jameson, F. 2003. "The end of temporality." *Critical Inquiry,* 29 (Summer): 695–718.

Jay, M. 2005. *Songs of Experience: Modern American and European Variations on a Universal Theme.* Berkeley: University of California Press.

Jenkins, H. 2004. "Game design as narrative architecture," in N. Wardrip-Fruin and P. Harrigan (eds.), *First Person: New Media as Story, Performance, and Game*. Cambridge, MA.: The MIT Press, pp. 118–30.

Koepnick, L. 2004. "Photographs and memories." *South Central Review*, 21, 1 (Spring): 94–129.

Lefebvre, H. 1991. *The Production of Space* (trans. D. Nicholson-Smith). Oxford: Blackwell.

Lefebvre, H. 1992. *Critique of Everyday Life, Volume 1* (trans. J. Moore). New York: Verso.

Lefebvre, H. 2002. *Critique of Everyday Life, Volume 2: Foundations for a Sociology of the Everyday* (trans. J. Moore). New York: Verso.

Lefebvre, H. 2004. *Rhythmanalysis: Space, Time and Everyday Life* (trans. S. Elden and G. Moore). London: Continuum.

Lefebvre, H. 2006. *Critique of Everyday Life, Volume 3: From Modernity to Modernism* (trans. G. Elliot). New York: Verso.

Mergenthaler, V. 2006. "Kreisfahrten: überlegungen zum ästhetischen potential eines filmischen 'stilmittels'." *Zeitschrift für Ästhetik und Allgemeine Kunstwissenschaft*, 51, 2: 269–86.

Michon, P. 2002. "Strata, blocks, pieces, spirals, elastics and verticals: Six figures of time in Michel Foucault." *Time & Society*, 11, 2/3: 163–92.

Nabokov, V. 1969. *Ada, or Ardor: A Family Chronicle*. New York: McGraw-Hill.

Rings, G. 2005. "Zum Gesellschaftsbild zweier zeitgenössischer Märchen: Emotionale und kognitive Leitmotive in Tykwer's *Lola rennt* und *Jeunet Les fabuleux destin d'Amélie Poulain*." *Fabula*, 46, 3/4: 198–216.

Schlipphacke, H. 2006. "Melodrama's Other: Entrapment and escape in the film of Tom Tykwer." *Camera Obscura*, 21, 2: 108–43.

Töteberg, M. 1998. *Tom Tykwer: Lola rennt*. Reinbek: Rowohlt.

Töteberg, M. 1999. "*Run Lola Run*: die karriere eines films." In M. Töteberg (ed.), *Szenenwechsel: Momentaufnahmen des jungen deutschen Films*. Reinbek: Rowohlt, pp. 44–9.

7

Infernal Affairs and the Ethics of Complex Narrative

Allan Cameron and Sean Cubitt

The opening images of *Infernal Affairs* (Andrew Lau Wai Keung Lau and Alan Mak Siu Fai, 2002) offer an oblique rendering of hell. Against a black background, a series of Buddha figures skirt the edges of the frame, to be replaced by the fierce brows and distorted maws of gargoyles. This is an image of descent, but as these nightmarish features surface through layers of darkness and smoke, the orientation of the movement becomes unclear. Is the camera still descending, or is it traversing the statues laterally? This initial sense of disorientation captures much about the formal and thematic direction the film will take. The film's Chinese title, *Mou gaan dou*, and opening quotation (from the Nirvana Sutra, verse 19), refer to the lowest level of hell in Buddhist mythology, "Continuous Hell."[1] Similarly, the rest of the film will be oriented around a spatial and moral hierarchy of levels. Yet we also argue that this hierarchy is undermined by a countervailing insistence on lateral orientation that is linked to the film's complication of ethical questions. In relation to its complex network of duplicitous characters, simultaneous actions, and technologically mediated communications, *Infernal Affairs* challenges its viewers to orient themselves both cognitively and ethically.

Released in 2002, *Infernal Affairs* is set in contemporary Hong Kong, five years after reunification with China. The Special Administrative Region maintains its distinctiveness, firstly in its use of Cantonese as opposed to the governmental language of the People's Republic, Mandarin; and secondly in the urbanity of its protagonists, whose knowledge of their city is integral to both their self-image and the plot. That the film's initial invocation of Buddhism coexists with its insistence upon its contemporary urban context should not, however, be seen as contradictory. As David Morley argues, "we have to begin to entertain the possibilities for a wide variety of (not necessarily secular or Western) modernities, in different parts of the globe, where science and magic, along with technology and tradition, may be mixed together in many new ways" (2007, p. 326). The intensely local modernity of Hong Kong, caught between the dying British empire and the emergent economic superpower of China, traversed by trans-Asian cultural flows, is the basis for a figuration of contemporaneity which is on the one hand utterly particular, and on the other deeply informative about the dialectics of modernity: the persistence of history, the limits of technology and rationality, and the clash not of civilizations but of loyalties at a moment as historically significant as the arrival of Protestantism is to the disturbed loyalties at the heart of Shakespeare's *Hamlet*.

The narrative centers on two young men. Ming (Andy Lau) joins the police as a spy for the triads and rises in the ranks, gradually acquiring the culture and values of the Hong Kong police force. Yan (Tony Leung) is a cop who is sent to infiltrate the triads, and who gradually finds his loyalties eroding under pressure of the lie he is forced to live. The structure of paired characters is mirrored in the supporting cast. Yan's police contact Superintendent Wong (Anthony Wong) is paralleled by Ming's triad boss Sam (Eric Tsang), while psychologist Dr Lee (Kelly Chen) and novelist Mary (Sammi Cheng) are romantic interests for Yan and Ming, respectively. The mirrored structure is further reinforced by the fates of the characters: Sam's death follows on from Wong's, while both women uncover their partner's true identity only at the end of the film. Though in some respects the narration is quite straightforward, it also proceeds according to a logic of mirrored experiences, situations, decisions, and actions. The structure is marked by police procedural and gangland cunning, coded messages, double crosses, and mistaken identity, rather than syntagmatic complexity. This intricate arrangement of characters and events governs, in turn, the narration's rapid traversal and linking of physical locations. Viewers must keep track of Yan and Ming's subterfuge, in which each pretends to be what he is not, while also following the complex series of coded communications among these infiltrators and their respective organizations.

Decrypting the City: Complexity and Terminal Identity

As befits a film which depends on contemporary, highly technologized police procedures for much of its narrative, *Infernal Affairs* can be seen as a techno-thriller. By wedding its technological base to a discourse surrounding questions of identity and subjectivity, *Infernal Affairs* takes up, to some extent, the role once performed by postmodern science-fiction films such as *Blade Runner* (1982) and *Total Recall* (1990). In particular, it articulates Scott Bukatman's notion of "terminal identity," which he defines as "a new subject-position to interface with the global realms of data circulation, a subject that can occupy or intersect the cyberscapes of contemporary existence" (Bukatman 1993, p. 9). This terminal identity involves "both the end of the subject and a new subjectivity constructed at the computer station or television screen" (ibid.). In *Infernal Affairs*, terminal identity is manifested via the characters' constant use of computer screens, broadcast devices, mobile phones, CCTV, and surveillance microphones in order not only to realize their goals but also, more directly, to survive. In this technologized, information-rich environment, the characters must be able to read technological codes, clues, and signs in order to outflank the other team, even reverting to pre-electronic modes of communication like Morse code (used by Yan to communicate with Superintendent Wong). Indeed, a surprising number of their coded communications are sonic, most importantly Morse code, but also, for example, the Mandarin song "Forgotten Time" (a reminder of Yan and Ming's meeting in a stereo store at the beginning of the film) that reappears in the last living-room sequence and is readily interpretable by Ming as Yan's signature.

At the same time, Yan and Ming's imbrication in the technologized environment of contemporary Hong Kong facilitates the erasure of a fixed individuality, generating instead fluid identities. In *Infernal Affairs*, Hong Kong identity (as in many pre-1997 films) is itself imbued with a sense of global connectedness, and also with technological know-how. Hong Kong in the film is a veritable screen city – movie screens, large-scale public screens, computer screens, department store video screens, surveillance screens, the "third screens" of laptops, mobiles, iPods, and PDAs. Hong Kong is defined by its high-tech environment, and by an emphasis on the vertical, not only in the singular framing to encompass large-scale skyscapes but in the characters' ability to scan digital maps offering a bird's-eye perspective on the city. A series of rooftop meetings afford prime views of the Hong Kong cityscape, while also recalling similar scenes from *The Matrix* (Andy and Larry Wachowski 1999), *Blade Runner*, and other science-fiction precursors of the techno-thriller. As in *The Matrix*, an ability to "read" the technologized city is associated with an elevated perspective.

In *Infernal Affairs*, the characters who cannot manage this vertical perspective are the ones who die first: Superintendent Wong is hurled from the top of a building after being caught on the wrong floor at the wrong time, while Sam (the leader of the crooks) is shot in a multi-level car park. These older characters misread the city, its levels, and its spatial, temporal, and technological codes. They are not as "wired" as Yan and Ming (who make the most direct use of computers and communication devices); not fast, flexible, or mobile enough. In this respect, *Infernal Affairs* is in accord with contemporary Hong Kong's tendency to narrate its globalized urban location via a stylistic emphasis on speed. These films, argues Esther Yau, "equally anticipate and register the impact of a high-speed race for profit against the barriers of time and space" (2001, p. 4). At crucial moments, Sam and Wong's lack of speed and adaptability is marked by sonic codes: the ting of an elevator and the ring of a cell phone provide death knells for Wong and Sam respectively. Not coincidentally, Wong and Sam are also the most stable characters, with the least fluid identities: one is clearly a cop, the other clearly a crook, representatives of an older order in which loyalties, identities, and codes of justice were still available (although *Infernal Affairs* II and III go on to complicate this distinction by suggesting a more morally complex past for Wong). At this juncture, the generational gap evokes Zygmunt Bauman's *Liquid Modernity* (2000), in which he argues that the present historical moment is defined by the devaluation of heavy and permanent resources, and a corresponding emphasis upon streamlining, speed, flexibility, and disposability. Accordingly, identity itself becomes a disposable asset in *Infernal Affairs*.

Infernal Affairs foregrounds the relationship between terminal identity and narrative legibility. The two key women in the story both make use of computers, but not for technological surveillance or detection: Ming's fiancée, Mary, is writing a novel on her laptop, while Dr Lee, Yan's romantic interest, is a psychiatrist who occasionally plays solitaire on her office computer. Crucially, their old-fashioned, psychologically derived methodologies can find no purchase with the elusive Yan and Ming. Mary is working on a story about a man who has 28 different personalities, but she cannot figure out whether her main character is good or bad. Similarly, Dr Lee is largely unable to divine Yan's true nature. Terminal identity escapes these old-fashioned approaches. The welcoming bed and psychiatrists' chair associated with these characters provide a comfortingly domestic home for the body, but the mind is elsewhere. Apparently, when viewed in relation to these "feminine" spaces, terminal identity is also an index of masculinity.

The challenge to the speed and flexibility of the characters in *Infernal Affairs* is also extended to the audience. Starting with a framing flashback showing Yan and Ming as cadets at the police academy, the film sketches their history in swift, elliptical fashion. By the time the adult Yan and Ming are introduced after the main title-card, a significant amount of plot information has been presented in a very short period of time, testing the viewer's cognitive abilities. As Yan and Ming perform their fake roles (of triad member and police detective, respectively), the quick setups and reversals of the plot demand an active and alert audience. "Can you keep up?" the film seems to ask. Spectatorship thus becomes a type of information management, just as the characters' plots, ambushes, and double-crosses are also enacted through information management. This applies also to the use of flashbacks in the film. The turn from color to grayscale, and the frequent use of jump-cuts in reprised scenes, as well as the reinsertion of echo-tracked voices as audio flashbacks, at once suggest the subjectivity of the memories evoked and their distance from accuracy, as the scenes acquire layers of meaning from their repositioning in the narration. At the same time, many of these flashbacks appear as rapid-fire barrages of narrative information, somewhat akin to the comical flashforwards in *Run Lola Run* (Tom Tykwer 1998). In a sense, we do not inhabit the times and spaces depicted in these flashbacks; we are never inside the flashback. Instead, we are made acutely aware of the flashback's status as a narrational and informational device. Indeed, their function as informational devices suggests further that the past exists only as a resource, not as a personalized cultural store from which an evolving identity draws its permanence.

Ultimately, terminal identity is made literal in the sense that one of the main characters apparently must die. This death is anticipated by the scene in which Ming deletes Yan's identity from the police computer system. After confronting Ming atop a skyscraper, Yan is challenged and then shot dead by a police officer who turns out to be another of Sam's minions. Descending in the elevator to the waiting contingent of uniformed police officers, Ming kills Yan's assassin, an act that serves on the one hand to avenge Yan's death but also, conversely, to conceal Ming's deception. The death of Yan reflects obliquely upon Hong Kong's own "terminal" identity in the wake of the 1997 handover to China, and the question of how, if at all, Hong Kong identity somehow survives Chinese assimilation. *Infernal Affairs* thus takes its place in the cycle of 1980s and 1990s Hong Kong films that evoke "both intimacy and unease" around the Hong Kong–China relationship (Teo 1997, p. 207), an issue that is dealt with even more directly in the film's two sequels.[2] Among post-1997 films, argues Sheldon Lu, anxieties around Hong Kong identity tend to be refigured as an embrace of flexible identity (2000, p. 276; 2001, p. 137), a notion that is particularly relevant here.

In *Infernal Affairs*, a sense of ambivalent retrospection surfaces at the end of the film, as Yan's identity is effectively subsumed by Ming's (becoming the yin to his yang), a point made all the more clearly by the fact that their endings appear interchangeable. Here, the evil twin wins, but turns out to have a good heart, which is identifiable or interchangeable with Yan himself, who seems to live on despite the death of the body. Conversely, Ming's killing of his erstwhile comrade-in-arms may also suggest his ongoing instinct for self-preservation: it allows him the pretense of preserving his good conscience while keeping him, ostensibly, on the right side of the law. Unlike Superintendent Wong, who displays a clarity of principle and purpose in this first film of the trilogy, Ming is saved only in that he is not discovered. The lie preserved maintains the disjuncture of terminal identity from any measure of reality, where the existence of the real is the prerequisite of both responsibility and justice.

This sense of disjuncture is further heightened by the existence of an alternative ending for the mainland Chinese version of the film. Here, the filmmakers, without any extra setup, reverse the ending by having Ming arrested for his crimes and apparently preserving Yan's life (he is sitting up with his eyes open exactly as in the Hong Kong ending, but appears to be given a point-of-view shot of Ming being marched away). This ending makes a belated attempt to iron out the moral ambiguities, evidently for the benefit of the Chinese authorities. It also serves to anchor the shifting identities of the characters: the "good" Yan survives, while the "evil" Ming is duly caught and punished. Here, then, "one country, two systems" (the Chinese government's promise that Hong Kong can remain a semi-autonomous political and economic sphere after the handover) is paralleled by one country, two endings. Yet the alternative ending's attempt to stabilize the moral meaning of the film gives rise to the sense that this is only one among an array of possible endings. Providing the justice which narrative closure demands, it reveals the lack of a sense of justice in the film that precedes it. The fragile and indeterminate status of Hong Kong democracy thus frames the film's moral ambiguity. In this confusing state of flux, perhaps morality itself becomes unrepresentable – subject to the state of "disappearance" that Ackbar Abbas describes as characteristic of Hong Kong culture in the context of its colonial past and neo-colonial present (1997). The fluidity of the characters thus anticipates the narrational and ethical fluidity of the film itself, which becomes chameleonic, adapting itself to its political context.

Terminal Ethics

The first fully realized encounter between Yan and Ming occurs in an audio and electronics store where Yan is working (they have already met in the past as police cadets). Here, Yan demonstrates some stereo equipment for Ming. The scene suggests not only two halves of a single system (reinforced by a symmetrical shot of the two men sitting in front of an array of speakers), but also a union of technological know-how and feeling. While Yan recommends a high-quality Hong Kong-made tube amplifier, Ming is able to locate an audio cable that further sweetens the sound of the music. Together, they sit and listen to a Mandarin pop song, connected by their appreciation for the music and their shared technical knowledge. "In a word, transparent," says Yan of the amplifier's sound quality, a comment that reflects ironically upon the mutual opacity of these two characters, neither of whom recognizes the other as the "mole." The sense of balance and easy camaraderie between these characters inflects them with an air of benevolence, despite the cold and merciless contest in which they are about to engage. Nonetheless, upon their next meeting, much later in the film, Yan asks Ming about the tube amp he purchased, commenting that it takes time to warm up: a process which, unlike hardwired and cold electronics, overcomes the division between information and warmth. Here, the sense of fluid identity – a signal inside a system – is grounded in a kind of "human" warmth and goodness. Yet given their later actions, this "goodness" must be considered apart from any genuine system of ethics. Both Yan and Ming must negotiate complex and interconnected systems of codes, yet neither of them is ultimately able to isolate a code of conduct.

Given the lack of a hermeneutic within the film itself, either in the form of a code to live by or of a code to interpret the central characters, the theme of terminal identity thus goes one step further, becoming terminal identification. For the audience, there is no character who provides a moral center for the film. We may perhaps identify with Yan, but if so we lose: the "evil twin" wins instead. Yet Yan's death, paradoxically, then becomes the occasion for a final sympathetic investment with his "twin," Ming. In order to get through the film with our sense of narrative balance and order intact, we are thus invited to take a pragmatic perspective on identification – to foster a fluid mode of identification that can match the characters' fluid identities. Although Wong and Sam both inhabit more clearly defined roles (cop and crook, respectively) than Yan and Ming, both in their own ways attract the audience's loyalties: Sam, as played by Eric Tsang, is a thoroughly charismatic gang boss, while Wong carries an air of quiet integrity (the latter's clarity of motive will be made far more murky in the two sequels, but it is never questioned here). Crucially, neither man provides a monopole around which the film's moral universe can be gathered into a coherent whole.

In the absence of a clear moral and identificatory center, responsibility for completing the narrative falls to the audience. Indeed, this responsibility is delivered to the audience on two levels. On the one hand there is the cognitive task of filling in the plot holes and providing a coherent explanation for the events and the actions of the characters. On the other is the far more demanding task of rounding out the film's moral sphere. The lack of a moral center in the narrative itself invites, indeed, given its genre precedents demands, the audience to provide this center. Yet the density of the narrative challenges the moral task, to the point where we may abandon the latter in order to survive the film. In other words, we may be punished for our dedication to a certain moral position or character, either through the death of those characters who most clearly embody a morally justifiable or at least coherent principle of action, or through the either-or dilemma posed by the fact that if the narrative makes sense, the morality does not, but if the morality makes sense then the narrative does not. So, the film may place responsibility upon us to provide moral judgments, but our freedom to do so is challenged by the twists, turns, and contradictions of the narrative.

In place of ethics, it may well appear, we are offered an aesthetic: of personal systems of morality generated in the loneliness which only great cities can engender. Such a conclusion cannot but recall Walter Benjamin's (2003, p. 270) strictures on the aestheticization of politics under Nazism – an anti-democratic and fundamentally amoral pursuit of aesthetic wholeness purchased through a carefully mediated control of information resulting in the technologically assured erasure of truth. We have already noted the generational distinction between those who understand or fail to understand the vertical dimension of the urban landscape. Writing of an earlier generation of Hong Kong films, Esther Yau notes that they "demonstrate a skillful adaptation of the ideological codes and functions of Hollywood to a context in which the public's preoccupations are survival and upward mobility" (1994, p. 181). Such films often "rationalize the modes of existence available within the social context as much as express, often in narrative terms, the breakdown and redefinition of these modes" (ibid.). Linking this mindset to Britain and China's economically motivated accommodation with regard to Hong Kong, Yau goes on to suggest that "the political identity of Hong Kong is thus the product of a pragmatic kind of complicity conducive to ideological ambivalence or dubiety" (pp. 183–4). Writing during the run-up to the restoration of Hong Kong to Chinese rule, Yau notes the ambivalence of "1997 consciousness," whose particular relevance to this analysis of a film made six years after the new regime came in concerns the destabilization of not one but two modes of social and spatial orientation. For Wong and Sam, the world offers a place, one that has to be attained, but which preexists the person who occupies it: gang boss, police superintendent. Ming and Yan belong to a generation for whom upward mobility is the central experience, based on the power of the Hong Kong economy in the later years of British rule, during which a discredited colonial regime embarrassed itself by demanding from the Chinese a democracy they had never themselves extended to their subjects.

The film's aestheticization of upward mobility exists in ironic counter-point to systems of spiritual morality, which tend to be predicated upon a vertical orientation. In tune with the lowest level of hell named in the film's title and opening epigraph, morality and spatial elevation go hand in hand. Accordingly, rooftop real estate in the film is the domain of the police. Wong and Yan, for example, stage their covert meetings in these locations. Upon working his way up to the Department of Internal Affairs, Ming is invited to hit golf balls from the top of the building. By the end of the film, when he has his climactic elevated confrontation with Yan, Ming is prompted to ask: "Do all undercover cops like rooftops?" Yet Ming's infiltra-tion of the police force severs the link between this vertical hierarchy and the moral hierarchy that it appears to underwrite (in which criminals belong in the underworld, while cops overlook the city from on high). The invo-cation of Buddhist mythology thus serves to emphasize the emphatically secular and amoral world in which the characters appear to rise and fall.

Yet what is striking about the aestheticization observable in *Infernal Affairs* is that while the narrative contains many vertical motifs, the film is, styl-istically speaking, wedded to horizontal mobility. The camera is rarely still, dollying in or out of shots, panning across a room, and when holding a face in frame, often enough observing that face through the windshield of a moving vehicle. Similarly, Ming's office environment is surrounded by internal windows. This suggests not only the tension between such a space of transparency and the opacity Ming must maintain with regard to his motives; crucially, it also suggests that this tension is played out along a horizontal plane, traversed laterally by light and information. In this context, in which speed and light are one, united as "the shifting appearances of momentary and false transparencies," the spatial integrity of the film's locations is challenged: "the glance is at once site and sight" (Virilio 1991, p. 62). In a city of screens, horizontal mobility holds sway. A lateral orientation is also suggested by the film's insistence upon sonic metaphors and codes. Both stereo and surround sound systems, after all, differentiate sounds in terms of direction and volume but not spatial elevation in relation to the listener. Therefore, if the stereo system at the beginning of the film provides a metaphor for Yan and Ming's parallel destinies, then it suggests not upward mobility but rather circulation within a horizontal system.

This horizontality, we believe, belongs to a newer mode of social aspiration that supersedes the myth of upward mobility, which is undermined in the film by Yan's progressive entrapment in the underworld and subsequent death, by Ming's rise to the top upon false premises, and by the sense that this achievement will be haunted by the ghost of his departed double (indeed, *Infernal Affairs* III [2003] plays heavily upon Ming's sense of guilt, to the point where he suffers a breakdown and begins to identify himself with Yan). Thus, upward mobility is demonstrated to be a lie in two senses: that it never occurs, or that it occurs only unjustifiably. This moral and spatial leveling is suggested in particular by the scene in which Yan uncovers Ming's identity as the mole. When Ming leaves his glass-walled office for a moment, Yan begins to snoop around, triggering an interaction between the two characters that is conducted indirectly via a type of narrative cryptography, a spatio-temporal circulation of oblique codes and communications. Recognizing his own handwriting on an envelope on Ming's desk, Yan looks through the window at Ming, and sees him tapping a document against his leg. This triggers in turn a very rapid grayscale flashback: a following shot from Yan's perspective of the "mole" displaying the same mannerism. Returning to his office to find it empty, Ming gazes through the glass at the exposed envelope, realizing he has been discovered. Here, a series of shots organized around horizontal camera movements and point-of-view shots through glass serve to level the protagonists spatially, and implicitly morally too.

That Yan's realization occurs as a flashback suggests, furthermore, a lateral movement through time, in which cyclical patterns of behavior and event are replayed. A similar effect is achieved by the repetition, at the close of the film, of Yan's expulsion from the cadet school. The scene is replayed in grayscale, but intercut with color shots of the adult Yan and Ming. Ming's adult persona responds again to the question "Who wants to trade places with him?" (referring to the departing Yan) with the words "I do." Of course, by the end of the film, Yan is dead, and the desire to trade places has an entirely different sense, that of a desire, we might say, for a narrative closure that the basic imposture forbids. As suggested by the film's prologue and epilogue, the characters are thus condemned to a circuitous progression through a Continuous Hell, an exteriority which implies that no self-improvement is possible once a path of destiny has been chosen. This may imply, on the one hand, that the characters are effectively outside of history ("He who is in Continuous Hell never dies," reads the concluding quotation). On the other, it may suggest that Yan and Ming are, like Hong Kong itself, confined by the terms of a specific history that appears to offer no exit. In any case, the amoral universe of urban Hong Kong in *Infernal Affairs* constitutes a Continuous Hell in which cycles always return, and where apparent success, like apparent failure, is merely a rise or fall on the same wheel, at equal heights, merely moving in different directions.

Democracy and Disorientation

As Jonathan Beller observes, "In the commercial cinema, you must narrativize whatever postmodern intensities are there to be experienced" (Beller 2006, p. 153). In simple narratives, the intensities associated with the ethics of decision making tend to be narrativized through such recognizable causal arrangements as the "felicitous calculus" of the utilitarians, whereby the maximum happiness arising from an act is the basis for deciding whether the act is a good one or not. Thus, the killing of enemy soldiers is good if it produces the defeat of the enemy's leader. In *Infernal Affairs*, the complex address to viewer loyalties undermines such a calculus. For example, although the death of Wong is clearly a wrong, Sam's death at the hands of his erstwhile mole Ming cannot represent victory, or the triumph of the good, because Ming's motive is largely one of self-interest. Arguably, audiences are not encouraged to want the death of any of the characters who die in the film, and no death gives us the kind of narrative closure that death so frequently affords in normative cinemas. In the culminating rooftop confrontation, Ming is silently ambushed by Yan. Where previously sound cues had indicated the imminence of death, Yan's gun appears silently pressing into Ming's back, with the softest of clicks as the safety is taken off. As the dialogue proceeds, a critical moment of ethical choice arrives when Ming asks for a chance to turn over a new leaf. Yan replies, "Good. Try telling that to the judge." A beat. Ming: "You want me dead?" Yan: "Sorry, I'm a cop." Ming: "Who knows that?" Here, Ming hints at the flimsiness of Yan's institutionally sanctioned moral code, connected in turn to the tenuousness of his professional identity.

Although there will be at least two more narrative twists before the film ends, this is the ethical crux. Here, a series of six swift jump cuts and a track-out frame Yan with his gun to Ming's forehead, emblematizing a judicial system that will only execute, the culmination of a moral code based on a trust that no longer exists, and the main characters' mutual loss of faith in the notion of their shared experience. Acted out above the city streets is a minimalist reading of the terminal fate of any virtue ethics grounded on immutable principles, any value ethics, or even the felicitous calculus, in a world in which dissimulation leads directly to the loss of trust. It is here perhaps that the film most clearly reveals the moral complexities of which complex narration is capable. Unlike other recent films in which good men lost in complex systems struggle to find a moral root (such as *Syriana* [2005], *Lord of War* [2005], and *Crash* [2004]), *Infernal Affairs* clearly anchors its moral judgments in personal responsibility. It does so, however, in the full knowledge that in order to take such responsibility, its central characters must actually and fully exist as coherent and therefore action-capable agents. It is here that the film's moral universe collapses.

This collapse is a function not so much of a crisis of subjectivity per se: it would be inaccurate to ascribe a Western modernist individualism to Hong Kongers' experience of their own particular modernity. Rather, since narrative depends upon relationships between people, and here, we believe, narrative meets a limit point, then the inference must be that the collapse is not within but between, not subjective but inter-subjective. That collapse is the result of a regime of betrayal and camouflage that pervades the plot. It is strictly speaking interpersonal rather than either individual or social, belying both capital's myth of individual freedom and the Durkheimian myth of a social consciousness which, once recognized, provides the basis for religious awe and moral action. It is the isolation of each, not at the moment of death (each fatality in the film is in fact accompanied by a moment of recognition, either of or from a witnessing character), but in the moment of communication that dominates the film's framing, staging, and use of focus and lighting. In this sense too we are dealing with terminal identities.

This sense of isolation is characterized by, for example, the scene described earlier in which Ming's identity is revealed to Yan. Here, the revelation plays out through a scenario of mutual exclusion, in which first Yan and then Ming communicate indirectly, in the other's absence, via the clues in Ming's office.[3] It is further encapsulated in the moment on the rooftop when Ming, glimpsing Yan reflected in the window of a skyscraper, spins around to find only empty space, as if the reflection had been his own after all. Once again, one protagonist appears as a virtual reflection of the other. To the extent that ethics concerns a personal commitment to the other, in which alone one's own right to exist is confirmed (Levinas 1989), all drama that is based on the face-to-face meeting of characters depends upon that irruption of the Other to produce one's being. In *Infernal Affairs*, by contrast, the mutual otherness of the two main protagonists fails to take shape, in the absence of any interaction that might confront each with the other. When finally our protagonists meet in an unmediated way, other than through inference and clues, the initial sense each has that the other can confirm them in their reality is diffused and disappointed by the continuing subterfuges. In this sense, both characters are denied the kind of truth to themselves that can only derive from their truth to the other, from the capacity each has to draw out the truth of the other from their initially unknowable physiognomies. It is a question for narrative film of the status of truth.

The question raised by *Infernal Affairs* concerns specifically the relations between truth and fiction or, rather, between the loss of truth experienced by both protagonists, and the sense that any audience will have that they are watching a fiction. The moral argument of the film becomes apparent in the failure of either Yan or Ming to grasp the complexities of their condition – that only in communication between them can an ethical relation be secured. Ming is prepared to ask for that recognition, but from a position in which he has already forfeited the trust on which interpersonal ethics can alone be founded. Yan in response refuses the invitation, calling on a morally superior, logically precedent, and socially binding concept of Law in which, however, neither can believe. As a result, it is the viewer who must take responsibility for the truth, while the characters blunder toward the dénouement in a thickening fog of deception.

The question then concerns truth's displacement from either a protagonist or an authorial voice toward a spectator who is, finally, just that – one who watches but is unable to act. What orders of truth can we expect, and on whom does responsibility for them devolve? If responsibility is as much a quality of democracy as is freedom, then a complex narrative is democratic to the extent that it works only when an audience or an audience member is ready to take over from the producers the job of completing the work. The complex narrative of the film raises the possibility that truth conditions change historically and biographically, but that under such pressure, a new gap opens between truth and action. That gap is the place of communication, but here such communication is always at a distance, and always subject to dissimulation and disguise, to the extent that even the face-to-face meeting is poisoned by its antecedent mediations. Perhaps more importantly still, the mounting array of betrayals and lies that sever the protagonists from any moral universe grounded in the recognition of an other leaves the viewer far more uncertain of their own commitment to the characters than would be the case in a less complex narrative – such as, for example, the US re-versioning of *Infernal Affairs*, Scorsese's *The Departed* (2006).

The difficulty becomes more intense as we try to fathom the democratic elements of the narrative–narratee relation. For the narratee to respond with an adequate moral evaluation of the film's fictive actions, there must be some sense of responsibility to the fictional others who play out their time on the stage. Firstly, however, this responsibility is made difficult by the characters' resistance to becoming fully real, stemming from the complexity of the narrative. Secondly, Yan and Ming's equivalence in terms of the parallel lies each must live, in itself ostensibly democratic, in fact dedifferentiates them, giving us the impression that both are equals not only in their lack of truth to the other and thence to the self, but also to us as viewers. Thus our otherwise culturally sanctioned role in interfacing with artistic texts, to make judgments and undertake creative and intellectual tasks not completed by the text itself, is frustrated by the lack of that difference into which we might insert ourselves. In effect, the spectator is drawn into the same dedifferentiating and vertiginous lack of reality that we observe in Ming's anxious moments scouring the terminal rooftop for his other. Has he jumped at his own reflection? Has he jumped at the reflection of the spectator? Are we jumping at our own reflection?

Democracy refused in two formal modes by the British and by the Chinese returns as a disorientation, in which the specifics of the ethics of trust common to Cantonese culture as reflected in Hong Kong film are undercut and themselves betrayed by a democratizing process which, in denying difference, denies that recognition of the other as other on which trust must be founded. The physical connection, instead of appearing as mediation, the common ground on which these primal ethical and communicative channels can be opened, appears as blockages, technological interference, and the grounds not of truth but of deception. Having opened this Pandora's box, however, the film cannot close it. The collapse of the interpersonal embraces also the spectator, drawn into this loss of the distinction that mediation provides.

This is perhaps why the film strikes us as so poignant, and so aesthetically pleasing. The duels that, from Hegel to Levinas, are at the heart of the interpersonal roots of the social, here are irreconcilable and unwinnable. They are not formative of truth but deforming, and yet that deformation is also informative, almost to surfeit, as we navigate the double-crosses to the conclusion (only to have them reopened and mirrored over again in the remaining films in the trilogy). The excess of information itself becomes a quality of this strange democratization of the narrative, as it is of the new urban societies of the twenty-first century. Typically, we hope for a film to become an agent, an Other with which we dialogue; but here the internal dedifferentiation of the characters spurs a second, external dedifferentiation. That it meets with such recognition as a popular success is due to a different order of truth: one that depicts epic, heroic, ethical failure as a characteristic quality of our times. That in passing it thus unveils the simplistic and truly ahistorical ethical principles of simple narrative is only a bonus.

Notes

1 Literally, "Mou Gaan Dou" means "No Way Out," which explains why the title is a reference to the lowest level of Buddhist Hell.

2 In particular, the connection between narrative complexity and Hong Kong's uncertain political identity is a much-noted feature of Wong Kar-wai's films (see for example *Chungking Express* [1994] and *2046* [2004]); their obsession with Hong Kong's disappearing identity is mirrored by a focus on time, flux, ephemerality, delivered via an aesthetic of visual and narrative complexity. Interestingly, Christopher Doyle, Wong Kar-wai's much-praised cinematographer, is credited as a "Visual Consultant" on *Infernal Affairs*.

3 A related sense of mutual dislocation colors the opening scene of *Infernal Affairs II* (2003). In this dialogue scene, not only do the voices occupy different speakers, but the ticking clock in the background also flicks from one side of the screen to the other as the eyelines intercut. This rigorous dualism is paralleled by the dialogue itself, in which neither Wong nor Sam is capable of communicating with the other, despite the earnest wish of both to make the connection.

Bibliography

Abbas, M. A. 1997. *Hong Kong: Culture and the Politics of Disappearance.* Minneapolis: University of Minnesota Press.

Bauman, Z. 2000. *Liquid Modernity.* Cambridge: Polity.

Beller, J. 2006. *The Cinematic Mode of Production: Attention Economy and the Society of the Spectacle.* Hanover, NH: Dartmouth College Press.

Benjamin, W. 2003. "The work of art in the age of its technological reproducibility: Third version," in H. Eiland and M. W. Jennings (eds.), *Selected Writings,* vol. 4, *1938–1940.* Cambridge, MA: Bellknap Press/Harvard University Press, pp. 251–83.

Bukatman, S. 1993. *Terminal Identity: The Virtual Subject in Postmodern Science Fiction.* Durham, NC: Duke University Press.

Levinas, E. 1989. "Ethics as first philosophy" (trans. S. Hand and M. Temple), in S. Hand (ed.), *The Levinas Reader.* Oxford: Blackwell, pp. 75–87.

Lu, S. H. 2000. "Filming diaspora and identity: Hong Kong and 1997," in P. Fu and D. Desser (eds.), *The Cinema of Hong Kong: History, Arts, Identity.* Cambridge: Cambridge University Press, pp. 273–88.

Lu, S. H. 2001. "Hong Kong diaspora film and transnational TV drama: From homecoming to exile to flexible citizenship." *Post Script,* 20, 2/3: 137–46.

Morley, D. 2007. *Media, Modernity and Technology: The Geography of the New.* London: Routledge.

Teo, S. 1997. *Hong Kong Cinema: The Extra Dimensions.* London: BFI.

Virilio, P. 1991. *The Lost Dimension* (trans. D. Moshenberg). New York: Semiotext(e).

Yau, E. 1994. "Border crossing: Mainland China's presence in Hong Kong cinema," in N. Browne, P. G. Pickowitz, V. Sobchack, and E. Yau (eds.), *New Chinese Cinemas: Forms, Identities, Politics.* Cambridge: Cambridge University Press, pp. 180–201.

Yau, E. 2001. "Introduction: Hong Kong cinema in a borderless world," in Esther C. M. Yau (ed.), *At Full Speed: Hong Kong Cinema in a Borderless World.* Minneapolis: University of Minnesota Press, pp. 1–28.

8

Happy Together? Generic Hybridity in *2046* and *In the Mood for Love*

Gary Bettinson

In this chapter I argue that adventurous storytelling in Wong Kar-wai's *2046* (2004) and *In the Mood for Love* (2000) arises predominantly out of an elaborate engagement with popular genre. I begin by arguing that narrational ploys in *2046* act self-consciously to disorient and misdirect the viewer: the film's ambiguous combination of melodrama and science fiction draws the viewer into errors of comprehension. Later I suggest that *In the Mood for Love* discreetly meshes together two disparate genres, resulting in a narration shot through with story gaps, unreliable cues, and retardations. I go on to sketch the ways in which both films alight upon a convention of melodrama, arguing that *2046* – a putative sequel to *In the Mood for Love* – cannot justify its complex generic strategies to the same degree as its more celebrated predecessor. Finally, I identify Wong's generic tactics in terms of a fundamental cinephilia, and point to what I suggest are the most pertinent and proximate contexts for Wong's generic and narrational experimentation.

Storytelling in both films is seldom gratuitously complex. Typically an obliquely staged action or a story ellipsis will be motivated by textual elements; often the unorthodox device will execute narrative functions, retarding, advancing, or providing commentary upon story action. I try to show that *In the Mood for Love* and *2046* justify even their most idiosyncratic narrational maneuvers by generic or compositional devices of motivation. The chapter also attempts to characterize the narrative functions performed by such maneuvers, along with the particular effects they engender.

Changing Minds: Complex Narration in *2046*

At the beginning of *2046*, Tak (Takuya Kimura) is traveling on a train departing from the year 2046, a year which attracts time-travelers who seek reclamation of lost memories. It is also a temporal space in which the forces of change are retarded. In 1963 Chow Mo-wan (Tony Leung Chiu-wai) pursues but is rebuffed by Black Spider (Gong Li), a professional gambler in Singapore. In 1966 Chow encounters Mimi (Carina Lau), who mourns the death of her playboy lover. After Mimi is violently attacked by a jealous admirer (Chang Chen), Chow learns that the assault occurred in room 2046 of Hong Kong's Oriental Hotel. The room number resonates with Chow, and he rents the adjacent room. There he writes a futuristic story entitled "2046." Later Chow solicits the attentions of Bai Ling (Zhang Ziyi) and a tempestuous affair ensues; but when Bai Ling becomes too emotionally dependent on him, Chow backs off. An ongoing feud between the hotel manager and his daughter, Wang Jingwen (Faye Wong), prompts Chow to intervene: he becomes a go-between in the affair involving Jingwen and her Japanese lover, Tak, of whom Jingwen's father disapproves. In 1970, Bai Ling inadvertently triggers Chow's memory of Black Spider, whose real name, Su Lizhen, reminds the protagonist of a past love. Chow rejects Bai Ling's overtures and taxis home alone.

2046 opens in the epoch of the film's title, and its post-credits sequence establishes a spectacular artery of futuristic roads and rail-tracks. Tak's voiceover dialogue accompanies enigmatic imagery of color-streaked tunnels, cavernous monoliths, and female robots. The plot then moves to 1963, though at this stage a lack of expository markers prevents us from determining the spatio-temporal context of the action. (A viewer familiar with *In the Mood for Love* may be able to infer a broad narrative context by certain echoic elements of the *mise-en-scène* [lighting, setting, etc.], as well as by the figure of Chow.) An inter-title provides the transition between the two scenes but is too abstract to orient us to the narrative context of our new setting. To compound our disorientation, Wong Kar-wai starts the second scene *in medias res* as Chow and a female intimate converse cryptically about promises exchanged during a prior unseen encounter. Combining repressive story exposition with an unspecified temporal and spatial context provokes the viewer's curiosity about narrative action: Who are the figures in this scene? How are they related? When and where is this action set?

Most strikingly, the juxtaposed scenes exhibit a highly disjunctive use of genre. There is a staggering lack of explicit causal, temporal, or spatial links between the two opening scenes, which generates ambiguity and in turn engages our curiosity. (How) are the two scenes related? Wong will sustain this ambiguity throughout the first 24 minutes of the film, so that the two plotlines unfold in uncertain relation to each other. Such ambiguity sets the viewer on the path to inference-making. Among the various hypotheses we are likely to hold in balance is that the two plot strands are unconnected, unless perhaps in broadly symbolic or thematic ways. Principally, though, the spectator will search for causal connections between the lines of action. Several factors may prompt us to regard the science-fiction plot as a "frame" narrative which encloses and articulates the 1960s action (which we regard as an "embedded" narrative). Plot order is one such factor: the film opens in 2046 and subsequently switches to 1963, an anterior maneuver which may hint at a flashback structure. The flashback hypothesis is strengthened by the presence of Tak's voiceover narration in the opening scene, which we may assume to bracket the 1963 scene as well as the futuristic action. And we might expect the embedded plotline to elucidate several oblique enigmas set up by the film's opening sequence (Why did Tak leave 2046? Did the woman he refers to ever truly love him? Will Tak discover the woman's secrets?).

The spectator's flashback hypothesis will be attenuated and eventually disqualified by subsequent events. An attenuating factor is the narration's refusal to anchor the 1960s action to Tak's voiceover commentary; and the introduction of Chow's voiceover during the 1960s scenes weakens our flashback inference still further. It is fully 24 minutes into the film before we can unequivocally determine the proper connection between the plotlines. Now both story strands are revealed to be causally linked: as Chow conveys in voiceover that he is writing a science-fiction novel entitled "2046," the narration provides visual fragments of futuristic action. The narration's communicativeness here allows us to confidently relate the film's science-fiction plotline to Chow's subjectivity.[1] At the same time, this new information countermands our initial flashback hypothesis, reversing our assumption that the futuristic scenes constitute a frame narrative that "narrates" an embedded 1960s storyline. Moreover, we are forced to recast what we have taken to be a "real" story universe (the 2046 sequences) in terms of a fictional milieu dreamt up by Chow. Until now (and given that *2046* initially announces itself as a science-fiction film) we are given no reason to regard the futuristic world as any less ontologically stable than the film's period setting. All of these factors function to mark the narration as predominantly repressive, apt to foster inappropriate and erroneous assumptions.

The overt juxtaposition of melodramatic and science-fiction genres in *2046* strikes a disjunctive note, particularly during early phases of the action.

As the film progresses, however, these genre elements gradually cohere in each of the main plotlines. Emotion is the common link between the genres, and it becomes central to both parallel stories. Without abandoning its futuristic iconography, the science-fiction plotline settles down into an essentially melodramatic narrative invoking sentiment, romance, and thwarted desire. The melodramatic line of action reciprocally broaches what genre specialists agree is a favorite theme of science fiction: the notion of "humanness" (Neale 2000, pp. 102–3; King and Krzywinska 2002). *2046* limns Chow's everyday existence as robotic. This analogy holds good for Chow's mechanistic tendency to shut down his emotions, and to repel the emotions of others. An assembly line of women bears witness to Chow's repudiation of emotional commitment. He values alcohol for its anesthetic effects ("It makes things easy"). His existence is also robotic in its commitment to routine: Chow is locked into an automated pattern of behavior. (It is not incidental that his diegetic writing fabricates a universe in which "nothing ever changes"; such a place offers utopian comfort for a protagonist seeking habituation and permanence.) Chow traces an arc of character development which guides him toward an acceptance of emotion (he develops romantic attachments to Jingwen and Su Lizhen) and change (he shrugs off old routines). In other words, indelibly *human* aspects of life force their way into Chow's acceptance. By organizing plot material around themes of emotion, Wong is able to harmonize two initially discordant genres.

Science fiction violates ordinary standards of realism, and *2046* exploits this norm to motivate a double character strategy: several of the film's performers play futuristic characters as well as their twentieth-century counterparts. Agents with identical physicalities routinely populate the universe of science fiction – think of François Truffaut's *Fahrenheit 451* (1966) as another example allied to art cinema. Moreover, Wong can motivate his film's science-fiction devices diegetically, by subjectivizing the futuristic plotline. *2046* justifies its fantastic genre iconography by harnessing it to Chow's outlandish imagination. Despite the bizarreness of the world he envisions, Chow weights his fictive universe with data from his own life ("I made up the whole thing," he says, "but some of my experiences found their way into it"). By making the protagonist a writer who is apt to novelize his real life, Wong can further justify placing several of the film's performers in dual roles.

The film's narration will complicate its pattern of doubling by yoking Chow's future self to the physical attributes of a different character. The

Chow of 2046 is identified by the bodily traits of Tak. In story terms, it is plausible that Chow should envision himself as Tak, given that he identifies with the Japanese character's romantic affection for Jingwen. But the narration delays overt signaling of this conflation of characters, so that for much of the film we inappropriately individuate Chow and the time-traveling Tak as separate characters. The late-arriving information (coming after an hour and ten minutes of screen time) forces us to make a host of reassessments and qualifications. First, we must re-identify Chow on the basis of entirely new bodily features: "Chow," we now discover, is individuated in the film by two contrasting physical specificities. (At the same time, we must discriminate Chow's "imagined" body from his "actual" body.) Second, we must revise our understanding of earlier sci-fi action involving Tak. The time-traveler's subjective state must now be retroactively understood as representing the attitudes, emotions, and beliefs of Chow. Complicating matters still further, the narration asks us to ascribe a different cluster of psychological traits to Tak in each of the film's two main time zones: despite their bodily continuity, Tak's past and future incarnations are not harnessed to a single psychology.

Deviously, the narration suppresses cues that might alert us to Chow and Tak's synonymity. In the film's opening sequence, Tak's voiceover dialogue (spoken in Japanese) overlays images of a futuristic cityscape. Later, the same stretch of dialogue is repeated and is once again accompanied by science-fiction imagery, but now *Chow* intones the dialogue (in Cantonese). By this stage, the narration has revealed Tak to be Chow's simulacrum, and thus the iterated phrase spoken by Chow compounds our understanding that both characters are interchangeable figures. But the more communicative iteration also exposes the repressiveness of the initial voiceover, which in retrospect is seen to hold back fundamental character information. Nothing in the opening sequence cues us to the protagonist's shifting identities. However, narrational sleight of hand is here justified at a diegetic level: since Chow literally "authors" the 2046 universe and envisions its visual dimensions, it is conceivable that he also "envisions" its sonic dimension, including the vocal characteristics of his characters. In this case, a repressive storytelling tactic can be justified in terms of the fantasy constructions of the novelist-protagonist.

Bodily resemblances encourage us to compare characters across the film's two distinct plotlines. The narration does not merely ask us to comprehend the future action *in its own right* (itself a demanding task, given the action's elliptical and enigmatic procedures); we must also grasp story action in the 2046 narrative as echoing and illuminating character psychology and relationships in the parallel plotline. Chow's romantic attraction to Jingwen is communicated most strongly – though, because "narrativized" by Chow, most obliquely – during the science-fiction scenes between Tak and the android. As well as keeping pace with current action, then, the viewer must constantly cross-reference characters and action across the parallel lines of action. Failing to determine the appropriate connections between characters, and to map the emotions and attitudes of an agent onto his or her parallel counterpart, risks losing track of character relationships in the 1960s sequences.

Both *2046* and *In the Mood for Love* weave repetitive patterns of story action, and here again compositional motivation anchors the narration's play with form. As we will see, obsessive reenactment justifies much of *In the Mood for Love*'s motivic action (i.e., action which, through formal repetition, acquires the function of a motif). *2046* motivates its repetitive action diegetically as well. Actions that we witness in the 1960s plotline are subsequently restaged in the 2046 narrative – a strategy which not only calls attention to the narration's motivic patterning, but also corroborates our belief that Chow builds his diegetic writing out of his real-life experiences.

However, though Wong motivates a surprising number of storytelling strategies by action within the story world, not every narrational strategy in *2046* can be accounted for by the diegesis or by generic convention. The film's ordering of story events, for instance, is outside the influence of any diegetic character or story action. No diegetic factor can justify the fact that, in plot terms, we are shown the 2046 universe *before* Chow decides to invent it. More generally, the narration asserts its autonomy by ordering story events in convoluted fashion. It is with considerable unpredictability that *2046* zigzags through its various time zones. The time-traveling trope of science fiction does not motivate this adventurous plotting either. It cannot, for example, account for the film's mazy trajectory within the twentieth-century plotline (e.g., its unpredictable shifts between 1963, 1967, 1970, and so on). Nor does science fiction motivate the narration's repressiveness. To be sure, many modern science-fiction films exhibit a repressive (or detective) narration (recall, for example, *Blade Runner* [1982], *12 Monkeys* [1995], and *Minority Report* [2002]). But detective narration in these films is motivated by an enigma and investigation set up in the films' story. In *2046* there is no such investigation to *generically* motivate the narration's ellipses, retardations, and deceptive stratagems. Occasionally refusing to mark temporal data explicitly (e.g., through inter-titles), the narration creates a labile sense of time by sliding between distinct time periods.

An unpredictable temporality also pervades *In the Mood for Love*, as does a highly repressive narrational style. If *2046* cannot textually motivate certain of its storytelling tactics, we shall find that *In the Mood for Love* provides greater justification for its various narrational strategies. Here, as so often in Wong's films, experimental storytelling begins with the director's cinephiliac engagement with genre.

Crimes of Passion: *In the Mood for Love*

In discussing *2046* I argued that a clash of generic styles creates a strong retarding and disorienting effect. More subtly, *In the Mood for Love* generates narrational complexity by tacitly imbricating two distinct genres. Wong has alluded in interviews to this generic layering, suggesting that a latent genre is operative beneath the film's surface melodrama. He reveals that *In the Mood for Love* was at first conceived as an exercise in Hitchcockian suspense, with the romance story of affairs and heartbreak merely a pretext for a virtual detective story.

> . . . instead of treating [*In the Mood for Love*] as a love story, I decided to approach it like a thriller, like a suspense movie. [The protagonists] start out as victims, and then they start to investigate, to try to understand how things happened. This is the way I structured this film, with very short scenes and an attempt to create constant tension. (Tirard 2002, p. 198)

This detective framework is discernible not only in the narrative structure of *In the Mood for Love*, but also, I suggest, in the film's *mise-en-scène*, iconography, and narrational point of view. A furtive detective paradigm recurrently snakes its way to the surface of the film, rupturing the conventions of melodrama and, most significantly, forcing us into errors of comprehension.

In the Mood for Love begins in 1962. Two strangers, Chow Mo-wan (Tony Leung) and Su Lizhen (Maggie Cheung), briefly cross paths at Mrs Suen's boarding house in Hong Kong. Mrs Suen leases a room to Su and her husband, while Chow leases the adjacent apartment for himself and his wife. Chow and Su establish a neighborly acquaintance, but begin to suspect their respective spouses of having an affair. The two characters grow curious as to how the affair began, and tentatively enact their spouses' initial overtures.

Gradually, the protagonists come to acknowledge their own mutual attraction, but determine not to act further on their desire. Gossip about their friendship soon percolates through the tenement building. Aware of his nascent feelings for Su, Chow takes a job in Singapore. Years later, Chow travels to Cambodia and visits the ruins of Angkor Wat, where he whispers a secret into a crevice in the ruins.

Synoptically, *In the Mood for Love* may seem to augur a fairly typical melodrama. Domestic conflict – the bedrock of the genre – is forecast by the story's marital betrayals, which prepare the way for impassioned confrontations within the central quartet of characters. Yet the narration largely banishes the spouses from the film, staving off melodramatic conflict, and exposing the adulterous figures as a kind of story armature on which to hang the activity of the main protagonists. More generally, the film will parade a host of narrational stratagems and gambits that cut against the grain of melodramatic convention.

How can we account for such unpredictable and apparently anti-generic storytelling in the film? I would posit the following explanation. Despite its explicit evocation of melodrama, *In the Mood for Love* tacitly animates and generally cleaves to the conventions of a distinct generic schema. The real locus of conflict in the film may be perceived at the level of narration, which negotiates a tension between melodramatic and detective modes of storytelling.

As Wong has hinted, *In the Mood for Love* may be understood as a virtual detective story, depicting the protagonists' investigation into a concealed infidelity. While the spouses' surreptitious affair constitutes the narrative "crime," the protagonists' post-mortem of the affair represents the narrative "investigation." In invoking the structure of a detective narrative, Wong also invokes the moral dimension of the detective universe. If the protagonists' play-acting is analogous to an investigation, the spouses' affair is attributed all the moral worth of a crime. (I am not arguing that the *film* confers this perspective on the spouses, only that it is the view shared by the protagonists.) It is their own simplistic morality that Chow and Su must confront when they become conscious of their illicit emotions, a revelation that occurs as they role-play the coquetry exchanged by their spouses. This restaging of the spouses' adulterous overtures literalizes a cliché of the detective genre: namely, that of retracing the criminals' movements (or reenacting the crime).

Mapping such tacit schemata onto the film allows us to expose familiar detective tropes, and ascribe generic motivation to apparently unconventional, anti-generic story action. Again, the protagonists' role-play provides an instance. If the protagonists intend their reenactment to be akin to a "detached" investigation, their intention backfires. Investigating the spouses' affair leads Su and Chow to identify with the extramarital desire they simulate.[2] This identification finds direct correspondence in detective fiction, where the close association of detective and criminal is a staple gesture. This results in a blurring of morality: the polarities of good and evil are collapsed, and the detective's moral identity threatens to be absorbed by the criminal's (or vice versa).[3] Against the film's *overt* melodramatic template, this role-play trajectory appears idiosyncratic and anti-generic. But by drawing on the film's *tacit* detective schemata we begin to discover quite traditional generic material. In this example, then, storytelling is not anti-*generic*; rather it hews to a generic paradigm that the film on the whole keeps hidden.

Tacit detective elements are brought palpably to the fore by the film's scenographic design. Noir iconography invades the *mise-en-scène*: ringing telephones and doorbells remain discomfitingly unanswered; cigarettes are obsessively smoked and function as ubiquitous markers of anxiety; and at night a perpetual rainfall pounds the lamp-lined streets of Hong Kong. An otherwise latent detective schema here parades on the surface of *In the Mood for Love*, and cues the spectator to search for other detective elements in the film.

Aside from story action and iconography, these detective elements become manifest in the film's narrational point of view. It is here that the film most consistently overturns conventional melodramatic storytelling. David Bordwell argues that a melodrama's narration is characterized by communicativeness and omniscience (Bordwell 1985, pp. 70–3). A melodrama will construct knowledge hierarchies which bestow epistemic authority upon the spectator. Edward Branigan has shown how hierarchies of knowledge allow us to "evaluate whether the spectator knows more than (>), the same as (=), or less than (<) a particular character at a particular time" (Branigan 1992, pp. 75–6). Melodramas predominantly cleave to the following pattern: S > C, where S denotes the spectator and C denotes the diegetic characters. In conventional melodrama, the narration creates a "disparity of knowledge" so structured as to situate the spectator on the top tier of the epistemic hierarchy. Consequently, the melodrama's narrative is presented with maximum transparency, mobilizing mainstays of the genre such as legibility of action and dramatic irony. By contrast, the detective film contrives a style of narration governed by opacity, repressiveness, and retardation. Omniscience and transparency are jettisoned. Even the investigation stage of the narrative is characterized by some degree of uncommunicativeness. In accordance with its narrative emphasis on concealment and mystery, the detective film harnesses its narration to the restriction of the viewer's knowledge. In Branigan's terms, the spectator and the protagonist tend to occupy the same strata in the hierarchy of knowledge (S = C), though sometimes the spectator will know even less than the detective (S < C).

In the Mood for Love's investigation is communicated with detective-style repressiveness. It is 26 minutes into the film before we are alerted unequivocally to the protagonists' suspicion of their spouses. (As with *2046*, Wong postpones the apparent crystallizing of story events until the third reel.) By this stage the film has strongly hinted at marital discord (Chow's wife invariably works late; Su's husband takes frequent and lengthy trips abroad). But the narration is extremely reticent in revealing both the spouses' affair and the protagonists' suspicion of it. Only when Chow first broaches the infidelity with Su is the viewer brought into knowledge of the crime and its incipient investigation. True to detective tradition, then, *In the Mood for Love* does not allow us "access to the detective's inferences until he or she voices them . . ." (Bordwell 1985, p. 67).

Revelation of the spouses' affair invites the spectator to retroactively sift through prior action. Now we are asked to reappraise earlier scenes whose proper context the narration has suppressed. For example, we must retrospectively assign a dual motive to a foregoing conversation between Su and Chow's wife: such scenes ought no longer to be construed as neighborly encounters, but as phases in an investigation. Although *In the Mood for Love* will concentrate our attention on present and future action involving the protagonists, narrational gambits such as this cue us to reevaluate *preceding* action in the film. We might assume, then, that the film adheres to the kind of temporal flexibility that Tzvetan Todorov argues is central to detective fiction (Todorov 1977, pp. 42–52). But contra Todorov, the retrospection ordered by *In the Mood for Love*'s narration does not encourage us to reconstruct the *crime* (i.e., the spouses' infidelity) so much as guide our attention to an earlier stage of the protagonists' *investigation* – thereby undergirding our assumption that the spouses are not the center of story interest.

The repressiveness of detective narration is also used to make the story events ambiguous. This is especially evident in the scenes of role-play, which often begin *in medias res* (thereby narrowing contextual hypotheses), and which present ambiguous cues to the performative nature of the protagonists' interpersonal exchange. Scenes of this kind initiate fluctuating hypotheses: Are the protagonists conversing "as themselves" or as the spouses they impersonate? The viewer must keep both possibilities in play while she waits for unambiguous cues to clarify the proper state of events. Once it has established the protagonists' penchant for performance, the narration can effect a play with our assumptions. It may, for instance, force us to recast ostensible role-play action as authentic dialogue between the protagonists – or vice versa. One strategy is to append a role-play scene to a "straight," non-simulated exchange between the protagonists, so that we mistakenly infer a continuation of unpremeditated character interaction. Just as *2046* undercuts our assumptions of objectivity (by subjectivizing the future universe), so *In the Mood for Love* undertakes ground-shifting tactics to render the authenticity of character action uncertain.

In the Mood for Love flaunts a narration that is restricted as well as repressive. Unlike melodramatic narration, which provides omniscient access to a cross-section of characters, the narration here is mostly restricted to the trajectory traced by one or both of the protagonists. The narration briefly deviates from this internal norm at an early stage in the film, before the spectator is made aware of the spouses' affair. Here our spatio-temporal attachment[4] to the protagonists is momentarily broken to grant us oblique access to the two spouses. Following an exchange with Su, Chow's wife (whose visual legibility is obscured by distant, out-of-focus, and back-to-camera framings) is heard to say to an off-screen male figure: "It was your wife." Abrasively, the narration then cuts to new action.

The narration here is *at once* communicative and repressive. Character dialogue is fairly communicative, cueing the spectator to infer an illicit relationship between the spouses. Yet both the brevity of the moment and its oblique visual treatment disorient and quite probably distract the spectator from the dialogue's import, causing us to miss or misconstrue essential story information. We may, for example, be unclear as to the identity of the man and the woman in the scene, particularly since the imagery does not present them legibly. (Su's husband is not shown even in oblique fashion; and in typical noir style, a large object – in this case, a lamp – ominously dominates the foreground of one shot, obstructing our view of Mrs Chow.) This oblique visual treatment of the spouses prevails throughout *In the Mood for Love.* Insofar as they appear corporeally in the film at all, the spouses are invariably obfuscated by repressive framings or by obtrusive objects in the *mise-en-scène.* The narration's uncommunicative presentation of these characters further sharpens our assumption that the spouses are not the film's central "interest-focus."[5] Still, the prospect of the spouses emerging more prominently into the action is not closed down: the narration refuses to foil our expectation of melodramatic conflict.

Repressing access to a character's physicality is a strategy more common to detective narration than to melodrama. However, if in the detective film such a strategy arouses and ultimately satisfies our desire for the concealed figure to be "unmasked," no such satisfaction is afforded the viewer of *In the Mood for Love*. The spouses are not concealed so that they may be subsequently unveiled at a later climactic stage in the narrative. Moreover, any sense of mystery in this regard is largely attenuated because the spouses are not anonymous figures: the spectator knows them as the husband and wife of the protagonists, while the spouses are of course fully visible to Chow and Su. We therefore come to realize that there will be no significant narrative revelation if the spouses are presented to us in a legible fashion (that is to say, without visual obfuscation) – which, in fact, they never are.

What, then, is achieved by shrouding the spouses in obscurity? Most significantly, I would argue, the physical void represented by the spouses means that they are more effectively supplanted – in the mind of the spectator – by the protagonists who undertake to simulate their activity. For the spectator, then, the adulterous couple becomes synonymous with, and thus inseparable from, the main protagonists.

A fallout of this conflation is that character individuation becomes hard to execute. Stylistically *In the Mood for Love* assists this effect, furnishing visual compositions that sometimes encourage a confusion of its two pairs of characters. Two contiguous shots provide an example. In the first shot, a woman sobs while taking a shower. We see the woman through her mirror reflection. She is turned away from the camera, which frames her obliquely from a high angle; furthermore the dimly lit, out-of-focus composition serves to muddy our visual hold on the woman. The second shot frames a man's hand in close-up, tapping on the door. As the image fades to black, the sequence comes to an end. Narrational point of view is hardly melodramatic, or communicative, here. Who are the figures in these shots? Is the woman in the shower Su or Chow's wife? Does the hand at the door belong to Chow or to Su's husband? A repressive detective narration retards and lays bare character individuation: because we have not been granted an adequate purchase on the spouses' physical appearance, and because of the narration's repressiveness, we are unable to individuate the characters

with confidence. Consequently, in an important sense, the central protagonists become indistinguishable from the spouses. According to Wong,
"at first I wanted to have all four characters in the film played by Maggie
[Cheung] and Tony [Leung], both the wife and Mrs. Chan, and the
husband and Mr. Chow" (quoted in Brunette 2005, p. 130).[6]

This putative interchangeability is also connoted by the gifts from
abroad that the spouses present their partners. In a searching conversation,
Chow hints that Su's handbag is strikingly similar to the one owned by his
wife; Su observes that her husband owns a necktie precisely identical to
the one worn by Chow. At last, the protagonists reveal that the respective
items were gifts from their spouses, who had each purchased the items during a business trip overseas. This sartorial duplication thus creates more
correspondence between the protagonists and their adulterous doubles: Chow
and Mr Chan wear identical ties and Su and Mrs Chow shoulder similar
handbags. Wong provides the payoff for all this doubling later in the film.
By exploiting our awareness of these sartorial likenesses, the filmmaker undermines our already tentative grasp of story action. Consider the scene in
which Su rehearses a confrontation with her husband. The scene begins with
characteristic uncommunicativeness. Exposition of the narrative space,
and of the characters within the space, is eschewed in favor of a single long
take, which frames Su clearly in a medium shot. Crucially, the narration
doesn't provide facial access to the man that Su addresses (who, though
visible in the foreground of the frame, is turned away from the camera).
Once more we are denied adequate knowledge of the narrative context, and
thus we aren't sufficiently *au courant* to realize that Su's "confrontation" is
merely a performance and that the man she addresses is not her husband,
but Chow. That Su confronts the obliquely positioned man about an infidelity reinforces our assumption that the man in the shot is Su's husband.

Moreover, the repressiveness of the composition, together with our belief
that Chow and Mr Chan are physically alike (i.e., they are attired similarly),
tricks us into a mistaken inference. (The composition also sustains the pattern of obscurely rendering [whom we assume to be] Su's husband, thus
further encouraging us to form the incorrect inference.) It is only when
the narration provides us with the previously withheld reverse-shot of Chow
that we are made to realize our error. At this point, we are forced to revise
our understanding of the narrative situation, the characters' relationships,
and the authenticity of the emotion expressed by Su.

This scene's repressive detective narration generates several hermeneutic possibilities among which the spectator oscillates. The fact that the

narration has misled us previously does not prevent us from succumbing
once more to its deceptive maneuvers. Here, we must attempt to determine the epistemic status of the action. We initially hypothesize, I would
suggest, that Su is confronting her husband about his alleged infidelity.
This hypothesis is facilitated at once by the limited situational context
provided for the viewer, and the oblique way in which the "husband" is
positioned in the frame. At last, we might suppose, the film brings to fruition
our generic expectation of marital conflict. But our hypothesis here is eventually contradicted by the narration's communicative cut to the man's face,
revealed to be Chow.

This communicativeness, while canceling out one hypothesis, triggers new
ones. We must now speculate that Su is confronting Chow with respect
to an off-screen affair that she suspects him of being involved in. This hypothesis engenders several further conjectures, none of which the spectator
can corroborate at this stage in the narrative. If Chow is having an affair,
why is Su distressed? Is her distress an expression of sympathy for Chow's
wife? Is Su upset that she herself is not the object of Chow's affections? Or
have Chow and Su been engaged in a romance of which the spectator has
not been aware, and to which Chow has now been unfaithful? The narration's ellipticality encourages us to "fill in" missing action by inferring a
greater development in the protagonists' relationship than we have witnessed.

Finally, the spectator – still reeling from the narration's deceptive
gambit – must balance these conjectures against a broader hypothesis: namely,
that the protagonists' activity is merely the latest stage in their ongoing,
obsessive rehearsal. Our comprehension of the scene is thus constantly in
flux. We have constantly to revise our assumptions concerning the protagonists' relationship, and to imagine what has occurred during those
narrative periods that the film elides. Moreover, the film's generic shape-
shifting comes palpably into play in this sequence: what at first appears to
be a situation conventional to the melodrama – a moment of domestic
conflict – is revealed to be something rather more unusual and elusive. The
scene's apparent melodramatic content, then, is disarrayed by a detective
narration that is both reticent and misleading.

Contingency, Motivation, and Cinephilia

In the Mood for Love not only hybridizes its melodramatic narrative with
detective conventions; it also undertakes to rework certain hallmarks of the

melodrama. Principally, the film flouts the melodrama's legible and force-
ful expression of character emotion. Su and Chow conservatively subor-
dinate emotional display to the prevailing mandates of their social milieu
(i.e., cultural "display rules" prescribing outward composure, decorum,
and impassivity). By substituting "excess" with "restraint," *In the Mood
for Love* inverts the melodrama's characteristic emphasis on emotional expres-
siveness. In melodrama, it is customary that the protagonist's affective state
– inferably bubbling away at the surface – pours out into the expressive
design of the diegesis. *In the Mood for Love* adopts this principle, but
here the *mise-en-scène* reflects a character type not given to outward,
"excessive" displays of emotion – characters whose affective states remain
firmly corseted. Thus Su is dressed in close-fitting *cheongsams* (traditional
Chinese dresses), the protagonists are confined by the cramped interiors
of their apartment building, and an incessant rainfall delivers the pathetic
fallacy, lamenting the unfulfilled romance that the protagonists themselves
cannot openly mourn. Not incidentally, these latter two motifs have greater
congruence with the visual iconography of film noir than with melodrama.

Both *In the Mood for Love* and *2046* evoke the melodramatic convention of contingency. As ingredients germane to the melodrama, chance and
coincidence are strategies for motivating action and eliciting surprise.
An effective melodrama will make economical if judicious use of these
strategies – all the better to preserve the semblance of causal logic and narrative plausibility. Acausality "acts upon" the protagonist (Elsaesser 1996,
p. 75), thereby positioning her as a victim of providence. Not so much
purposefully maneuvering through a causally prepared chain of events as
buffeted between a sequence of chance incidents, the melodramatic hero
is thrust inexorably closer to the dire conclusion that fate has prepared for
her. Conventionally, then, the trajectory of the melodramatic agent is
overlaid with a sense of the inevitable and the inescapable: no amount of
effort or artfulness will emancipate the protagonist from her predetermined
course.

Several moments of coincidence assail the protagonists of *In the Mood
for Love*, and the film itself employs this generic trope quite self-consciously.
On several occasions the characters are made to remark upon the dis-
quieting presence of coincidence. Baring the device of coincidence gives
emphasis to the protagonists' position as *subjects*, both of fate (in narrative terms) and of fiction (in narrational terms). In other words, the
salience of coincidence, as both story event and plot device, underlines the
vulnerability and lack of agency peculiar to the protagonists. At a narrative

level, however, the film will subvert its apparent positioning of the protagonists as victims of fate.

Coincidence is evoked conventionally in the opening phase of *In the Mood for Love*. Chow and Su convoy their possessions into their new apartments at a coincidentally concurrent time.[7] Character dialogue ensures that the coincidence is well marked: "What a coincidence! Moving in on the same day!" Already our generic expectations are animated: we are likely to read into these opening scenes something more than simply a succession of plain coincidences.

Separately choosing the same day on which to move apartments, the film's romantic protagonists are, we infer, already unassailably "attuned" to each other, and thus perfectly compatible as an ideal partnership. (This reading relies on the inferred presence of a predestined order of things, which I have noted teleologically orders the melodramatic universe.)

Engendered by these opening scenes, then, is a set of generically informed inferences and assumptions. The rest of the film, however, invokes coincidence in a way that aims to dislodge our generic assumptions. If we have been tracking the film's coincidences, we begin to realize that the protagonists disingenuously adduce coincidence for events which they know to have a firm basis in causality. The phrase "What a coincidence!" is the most repeated line in the film, and yet the accuracy of the remark becomes increasingly suspect with each repetition. Gradually the phrase comes to expose the protagonists' willingness to live inauthentically, to cede responsibility to invisible (ideological, metaphysical) forces, and to negate their personal desires and beliefs. Denying personal responsibility, the protagonists sign quite logical situations over to fate by intoning this phrase. In no sense are the protagonists "acted upon" by capricious phenomena outside their control; rather their repression is largely of their own design, since the existence of fate can no longer be deemed the prime mover of the protagonists' inability to act. Once again, what strikes us initially as generic convention – the evocation of coincidence – emerges, on closer inspection, as something quite different (in this case, generic subversion). If the viewer is to fully grasp the film's intricacies of storytelling, then, she must mine its apparently conventional generic elements for clues to character psychology and story action.

2046 revives the "What a coincidence!" dialogue, but (as with some of the film's other allusions to *In the Mood for Love*) it falls short of capturing the phrase's original raison d'être. Far from staking out character traits, the appropriated utterance now functions denotatively as a fragment of incidental dialogue, and transtextually as an instance of authorial citation. As such, it serves neither the melodramatic function of foregrounding acausality nor the function of exposing character traits. More generally, *2046* recycles old motifs while diminishing their degree of justification.

Consider *In the Mood for Love*'s appropriation of a Nat King Cole song. As Chow prepares to leave for Singapore, he asks Su: "If there's an extra ticket, would you go with me?" This dialogue constitutes a dangling ellipsis, since Su makes no reply. Instead the aural track is dominated by Nat King Cole's "Quizas, Quizas, Quizas," the refrain of which significantly translates into English as "Perhaps." The lyric may be understood as representing Su's thoughts in response to the question posed in dialogue. More generally, the ambiguity conveyed in the lyric is entirely apt for the undefined relationship between the protagonists, and successfully sustains the suspense that the scene aims to evoke. In addition the song fulfills an affective purpose, establishing and augmenting mood. *2046* establishes sonic continuity with *In the Mood for Love* by making motivic use of another Nat King Cole ballad, "The Christmas Song." Some important narrative functions are performed by the song's usage, which designates a specific time of year, operates motivically to highlight developments in story action, and contributes to mood-setting. But in contrast to *In the Mood for Love*'s deployment of Cole's music, "The Christmas Song" fails to comment on character relationships or to convey subjective states.

Dense intertextuality invites the viewer to situate *2046* with respect to Wong's earlier work (most particularly, *In the Mood for Love*). Indeed, cinematographer Christopher Doyle has described *2046* as "a compendium film" (quoted in Walters 2005, p. 86), a kind of elaborate suite of favorite themes, forms, and styles. The film's (self-) citation and repetition, often excessively showcased, might lead one to infer artistic stagnation. But regardless of whether this is the case, such qualities can be assimilated "positively" into the film's overall storytelling armory. The dense intertextual allusiveness of *2046* solicits an additional layer of comprehension from the viewer schooled in Wong's previous work. For such viewers, the process of unraveling *2046* includes determining in what ways the film cross-fertilizes with other films in the director's oeuvre.

Irrespective of its allusive qualities, *2046*, as we have seen, possesses its own intrinsic formal tactics, many of which depart flagrantly from orthodox storytelling norms. Yet, *In the Mood for Love* coordinates a greater range of motivation devices than does *2046*. Both films foreground repressive narrations that hold back narrative information, encouraging us to plug gaps in the story while refusing to validate any of our competing hypotheses. Storytelling of this sort can be justified in both films by norms of art cinema narration, and by the signature traits of the film author. But whereas *2046* cannot motivate narrational repressiveness by its melodramatic or science-fiction schemata, *In the Mood for Love* can justify its narrational strategies generically, since it dovetails both narrative and narration with the norms of detective fiction.

The generic gambits in *2046* and *In the Mood for Love* point us, finally, to the filmmaker's implicit cinephilia, which in turn enables us to sketch in pertinent contexts for Wong's filmmaking. Primarily, there is the 1960s European art-cinema context: Wong admires such auteur cineastes as Truffaut and Jean-Luc Godard, whose films have exemplified the practice of bending popular genres to personally expressive ends.[8] The genre mixing germane to Hong Kong mainstream cinema provides a secondary, albeit more proximate, reference point. Approaching traditional genres with both affection and irreverence, the film-obsessed auteur produces ostensible genre films that assault or travesty generic norms. Characterizing Wong in these terms also helps us make sense of the bold allusive strokes evinced in *2046*: the cinephile-auteur celebrates his own work as well as that of other filmmakers.

I have argued that complexity in *2046* and *In the Mood for Love* largely arises out of a cinephiliac play with genre. Overlapping genres permeate *In the Mood for Love*, whose style, structure, and story are shot through with detective conventions; and *2046* mobilizes a collision of generic schemata, only to smooth down this conflict once the narration becomes more communicative. Both films prompt us to probe generic convention. What looks like fidelity to generic norms may come into focus as generic subversion; likewise, apparent deviation from generic norms may, on closer inspection, emerge as an oblique or tacit adherence to convention. Moreover, story comprehension in both films is complicated by gambits of character individuation, firmly rooted in generic motivation (the detective film's affinities between investigator and criminal; the science-fiction film's populace of clones and androids). Indeed, many of the films' bold narrational procedures are motivated generically and/or diegetically; in other words, the films provide strong compositional justification for their experimental techniques. As I have pointed out, not every aspect of adventurous storytelling in *2046* and *In the Mood for Love* is attributable to the filmmaker's ambivalent commerce with popular genre. But I have aimed to show that, in both films, Wong's engagement with genre constitutes an extremely fertile source of narrational complexity and experimentation.

I would like to thank David Bordwell, Murray Smith, and Catherine Grant for their cogent comments on an earlier version of this chapter. Any faults that remain are, naturally, due to me.

Notes

1   Given the opening vista's hyper-stylization of Hong Kong skyscrapers and neon signs, we might take the futuristic cityscape to evoke what Warren Buckland calls a "possible world"; that is, a world which represents "a modal extension of the 'actual world'" (Buckland 1999, p. 177). We might suppose, in other words, that 2046 is a projected milieu which exists in causal (albeit temporally distant) continuity with the 1960s Hong Kong we see later in the film. But this hypothesis is invalidated by the revelation that 2046 is harnessed to a character's interior subjectivity. As a reification of Chow's diegetic writing, 2046 is "a purely imaginary world that runs parallel to, but is autonomous from, the actual world" (ibid.).

2   A kind of ambiguous double relationship is implied in the protagonists' mutual attraction: has Su fallen in love with Chow, or the character he incarnates (which is, paradoxically, Su's own husband)? Is Chow attracted by Su, or merely by his wife's "copy"?

3   A parallel scenario pertains to *In the Mood for Love*'s protagonists, whose close identification with the spouses destabilizes their own sense of moral propriety (e.g., their convictions of marital fidelity).

4   I am borrowing the term "spatio-temporal attachment" from Murray Smith (1995). Smith's term "concerns the way in which the narration restricts itself to the actions of a single character, or moves freely among the spatio-temporal paths of two or more characters" (1995, p. 83).

5   The term "interest-focus" derives from Seymour Chatman. It denotes the figure or figures in a narrative whose point of view we share (at least temporarily), and with whom we are encouraged to identify to some degree (Chatman 1990, p. 148).

6   That Wong would occasionally enlist Tony Leung and Maggie Cheung to act as (off-camera) stand-ins for the husband and wife characters would seem to confirm that Su and Chow are meant to *embody* for us their respective counterparts.

7   During this sequence, which is overlaid with a comic atmosphere of pandemonium, the characters' possessions are mislaid and delivered to the wrong apartment: a foreshadowing, therefore, of the confusion of personal items –

e.g., Chow's necktie, Su's handbag – that will harvest more dramatic effect later in the film.

8   Like Wong, both Godard and Truffaut subject the science-fiction genre to less than reverential treatment. Godard's *Alphaville* (1965) yokes the genre to noir iconography, while Truffaut presents a weirdly anachronistic vision of the future in *Fahrenheit 451* (1966), complete with 1930s-style fire engines.

Bibliography

Bordwell, D. 1985. *Narration in the Fiction Film*. London: Routledge.

Branigan, E. 1992. *Narrative Comprehension and Film*. London: Routledge.

Brunette, P. 2005. *Wong Kar-wai*. Urbana-Champaign: University of Illinois.

Buckland, W. 1999. "Between science fact and fiction: Spielberg's digital dinosaurs, possible worlds, and the new aesthetic realism." *Screen*, 40, 2 (Summer): 177–97.

Chatman, S. 1990. *Coming to Terms: The Rhetoric of Narrative in Fiction and Film*. Ithaca, NY: Cornell University Press.

Elsaesser, T. 1996. *Fassbinder's Germany: History, Identity, Subject*. Amsterdam: Amsterdam University Press.

King, G. and Krzywinska, T. 2002. *Science Fiction Cinema: From Outerspace to Cyberspace*. London: Wallflower Press.

Neale, S. 2000. *Genre and Hollywood*. London: Routledge.

Smith, M. 1995. *Engaging Characters: Fiction, Emotion, and the Cinema*. Oxford: Clarendon Press.

Tirard, L. 2002. *Moviemakers' Master Class: Private Lessons from the World's Foremost Directors*. New York: Faber and Faber.

Todorov, T. 1977. *The Poetics of Prose* (trans. R. Howard). Oxford: Basil Blackwell. (Original work published 1971.)

Walters, B. 2005. "Hong Kong dreaming." *Sight and Sound*, 15, 4 (April): 86.

9

Revitalizing the Thriller Genre: Lou Ye's *Suzhou River* and *Purple Butterfly*

Yunda Eddie Feng

Ang Lee's *Crouching Tiger, Hidden Dragon* (2000) introduced Chinese-language cinema to millions of movie viewers. However, *Crouching Tiger's* financial success and Oscar wins have narrowed the scope of Chinese-language fare in today's international circuit. Seeking huge profits and awards, Chinese directors have made wave after wave of mega-production swordsman movies such as *Warriors of Heaven and Earth* (He Ping 2003), *The Promise* (Chen Kaige, 2005), and *The Banquet* (Feng Xiaogang 2006). Zhang Yimou, once known for intimate dramas in rural settings, helmed three entries in the martial-arts derby – *Hero* (2002), *House of Flying Daggers* (2004), and *Curse of the Golden Flower* (2006). Regardless of the quality of these features, this trend skews general perceptions of Chinese cinema and leads major talents to participate in projects that feel routine and formulaic. The martial-arts genre has the potential to overshadow Chinese cinema the way that the samurai genre has overshadowed Japanese cinema.

Lou Ye, the writer-director of *Suzhou River* (2000) and *Purple Butterfly* (2003),[1] has not succumbed to the lure of the martial-arts genre. Instead, he tries to court Western audiences through the deployment of complex storytelling techniques within the thriller genre. Specifically, Lou is in direct dialogue with Alfred Hitchcock, whose name is essentially synonymous with thrillers. Lou subverts viewer expectations derived from collective exposure to Hitchcock's movies such as *The 39 Steps* (1935), *Secret Agent* (1936), *Rear Window* (1954), and *Vertigo* (1958). Through complex storytelling, Lou revitalizes the thriller genre by creating viewer ambivalence toward the subjective nature of narrative reality.

Lou Ye was born in Shanghai, China in 1965. He was a student in Beijing in 1989, so he witnessed the Tiananmen Square demonstrations first-hand.

Lou has been called a member of China's "Sixth Generation" of directors, though the term "Sixth Generation" is broad and un-defining in nature as it refers to a disparate group of moviemakers rather than to unifying aesthetics (Lim 2007). This is in contrast to the "Fifth Generation" directors, whose movies share similar characteristics partly because the directors worked on each other's movies. (For example, Zhang Yimou was once Chen Kaige's cinematographer.)

The Thriller Genre and Lou Ye

During the 1930s, Hitchcock directed six thrillers that established him as one of the leading moviemakers in the United Kingdom. *The Man Who Knew Too Much* (1934), *The 39 Steps* (1935), *Secret Agent* (1936), *Sabotage* (1936), *Young and Innocent* (1937), and *The Lady Vanishes* (1938) comprise the "thriller sextet" (Ryall 1986, ch. 6). A close examination of Hitchcock's "thriller sextet" reveals that the movies share similar structures, characteristics, and images. Hitchcock used the spy-thriller formula again several times during the American phase of his career. For example, *North by Northwest* (1959) is basically a remake of *The 39 Steps*.

A set of norms defines how Hitchcock's spy thrillers operate. These norms control how the narratives progress from start to finish. Except for fine details such as names, time periods, and locations, the norms basically remain the same in each member of the "thriller sextet." Of course, the thriller genre encompasses more than just espionage tales, but Hitchcock's formula is generally applicable to all thrillers.

Jerry Palmer defines a thriller by two components: a hero and a conspiracy (with the hero finding a way of defeating the conspiracy) (Palmer 1979, pp. 53, 82). The protagonist is usually the "wrong man," an individual who would have nothing to do with the conspiracies in the movie except for a case of assumed/mistaken identities. The spies have a MacGuffin, an object that initiates a plot but is of inconsequential value in and of itself. The villains conduct a manhunt for the "wrong man" protagonist, and the chase eventually becomes a double pursuit as villainous spies and misinformed authorities both look for the protagonist. The pursuits lead to close calls, evasions, capture and interrogation/torture, narrow escapes, and even turnabouts (the hunted becomes the hunter) (Barr 1999, pp. 132–86). Hitchcock's thrillers usually have a romance angle (the romance angle is common in movies with double narratives). "Nearly all of Hitchcock's films from this period develop a strong tension between male and female points of view, with the villain's perspective occasionally invoked to complicate matters further" (Rubin 1999, p. 82). The thrillers usually end with images that suggest that the male and female leads will live happily as lovers.

Lou Ye breaks Hitchcock's mold in several important ways. In Hitchcock's movies, "the thriller hero monopolize(s) the reader's sympathy and allegiance . . . It is therefore possible to have suspense even if the outcome is predictable or the solution already known; what is important is that the reader identify wholeheartedly with a hero who is perplexed" (Rubin 1999, pp. 11–12). *Suzhou River* and *Purple Butterfly* disperse attention to several principal characters. Most of these principal characters can be considered their respective movies' protagonists, though as they all commit reprehensible acts, none of the protagonists are clearly heroes or villains.

Suzhou River and *Purple Butterfly* share several themes that indicate a pessimistic world view in contrast to the general optimism of Hitchcock's oeuvre. Lou Ye depicts love and sex as destructive forces rather than ones that heal, perpetuate humanity, or at least give pleasure. In both movies, problems arise when one set of lovers crashes into the lives of another set of lovers, and most of these characters eventually die. In *Suzhou River*, two men are in love with two physically identical women; one man's efforts to reclaim his lover ruin the other couple's relationship. In *Purple Butterfly*, two pairs of lovers (at different times) go on dates before the men leave the next morning by train. Ironically, three of these characters first meet in a train-station shootout that initiates a series of killings throughout the rest of the movie. Lou's pessimistic worldview suggests that "positive" forces such as China's recent economic boom and patriotic heroism hurt more than they benefit people.

Lou's movies are character studies as opposed to plot-driven entities like Hitchcock's movies. In Hitchcock's thrillers, a MacGuffin initiates a manhunt, and the characters pursue each other to determine who ends up with the MacGuffin. Neither *Suzhou River* nor *Purple Butterfly* is interested in such mechanisms. Rather, they prefer to observe characters in episodic "real life" moments. In fact, while *Purple Butterfly* has an obvious MacGuffin, the movie gets rid of it quickly once its initial utility expires.

Lou Ye and Complex Storytelling

Lou Ye's use of complex storytelling further complicates and enriches the thriller genre. Hitchcock's thrillers use classical storytelling, with linear narrative progression. Both *Suzhou River* and *Purple Butterfly* have non-linear structures that confuse viewers, since significant portions of story information are elided and causal relationships are unclear when the movies jump back and forth through their chronologies.

The confusion caused by temporal instability is compounded by the movies' aggressive visual style, which is comprised of restless cameras and frequent, rough edits. The visual confusion also heightens narrative confusion since Lou gives viewers little opportunity to process the images. Upon first viewing, *Suzhou River* and *Purple Butterfly* seem to be comprised entirely of brief shots. However, on closer inspection, one sees that each movie has several long takes lasting more than a minute. These long takes are among the most important moments in these movies. Long takes create a sense of anticipation, alerting viewers that essential information or action is about to be revealed.

In *Suzhou River*, most of the long takes indicate when the unseen diegetic narrator is filming the on-screen action. In other words, these shots are optical point-of-view shots (we see the events directly through the character's eyes). In Edward Branigan's terms (Branigan 1992, ch. 4), the camera in these shots is "internally focalized (surface)," with the important detail that they are not accompanied by any reverse angle cutting that shows the audience whose look is being focalized/represented on screen. We know that these shots represent the look of a character within the diegesis because the camera interacts with other characters – they look into the camera and smile or wave, the camera is kissed, we see the character's hands on the frame lines, etc. These scenes are analogous to the camerawork in Robert Montgomery's *Lady in the Lake* (1947), the well-known Hollywood experiment that attempted to focus a film exclusively around a character's optical point-of-view shots (Branigan 1992, pp. 142–6). In *Purple Butterfly*, long takes signal that strangers will collide violently soon.

Suzhou River and *Purple Butterfly* differ in the way that they convey exposition. *Suzhou River* inundates viewers with exposition delivered via voiceover narration by a talkative diegetic narrator (who is unreliable because he is involved with and manipulates the movie's events) and dialogue from other verbose characters. The viewer has to filter out non-truths in order to understand the narrative. Further confusion is created by the use of handheld camerawork representing both the unseen diegetic narrator's optical point of view and the director's standard non-focalized shots of the events. Since the entire movie looks like it was shot by the same person (someone in the movie's diegesis), the viewer might wonder if the narrator's story can be accepted at face value. On the other hand, *Purple Butterfly* relies heavily on visual cues rather than verbal ones for narration. Therefore, audiences have to generate information on their own in order comprehend a movie filled with gaps. Also, *Purple Butterfly* does not rely on a diegetic narrator to tell its story, and the entire movie is comprised of non-focalized shots.

Suzhou River

Suzhou River grew out of Lou Ye's work as a producer on the *Super City* television series during the mid-1990s. Lou planned to contribute two segments, but he ran out of money. After receiving completion funds from European sources, Lou created an 82-minute feature film that combined the two scripts (Silbergeld 2004, pp. 45, 121). At the 2000 Viennale (Vienna International Film Festival), *Suzhou River* won the FIPRESCI Prize "for its realistic and documentary approach to thriller conventions, and its expressive use of narrative and cinematic structure" (FIPRESCI).

Suzhou River has four main characters: Mada (Jia Hongsheng), Mudan (Zhou Xun), Meimei (Zhou Xun again), and an unseen narrator (voiced by Lou Ye), who is a videographer.[2] Mada and Mudan represent one pair of lovers, and Meimei and the narrator another pair. Mada is a courier who frequently chauffeurs Mudan from place to place. Mudan disappears after Mada kidnaps her for ransom.[3] A few years later, Mada thinks that Meimei is Mudan. Meimei appears to be the "wrong woman," pursued by Mada. The double pursuit involves Mada trying to find Mudan while the narrator and Meimei attempt to determine if Mada is telling the truth. Initially, Mada believes that the other characters are in a conspiracy to hide Meimei's "real" identity, and the narrator wonders if Meimei and Mada are playing games with him. Mudan and Meimei are the obvious examples of mistaken identities, though the movie's suggestion that the narrator and Mada are the same person is also a case of mistaken identity.

Suzhou River has a bookend structure. However, the movie is not a simple A-B-A construct with clearly demarcated ends and beginnings. The movie intentionally conflates the past and the present to emphasize the four main characters' similarities as well as the confusion that they feel about their own identities after meeting each other.

The movie can be divided into seven segments. Segment 1 (0:00:00– 0:03:52) includes the opening credits, which appear on a black background.

Dialogue emanates from the soundtrack as the screen slowly fades to footage of the Suzhou-River vignettes that the narrator shot. In the dialogue, Meimei (unidentified at this point) wonders if her lover (the diegetic narrator, also unidentified at this point) will look for her the way that Mada searched for Mudan. (We later discover that this dialogue comes from Segment 6, toward the end of the movie.) The diegetic narrator (from now on, simply "the narrator") introduces himself and establishes the Suzhou River as the life force of one of Shanghai's industrial areas. Segment 1 ends with the movie's title appearing on a black background.

Segment 2 (0:03:52–0:10:16) establishes the relationship between Meimei and the narrator. Meimei tells the narrator about Mada, a man looking for a woman who looks like Meimei. This is the movie's diegetic "present."

Segment 3 (0:10:17–0:10:54) is a montage of footage taken from what looks like someone's balcony. The movie never makes it clear who shot this footage or what it is supposed to be. The two most likely inferences we can generate is that Segment 3 could represent the narrator looking at (or filming) his neighbors; or it could be a part of the Segment 4 flashback.

Segment 4 (0:10:55–0:38:20) is a flashback to the "distant past," where Mada and Mudan's story begins. The first shots in Segment 4 are visually contiguous with the footage in Segment 3. Here, the movie blurs the distinction between the past and the present. The camerawork also becomes more standard, since the narrator is not present, and is therefore not filming the scenes.

Segment 5 (0:38:20–0:53:50) is the "recent past." The events in Segment 5 take place chronologically after the events in Segment 4. Mada returns to Shanghai and begins meeting with Meimei, who looks just like Mudan.

In Segment 6 (0:53:51–1:19:28), the past catches up to the present. Mada meets with the narrator, thereby confirming what Meimei told him about Mada looking for a long-lost love. And with the narrator back in the picture, we occasionally see shots focalized around his optical perspective, although they are not systematically used, as they were in Segments 1 and 2. However, because previous segments show both the narrator and Mada peeking voyeuristically at Meimei while she changes clothes, the viewer wonders if the narrator and Mada are the same person, if Mada is a figment of the narrator's imagination, or if the entire story is a fabrication (perhaps a fictional movie that the narrator is shooting).

Segment 7 (1:19:38–1:22:17) is the end credits sequence, which does not have any visual or aural overlaps with Segment 6.

Jerome Silbergeld's *Hitchcock With a Chinese Face* (2004) includes one of the first in-depth scholarly critiques of a movie directed by Lou Ye. Silbergeld is primarily interested in how contemporary Chinese movies incorporate elements of Chinese paintings, architecture, statues, literature, and other art forms from the past. Of course, given *Suzhou River's* similarities to *Vertigo* and *Rear Window*, Silbergeld discusses Lou Ye's "replies" to Hitchcock's imagery, themes, and story/plot construction. For example, he compares Mudan's leap from a bridge into the Suzhou River to Judy's fall from the top of a bell tower in *Vertigo*. Silbergeld also compares the Shanghai Oriental Pearl Tower to the bell tower in *Vertigo*, though the Pearl Tower is more than simply a visual allusion.

The Shanghai Oriental Pearl Tower plays an important part in *Suzhou River's mise-en-scène*. The "Tower encompasses a dream world, a mighty transformation from the mundane and the ordinary" (Silbergeld 2004, p. 29). The camera often drifts toward the Tower on Shanghai's waterways, or the Tower appears in the background while the characters interact in the foreground. However, the camera and the characters never reach the Tower, which is located in the Pudong district. Pudong is Shanghai's recently developed financial district and is separated from the rest of the city by Huangpu River. Thus, the characters are permanently ghettoized in Shanghai's squalid districts. The Oriental Pearl Tower (and all that it represents) seems like a distant phantom, an illusion of the free-market success that dominates news headlines but is out of reach for the vast majority of Chinese citizens.

Lou Ye complicates *Vertigo's* structure when he reveals that the "real woman" did not actually die when everyone else thought she did. Silbergeld argues that the "double-disappearance in *Vertigo* . . . becomes a triple-disappearance in *Suzhou River*," which reverses Hitchcock's formula (Silbergeld 2004, pp. 30–1). The first disappearance is Mudan's leap into the Suzhou River. The second disappearance is Mudan's real death. The third disappearance is Meimei's abandonment of the narrator. While the three disappearances are indeed an extension of what occurs in *Vertigo*, Lou does not really reverse Hitchcock. In *Vertigo*, Scottie interacts only with the doppelganger, never with the "real woman." In *Suzhou River*, Mada interacts with both the "real woman" and the doppelganger. In both *Vertigo* and *Suzhou River*, the women whom Scottie and Mada love die. One could argue that Judy is the "real woman" for Scottie anyway since he never meets his friend's wife; thus, the real "real woman" dies in both Hitchcock's and Lou's movies.

Curiously, despite the movie's abundance of deceptions, betrayals, and deaths, Silbergeld feels that *Suzhou River* also reverses Hitchcock's cynicism. "Mada's quest for redemption inspires the mistaken female's spiritual awakening" (Silbergeld 2004, p. 16). Silbergeld's argument that *Suzhou River* has a "more idealistic trajectory" than *Vertigo* relies in part on Meimei's realization of the value of her relationship with the narrator versus Judy's death (Silbergeld 2004, p. 23). *Suzhou River* is not quite the uplifting story that Silbergeld believes it to be. Meimei asks the narrator if he would look for her the way that Mada searched for Mudan. The narrator says yes, and Meimei accuses the narrator of lying. The next morning, the narrator discovers that Meimei has left him, but instead of looking for her, the narrator (probably drunk as indicated by the camera falling on its right-hand side) takes a boat trip down the Suzhou River again, passively waiting for the next love story to drop into his life. As the narrator drifts toward the Oriental Pearl Tower, smoke fumes cloud his field of view. Unlike Hitchcock's "thriller sextet," the movie does not end with a shot of a man and a woman as a happy couple. (Even *Vertigo* once had a "happy" ending, with Scottie returning to Midge's apartment in some versions.) The imagery and the narrator's lack of initiative negate Silbergeld's claims. Moreover, Meimei is the least developed of the four principal characters. She is a cipher upon which Mada and the narrator project their feelings and dreams. The viewer also does not know what happens to Meimei at the end of the movie, so discussing her fate is pure conjecture.

Viewers may at times be confused regarding whose shots are on screen – the director's or the diegetic narrator's. This is especially true during Segment 3, when the movie segues from the "present" to the "distant past." In fact, a viewer probably does not even know that the movie is in the middle of a flashback during Segment 3. The conflation of the narrator's optical point of view (when he is present to participate in or observe/ shoot the action) and the director's objective/non-focalized shots (when the narrator is not present) emphasizes how similar the story's two principal male characters are. "Although the videographer-narrator himself is never quite seen by the audience . . . it is precisely this constrained viewpoint that by the end of the film becomes the chief object of scrutiny" (Silbergeld 2004, p. 37). Many of the long(er) takes can be construed as shots from the narrator's perspective, though even this rule is tested by the fact that Mada spies on Meimei in her dressing room in almost the exact same way that the narrator does. By extension, because the movie suggests that the narrator and Mada might be the same person, the viewer begins wondering if Meimei really is Mudan after all, if Meimei is simply playing a game with Mada in revenge for what he did to her. The differentiation between the diegetic narrator's focalized shots and the director's non-focalized objective shots can be made only after the viewer realizes – at the end of the movie – that the narrator has been "truthful." Still, even during subsequent viewings, some shots – like much of Segment 3 – remain of indeterminable origin.

Suzhou River's aural component is a key element of the movie's complex storytelling methodology despite cinema being a primarily visual medium. Before any images appear on-screen, the soundtrack plays part of a dialogue that is repeated and extended at the end of the movie. Then, the voiceover narration begins. Since the narrator is also a major character, he participates in many dialogue exchanges. The characters' talkativeness impedes rather than eases viewers' understanding of the story.

> The videographer's frequent narrative hesitations and uncertainties about where the story might go next not only hint that the film's many riverine twists and rhetorical turns are perhaps opportunistic fabrications designed to favor the narrator's own cause but also reflect his own weak attachment to objective reality and therefore challenge his assertion early in the film that "photographs don't lie." (Silbergeld 2004, p. 42)

The narrator uses suppositional words such as "if," "maybe," and "perhaps" that undermine viewers' trust in him because one has a difficult time ascertaining if the narrator is telling the truth, if the narrator believes what other people tell him, if the narrator is outright lying, or if the narrator is rambling as he makes up a fictional narrative (after all, the narrator is a videographer). During the tricky transition in Segment 3, the narrator says that he is as capable as the next person in inventing a story about doomed lovers. Even though the narrator says that he is not familiar with Mada's story, he is the one narrating the events that take place in Segments 4 and 5. At this point, one might feel that the narrator has contradicted himself.

Even though an alert viewer will be skeptical of the narrator's reliability, the movie's visuals are so closely identified with the narrator's vantage point that the viewer's general impressions of the other characters are filtered through the narrator's perspective. One finds oneself "agreeing" with the narrator's sarcastic assessments of Mada and Meimei, though the narrator retains some semblance of impartiality with regards to Mudan (which makes sense because the only time he ever meets Mudan is when he stands over her dead body). The other characters' viewpoints are also strongly presented, though a general atmosphere of distrust pervades. Since Mada betrays Mudan, the other characters and the viewer doubt Mada's statements. Meimei frequently expresses disbelief at what Mada and the narrator say to her. Until the movie's climax, no one knows for sure if the characters genuinely believe that the others are lying or if they pretend to think that the others are lying.

Lou Ye shies away from keeping the movie shrouded in uncertainty by literalizing Mada and Mudan's tale. Indeed, the voiceover's barrage of information, otherwise a method of confusion and concealment, gives away most of the story during Segment 1. The movie's climax – when the narrator and Meimei stand over Mada's and Mudan's dead bodies – eliminates the blurring of the characters' memories and identities. Thus, the viewer no longer wonders whether or not the narrator and Mada are the same person, whether or not Meimei and Mudan are the same person, and whether or not the entire story is a figment of the narrator's imagination.

Purple Butterfly

Purple Butterfly is Lou Ye's reworking of Hitchcock's spy thriller sub-genre. Xinxia (Zhang Ziyi) and Xieming (Feng Yuanzheng) are members of an anti-Japanese resistance group.[4] Itami (Toru Nakamura) is a Japanese intelligence agent. Xinxia and Xieming want to assassinate Yamamoto, Itami's boss. Xinxia and Itami were lovers in the past, so they use each other to accomplish their goals. Situ (Liu Ye) and Yiling (Li Bingbing) are non-political civilians, but they are victims of the clash between anti-Japanese and Japanese factions.[5]

Situ is the "wrong man" who is doubly pursued by spies (Xinxia, Xieming, and their associates) and the authorities (Itami and the Japanese, who effectively ruled China's seacoast during World War II). Xinxia uses another name ("Ding Hui") with her associates in Shanghai. The MacGuffin is a case with information about Japanese operatives in Shanghai. The main story concludes with a turnabout as Situ, fed up with being threatened by everybody else, hunts his persecutors.

Purple Butterfly can be divided into five segments. Segment 1 (0:00:00–0:14:40) is about events that take place in 1928's northeastern China. This segment includes the opening credits, which begin appearing on a black background and continue to appear as the narrative begins.

Segment 1.5 (0:14:41–0:14:48) is a long transition fade from Segment 1 to Segment 2. The transition fade might be jarring and confusing to some people because the image changes from horizontal panning over dead, bloody bodies lying in a street to a stationary shot of a man smiling and whistling while grooming himself in front of a mirror. At this point, the movie jumps from 1928 to 1931, from northeastern China to Shanghai.

Segment 2 (0:14:48–1:48:02) is the main body and can be understood independent of the rest of the movie. Segment 2 is about events that take place in 1931's Shanghai.

Segment 3 (1:48:02–2:02:39) is a flashback to a period prior to the train-station shootout, though this is not apparent until the end of the segment. The movie cuts abruptly to an extreme close-up shot of Xieming's face as he sits in a dark room waiting for Xinxia. The music that was playing at the end of Segment 2 is also cut off abruptly rather than used as a sound bridge between Segments 2 and 3. During a first viewing, one might think that Xieming survived the botched assassination attempt on Yamamoto.

Segment 3 is the movie's Achilles' heel. Running for approximately 12 minutes, Segment 3 forces the movie to double back on itself while yielding minimal results. The dialogue reveals emotions and motivations that can be inferred from words and actions elsewhere in the movie. In this regard, Lou Ye unwisely abandons the economy of narration and information delivery used elsewhere in the movie.

This segment also has a (too long) long take that shows Xinxia, Xieming, and Yiling in the same frame. This long take feels like an unnecessarily repetitive technical exercise after the long take in Segment 2's train-station shootout sequence. The Segment-3 long take confirms that Xinxia and Xieming are in the background of an extreme close-up shot of Yiling's face in Segment 2 as she sits in a cable car on her way to the train station. However, in the story's chronology, the characters inhabit the same spaces (the area in front of the laundry service and the train station) twice within a matter of minutes/hours, so whatever point the Segment-3 long take makes is simplistic and forced. Not clarifying that Yiling passed by Xinxia and Xieming on her way to the train station would have eliminated an unnecessary coincidence. Segment 3 can be removed altogether without diminishing the rest of the movie.

Segment 4 (2:02:39–2:05:00) is comprised of vintage documentary footage showing destructive Japanese actions in China. This segment has no direct narrative relation to Segments 1, 1.5, 2, 3, or 5. Thematically, Segment 4 reinforces a pro-Chinese/anti-Japanese sentiment.

Segment 5 (2:05:01–2:07:56) is the end credits sequence, which does not have any visual or aural overlaps with Segment 4.

The first narrational analyses of *Purple Butterfly* appeared at websites devoted to Chinese cinema. While not scholarly in nature, viewing guides at MonkeyPeaches.com and HelloZiyi.us are valuable resources, providing background historical information and clarifying visual/aural cues. HelloZiyi.us also provides rectificatory English-language subtitles for Itami's revelations during his dance with Xinxia.[6] The Palm Pictures Region 1 DVD's subtitles incorrectly have Itami stating that Yamamoto was killed by Xinxia's fellow resistance members, that he and Xinxia were both successful, and that they can go to Tokyo together. Itami actually says that Yamamoto returned to Tokyo safely and that Xinxia can never accomplish her mission. Moreover, Itami does not mention anything about Xinxia going to Tokyo with him. This is a significant piece of information because it reiterates the movie's pessimistic outlook.

Purple Butterfly is a series of fragments and moody montages, and Lou Ye repeats images so that viewers can make connections between actions that were interrupted while the movie shifts from one set of characters to another. After being the center of attention in Segment 1, Xinxia and Itami disappear for more than 10 minutes and 30 minutes, respectively. Xinxia's reappearance is not even immediately apparent; she and Xieming are blurred background figures in an extreme close-up shot of Yiling's face right before the train-station shootout sequence. Confusion is lessened once one realizes that long fades and complete editing breaks (i.e., edits without picture or sound bridges) denote temporal transitions and jumps throughout the movie's non-linear structure.

Purple Butterfly is short on expository dialogue and text. Captions that reveal the settings and times of Segments 1 and 2 appear two minutes after their respective segments start. Itami never tells anyone that he speaks Vietnamese in addition to Japanese and Mandarin Chinese. Therefore, unless one understands some combination of the aforementioned three languages, a viewer may not know that Itami converses with his landlady in Vietnamese. (Xinxia tells Xieming that Itami's landlady is Vietnamese, but this piece of information is insufficient to support a definite conclusion that Itami speaks Vietnamese. The only way to know that Itami speaks Vietnamese is to understand Vietnamese, too.) The lack of exposition is especially taxing on viewers who are unfamiliar with East-Asian languages, histories, and cultures. Such viewers may fail to distinguish Chinese characters from Japanese ones and may not understand why it was difficult for Chinese and Japanese people to be romantically involved with each other during the first half of the 20th century. Therefore, a viewer's comprehension relies heavily on inference generation from visual cues. Paradoxically, *Purple Butterfly's* lack of expository information makes it a more stable experience than *Suzhou River*. The movie does not question itself or its characters, so the viewer is unlikely to wonder if the images are falsehoods or dreams.

The lack of information is diegetic (what the characters do not tell each other) in addition to being non-diegetic (what the movie does not tell viewers), with the diegetic lack of information obviously amplifying the non-diegetic lack of information. As such, Lou Ye seems to be questioning the very usefulness and purpose of concrete information. When anti-Japanese and Japanese factions as well as Situ first meet, the factions do not bother explaining anything to Situ because they assume he is a resistance fighter. Later, after everyone finds out that Situ is an innocent bystander, Situ is treated as a pawn by both sides anyway. The movie indicates that what Situ knows or does not know is irrelevant; he is stuck between two forces determined to use him to destroy each other even though he has nothing to do with either side.

Despite the characters' (and the movie's) avoidance of words, not every uttered word is vital to comprehension of the narrative; some expository information is practically useless. For example, Xinxia's pseudonym ("Ding Hui") has little function, other than to reflect the secretive nature of espionage life, because the movie does not use Xinxia's two names as a source of confusion or mistaken identity. After they reunite in Shanghai, Itami quickly realizes that Xinxia is an anti-Japanese operative, regardless of what her name is. At one point, as Itami reminisces about the past, the soundtrack cuts him off by fading in music and fading out his voice. At another point, the anti-Japanese operatives hold a briefing that reveals details of Itami's training as a spy. However, this information also serves little purpose because Xinxia is already familiar with Itami's background and because the viewer has already observed Itami's ability to speak several languages. *Purple Butterfly's* visual-storytelling strengths negate the need for the characters or the movie to provide verbal commentary.

Since the movie does not reveal all of the characters' motivations, viewers have the opportunity to debate several permanent gaps. For example, at the end of Segment 2, Situ seeks out Itami in a Japanese dance hall. After shooting Itami, Situ points his gun at Xinxia's face. However, just before he shoots Xinxia, Situ lowers his gun to her right shoulder area. Situ's last-second hesitation piques some curiosity about his relationship with

Xinxia. Even if Xinxia never admitted to him that she was the one who shot Yiling, Situ knows that Xinxia is partially responsible for Yiling's death, not to mention his almost dying several times.[7] Situ still shoots Xinxia, so he has not forgiven her. However, since he does not destroy Xinxia's face, one wonders if he became enamored with her during the times that they spent together. The nature of the relationship between Xinxia and Situ depends on audiences' assessments of the characters' personalities. In giving audiences room to interpret the movie's subtleties, Lou Ye expands the viewing experience beyond *Purple Butterfly*'s running time.

Conclusion

Suzhou River and *Purple Butterfly* do not offer narratives that simply mimic previously told stories even though they remain identifiable as thrillers. This is achieved with severe temporal conflations or disruptions and the destabilization of the ability to perceive reality accurately (on both the characters' and the viewer's parts). As the characters wonder about each other's motivations and actions, the viewer's own inferences are thrown into doubt since Lou Ye avoids dramatic irony as much as possible. Lou's *Suzhou River* and *Purple Butterfly* are responses – and rebukes – to moviemaking that relies on reinforcing viewer expectations.

I thank Edward Feng and Elisabeth Ret for their support during the writing of this essay.

Notes

1   *Suzhou River* and *Purple Butterfly* are direct English-language translations of the movies' Chinese-language titles.
    Lou Ye's Filmography as a Director:

    Summer Palace (*Yihe Yuan*) (2006) – also screenwriter and editor
    Purple Butterfly (*Zi Hudie*) (2003) – also screenwriter and editor
    Suzhou River (*Suzhou He*) (2000) – also screenwriter
    Don't Be Young (TV movie) (1995)
    Weekend Lover (*Zhoumo Qingren*) (1995)

    Compiled from Silbergeld, p. 121 and "Lou Ye" entry.

2   Silbergeld, "A Note on Transliteration," p. x.

Following Silbergeld's lead, I use Hanyu Pinyin transliterations of the characters' names rather than the transliterations offered by English-language subtitles found on most film prints and DVD releases. Silbergeld explains the meanings of the characters' names in *Hitchcock With a Chinese Face.*

The narrator's name is uttered once, almost unintelligibly, by a police officer near the end of the movie (around 1:11:55). The narrator's name sounds like Li Jiqian or Li Jiquan. Without benefit of either Chinese subtitles or a Chinese-language script, I am unable to determine the narrator's exact name and if the narrator's name has any bearing on the movie's themes.

3   The English-language subtitles mistakenly translate "45 *wan*" RMB, the ransom amount, as "45,000" RMB. "45 *wan*" is actually "450,000" RMB, which Mudan thinks is not a lot of money for her life. Silbergeld repeats this error on p. 11 of *Hitchcock With a Chinese Face.*

4   Some journalists and movie reviewers have written that the title is the name of the anti-Japanese resistance group. However, none of the characters refer to the anti-Japanese group as "Purple Butterfly," though a butterfly pin on a suit jacket is used as an identifying mark and Yiling catches butterflies that fly into her apartment.

5   Continuing to follow Silbergeld's lead, I use Hanyu Pinyin transliterations of the Chinese characters' names rather than the spellings supplied by English-language subtitles on some DVDs. Therefore, I use Xinxia instead of Cynthia and Situ instead of Szeto. The use of "Cynthia" for Xinxia is potentially misleading, as it suggests that Xinxia has a predilection for Western practices – a suggestion that is not supported by anything else in the movie.

6   Meng Ye, *Purple Butterfly* Background Information (http://www.monkeypeaches.com/0206M.html#020623C), MonkeyPeaches.com, June 23, 2002. Accessed: February 1, 2007.

Meng Ye, *Purple Butterfly* Viewing Guide (http://www.monkeypeaches.com/030824A.html), MonkeyPeaches.com, August 24, 2003. Accessed: February 1, 2007.

"Governor Yu," *Purple Butterfly* Viewing Guide (http://www.helloziyi.us/Articles/PB_Guide_DVD.htm), HelloZiyi.us, 2005. Accessed: February 1, 2007.

"Governor Yu" *Purple Butterfly* Page (http://www.helloziyi.us/Movies/Purple_Butterfly.htm), HelloZiyi.us, 2001–2002. Accessed: February 1, 2007.

I confirmed Governor Yu's subtitles by listening carefully to Toru Nakamura's line deliveries and by watching the Zoke Culture Region 0, China DVD (released July 28, 2003), which has Simplified Chinese subtitles.

7   Perhaps Xinxia doesn't think or doesn't know if she shot Yiling, though the editing during the train-station shootout suggests that Xinxia is the one who killed Yiling.

Bibliography

Barr, C. 1999. *English Hitchcock*. London: Cameron and Hollis.
Branigan, E. 1992. *Narrative Comprehension and Film*. New York: Routledge.
FIPRESCI website (http://www.fipresci.org/). http://www.fipresci.org/awards/awards/awards_2000.htm. Accessed: February 1, 2007.
"Governor Yu." *HelloZiyi.us* (http://www.helloziyi.us/). "Governor Yu," 2007. Accessed: February 1, 2007. (HelloZiyi.us's webmaster wishes to remain anonymous for privacy reasons, though he is known as "Governor Yu" in Internet fora.)
Lim, D. 2007. "Lou Ye's generation next." http://www.villagevoice.com/film/0045,lim,19607,20.html (accessed: February 1, 2007).
"Lou Ye" entry (http://www.imdb.com/name/nm0521601/). IMDB.com, 2007. Accessed: February 1, 2007.
Meng, Y. 2007. *MonkeyPeaches.com* (http://www.monkeypeaches.com/). Accessed: February 1, 2007.
Palmer, J. 1979. *Thrillers: Genesis and Structure of a Popular Genre*. New York: St. Martin's Press.
Rubin, M. 1999. *Thrillers*. Cambridge: Cambridge University Press.
Ryall, T. 1986. *Alfred Hitchcock and the British Cinema*. Champaign: University of Illinois Press.
Silbergeld, J. 2004. *Hitchcock With a Chinese Face*. Seattle: University of Washington Press.

10

The Pragmatic Poetics of Hong Sangsoo's *The Day a Pig Fell into a Well*

Marshall Deutelbaum

Despite the apparent promise of its title, there is neither a pig nor a well in Hong Sangsoo's first film, *The Day a Pig Fell into a Well* (*Doejiga umul-e ppajin nal*, 1996).

Hong appropriated the title from a short story by John Cheever originally published in the October 23, 1954 issue of *The New Yorker* magazine and later included in a collection of the author's short stories. The story begins:

> In the summer, when the Nudd family gathered at Whitebeach Camp, in the Adirondacks, there was always a night when one of them would ask "Remember the day the pig fell into the well?" Then as if the opening note of a sextet had been sounded, the others would all rush in to take their familiar parts, like those families who sing Gilbert and Sullivan, and the recital would go on for an hour or more. (Cheever, p. 219)

Hong has never explained his reason for adopting the title, though it seems likely that the way in which the story of the unfortunate pig is related piecemeal by Cheever's characters mirrors how the film was written. Just as the recital of the events that happened on that singular day is stitched together from the specific detail supplied by each family member, Hong's film is the result of the combination of four scripts by four writers – supposedly students he assigned to the project – each of whom created a character and described the events the character experienced over the course of a day. Making adjustments as he saw fit to connect the characters to one another, Hong then edited the four accounts into the single script that became the blueprint for his multi-character/multi-plot film. The film, reflecting its genesis, is still divided into four parts, each of which follows a character over the course of a day as he or she interacts with, merely observes, or simply crosses paths with one or more of the other three.

The first part, primarily concerned with a modestly successful writer named Hyosup, also introduces two of the film's other main characters, Minjae, a young woman who loves and admires him unquestioningly, and Bokyung, an unhappily married woman whom Hyosup claims to love and with whom he is having an affair. Over the course of the day, he retrieves a manuscript from a publisher and meets Minjae at a coffee shop where she offers to edit it. He then meets Bokyung, taking her to a hotel to have sex. Afterwards, he leaves her in order to meet another publisher, then rejoins her for coffee at an art gallery. Finally, that night, he attends a dinner in honor of another writer. During dinner Hyosup becomes increasingly drunk and belligerent and, finally, is arrested and sentenced to five days in jail.

The second part introduces Dongwoo, Bokyung's overly hygienic husband, as he boards a bus for what will be a trouble-plagued business trip to Jinju. To begin with, the trip unexpectedly takes longer than it should after the passenger seated beside him throws up on his shoes. Then, because Dongwoo leaves the bus at its next stop to clean up, he has to take another bus and arrives late for his business appointment. However, the appointment never takes place that day because the manager he is supposed to meet never returns to his office. Between revisits to the office in hopes of having the meeting, Dongwoo first kills time in a restaurant, then visits a friend in his apartment. After the appointment is rescheduled for the following day, Dongwoo spends the night in a small hotel where he has sex with a prostitute. Because his condom breaks during intercourse, Dongwoo stops at a clinic the following morning where he learns that he will have to wait 40 days to see whether he has contracted a venereal disease as a result of the accident.

The film's third part follows Minjae as she buys a pair of boots as a surprise birthday present for Hyosup on the way to her job selling tickets in a run-down movie theater. While at work, she edits Hyosup's manuscript and, at one point, sneaks away to apply for a better-paying job dubbing video sound tracks. After work, she drops off Hyosup's manuscript at his publisher, and then buys a birthday cake, meaning to surprise him with it, too. She is the one who is surprised, however, because when she arrives at his apartment she finds Bokyung is there. Hyosup cruelly disillusions Minjae by telling her he loves Bokyung and means to marry her. He brutally rejects Minjae, pushing her to the ground. Minsu, one of Minjae's co-workers from the theater, who has followed her, observes this from a distance. He follows Minjae to a restaurant where he strikes up a conversation with her. Eventually the pair winds up in bed.

The fourth part begins in yet another morning as Bokyung, apparently having planned to go away with Hyosup, waits for him in a bus station. When he doesn't arrive, she leaves a message on his answering machine saying she'll wait for him for another 30 minutes. When he still doesn't appear, she goes to Hyosup's apartment, leaving a note wedged into the door when there is no response to her knock. After she leaves, Hyosup's neighbor takes note and reads it in her apartment. While sitting in a restaurant later in the day, Bokyung sees her husband walk by. She follows him to a clinic and tries to find out what he is being treated for. Then, after riding aimlessly on a city bus, she stops at a relative's shop where she naps, dreaming about how the people she knows act at her funeral. After leaving the shop, she stops at a photographer's studio where she insists upon buying, and then destroying, a formal portrait of her husband and herself with a small child. Still later, she returns to Hyosup's apartment, but again receives no reply. She sees that the note she left is gone and walks away. (We then see what she cannot see in the apartment: Minsu has killed Minjae and Hyosup.) In bed at home later that night, Bokyung struggles briefly before allowing Dongwoo to force himself sexually upon her. After her husband has gone out for cigarettes, Bokyung leaves another message on Hyosup's answering machine. The next morning, after reading the newspaper, Bokyung seems to be about to commit suicide, though we can't be sure because the shot of her on the verge of committing suicide – and the film itself – end abruptly.

The Day a Pig Fell into a Well is a striking departure in subject matter from what had been the norm for nearly a decade in the films known collectively as New Korean Cinema. As Jinhee Kim explains,

> The years between the mid-1980s and the early 1990s—a period marked by intense political upheavals and carefully measured cultural oppression—are now commonly referred to as the period of the New Korean Cinema. The bulk of films produced during this period are dependent on social context for the development of their plot, characters, and themes. Many proponents of this artistic movement saw film as a social institution that is obliged to portray the political realities of the marginalized classes such as factory workers, prostitutes, anti-government resistants, and persons from other neglected corners of society. (Kim 2002, pp. 11–12)

Recognizing the film's departure from the focus of New Korean Cinema, critics interpreted the discontinuities Hong left in the film's depiction of the characters' mundane reality as evidence of the social malaise that many people thought was the hallmark of the post-political Korea. As Michael Robinson explains this social shift:

> While the struggles of the 1980s led to the beginning of democratization and true civilian governance, cultural life thereafter seemed vacuous and purposeless to many who had devoted their life's work to opposing authoritarian rule. Some artists who expressed their sense of detachment in the new era of apolitical cultural life were roundly criticized as somehow giving up. Yet, such expressions captured what many felt was the existential crisis that had beset Korean culture in the 1990s. (Robinson 2005, pp. 24–5)

From this perspective, critics interpreted *The Day a Pig Fell Into a Well* symptomatically, as a fragmented, postmodernist work that presented the corrupting effect of modernization on Korea. As Eungjum Min, Jinsook Joo, and Han Ju Kwak explain:

> *The Day a Pig Fell into a Well* does not address directly the issue of modernization. Nevertheless, insofar as the social reality of modern Korea is considered the outcome of modernization, the film consistently shows how our lives in the postindustrial society have become fragile, dislocated, and confused. Viewed in the context of modernization, the film is a grim portrait of (post)modernity, filled with symptoms of disruption. (Min, Joo, and Kwak 2003, p. 147)

Consequently, they argue,

> The film attempts not to reproduce realist effects, but to urge the viewer to confront the fragments of reality per se. It deconstructs "our" traditional concept of reality by showing trivial details, which ceaselessly collide, intersect, and intermingle with one another in a closed structure. What it constructs, therefore, is not a tapestry of unitary reality, but the absence of such reality. (2003, p. 143)

Furthermore, they contend that in place of traditional narrative unity, clear psychological causality, and closure,

> The film uses various formal strategies to express disruption and disillusionment . . .

Its episodic narrative structure is a device which effaces temporal linearity. The adoption of a fragmentary narrative structure which enables the
shift of protagonists has the effect of suggesting not only the complexity of
modern life, but also the disjunction of it. (2003, p. 146)

Careful attention to details in the film, however, reveals that rather than
"efface temporal linearity," as the trio of critics declare, the film quietly
announces its temporal order to observant viewers through numerous wall
calendars whose progression of months – indicated by number, not name
– mark the narrative's four-month span: Hyosup's section begins in
September; the next two parts about Dongwoo and Minjae occur during
the month of October, perhaps on the same day, October 26. Bokyung's
section occurs during December. Although specific dates are impossible
to determine for the three parts other than Minjae's, the progression of
months tallies logically with events we see in the characters' lives.

With Hyosup sentenced to five days in jail at the end of the first part,
the third section must take place at least that many days later to give Minjae
time to finish editing the manuscript she received from him during the
first part and also allow Minsu, sentenced to five days in jail at the same
time as Hyosup, to return to work after serving his sentence. In fact, by
the date of October 26 that Minjae has circled on her calendar to mark
Hyosup's birthday, we can be sure that more than five days have elapsed
between the first and third parts. Wall calendars in the second part indicate that Dongwoo's trip to Jinju occurs in October. Intriguingly, of all the
characters, only Minjae and Dongwoo never meet or even cross paths. Despite
this, or perhaps because of it, internal evidence suggests that his trip may
also have occurred on October 26. When he telephones Bokyung from the
hotel in Jinju the night of his trip, he is puzzled to find that she is not at
home and leaves a message on the answering machine asking her to call
him when she returns home. Quite possibly, Bokyung is not at home because
she is at Hyosup's apartment, as Minjae discovers when she pays her
surprise birthday visit there in the third part. Analogously, the lovers'
quarrel that Dongwoo hears in the hallway outside his hotel room after he
makes the telephone call suggestively mirrors the quarrel that occurs at
roughly the same time of the night in the third section when Minjae discovers that Bokyung is with Hyosup.

At the end of the second part, Dongwoo is told that he will have to wait
40 days to see whether he has contracted a genital infection because his
condom failed. Dongwoo's visit to the clinic in the film's fourth part takes

place in December, about 40 days later. By paying attention to the wall calendars we can deduce from part three when part two occurs, then, retrospectively, understand from part two why part four occurs in December.
Rather than call the film fragmented, then, we might more accurately describe
the film's chronology as being linear with a great many gaps of all kinds,
none more puzzling than the formal photograph that Bokyung tears
up. It suggests a happier family life before the film begins and hints that
her alienation from her husband and willingness to have an affair with
Hyosup are the consequence of whatever may have happened to their child.

By focusing only upon the gaps in the realistic elements of the film's story,
critics ignore the significant cinematic choices Hong made in how to tell
or narrate these stories through his use of camera placement and editing.
These choices create additional gaps that cannot be explained by the film's
social context alone. Rather, the gaps are designed to wean viewers from
their habitual, virtually automatic habits of perception learned from years
of watching traditional narrative films. In other words, *The Day a Pig Fell
into a Well* is an example of pragmatic poetics, a perceptual model offered
by a first-time filmmaker to his audience in order to teach them to understand – or at least how to approach an understanding – of his personal
aesthetic. Hong expects viewers to do considerably more interpretative work
than traditional narrative films require.

Indeed, he signals their need for heightened attention during the film's
opening credits as the soundtrack moves from orderly language (a woman's voice heard announcing the imminent departure of a bus for Jinju),
through apparently random phrases (a man's muffled voice saying "Well
. . . let's start! Ready!" and a different woman's voice enigmatically intoning, " 'Blue, down!' 'Blue, raise!' 'Blue, don't down!' 'White, don't raise!'
'Blue, raise!' 'White, don't down!' 'Blue, don't down!' 'White, don't down!' "),
to sounds whose origins cannot be identified (a ringing bell, a whistle,
the opening and closing of a door, and the sound of knocking). Depending upon how well they have been able to remember these sounds, viewers
will recognize the bus announcement when it occurs in context at the
beginning of the film's second part, the enigmatic phrases when they are
spoken by Minjae in the film's third part as she dubs a video game, and
the final sequence of sounds when Bokyung makes them during her final
visit to Hyosup's apartment in the film's fourth part.

One can begin to appreciate Hong's program of perceptual reeducation
by comparing the narrative and narrational complexities of *The Day a Pig
Fell into a Well* with how the narrative and narration are handled in the

considerably more conventional multi-plot/multi-character Hollywood film, *Crash* (Paul Haggis 2004), the winner of numerous awards, including Academy Awards for Best Motion Picture of the Year, Best Screenplay Written Originally for the Screen, and Best Achievement in Editing. Everything that the characters do in *Crash*, as well as the situations in which they find themselves as they interact with one another, result from racial and ethnic discrimination and misunderstanding. The intensity of this single thematic and motivational focus is heightened by the story taking place in less than a day.

Crash's narrative is organized around the progressive development of a variety of situations related to its themes. For example, during an unnecessary late-night vehicle stop early in the film, Tommy Hanson, a white rookie policeman who believes himself to be racially tolerant, watches silently as John Ryan, his senior partner, sexually humiliates an African-American woman in front of her husband, Cameron Thayer. Later that day, disgusted by what his partner did, Hanson asks for and receives permission to drive patrol by himself when he resumes work that afternoon. As he begins work that afternoon, however, Ryan, who knows why his former partner will no longer work with him, warns Hanson that he really does not know himself. Ryan's cautionary warning is fulfilled late that night, when Hanson stops on his way home, to give a ride to a young African-American hitchhiker. As they talk, Hanson slowly comes to mistrust the young man. When he reaches into his jacket to show Hanson a religious statuette like the one on the dashboard of the car, Hanson assumes without sufficient provocation that the man is reaching for a gun and shoots him, thereby confirming Ryan's earlier warning about his latent racism.

The three stages of Hanson's experience reflect the well-established, three-part or three-act structure common to most Hollywood narratives. Thus Cameron Thayer, the television director who helplessly watched the sexual abuse of his wife during that night-time traffic stop, finds himself forced at work the next morning to reshoot a scene of the sitcom he is directing because its white star complains that a black actor delivered his lines in way that did not sound black enough. Thayer's argument with his wife moments later at lunchtime when she complains that he should have asserted himself when she was sexually touched while being searched the night before further accentuates his anger at believing that his survival depends upon acquiescing to white men in positions of authority. By the time he leaves work to drive home late that afternoon he is so thoroughly frustrated by the racial humiliations he has suffered in quick succession that he turns a minor traffic stop into a confrontation with police because of his need to finally assert his dignity. *Crash's* plot lines are so tightly interconnected that only Tommy Hanson's chance arrival at the scene defuses the confrontation, and in the process, as it were, allows Hanson to atone for his silence the previous night when he watched John Ryan humiliate Cameron by groping his wife. Later that night, however, when Hanson fulfills Ryan's warning, he realizes that his atonement was illusory. In contrast to *Crash*, the motivations and situations of the characters in *The Day a Pig Fell into a Well* are not tied to a single theme, nor are their plotlines intertwined to so thoroughly.

Just as they differ in their narrative structure, the films differ in their styles of editing. Unlike Hong's film, *Crash* not only adheres consistently to the long-established principles of continuity editing that audiences follow so effortlessly, at times it uses editing to smooth the transition from one plot to another by eliding the beginning of an action or sound at the end of a scene in one plotline with its apparent conclusion at the beginning of a scene in a different plotline. Thus the gun-shop's door that begins to swing open at the end of the film's first sequence, which introduces the plotline that follows a Persian convenience shop owner, seems to complete its opening at the beginning of the next sequence as two carjackers in a different plotline are introduced as they finish pushing open the door of a restaurant they are leaving somewhere else in Los Angeles. At the end of another sequence, a locksmith's van that backs out of a driveway late at night becomes a stolen SUV when it begins to move forward as the narrative switches to another plotline. Even though darkness and motion obscure the transformation of the vehicle, much of the illusory continuity that smoothes over the change of shot is created by a song on the soundtrack, begun in the van and continued in the SUV without a missed note.

Because *The Day a Pig Fell into a Well* frequently ignores the conventional patterns of continuity editing with which viewers are familiar, even the simplest spatial and temporal relationships between characters become surprising and even confusing. For example, a series of shots when Hyosup meets Minjae in the coffee shop in the first part are only partially edited in the traditional way: while Minjae reads a manuscript he wants her to edit, Hyosup gets up from their table, telling her that he is going outside. The next two shots show him outside the restaurant. The fourth shot returns to Minjae, reading. But 10 seconds after the shot begins, we hear Hyosup, off-camera, asking her what she thinks of the manuscript. The next shot reveals what the soundtrack has already signaled: contrary to the norms of classical practice that would have shown his return before he spoke (as would have been the case had the scene appeared in *Crash*), Hyosup has returned to the table and has been seated there since sometime before the second shot of Minjae reading.

This kind of retrospectively revealed temporal and spatial continuity occurs throughout the film. A particularly striking instance that ignores the protocols of continuity editing occurs in the second part after Dongwoo arrives late for his business appointment at the office in Jinju. After the secretary tells him to return after lunch, the next five shots, separated by straight cuts and lasting a minute, show:

1   Two men working in a restaurant's kitchen.
2   Dongwoo standing by a plate-glass window talking to his wife on the telephone.
3   A close-up of a carton of milk and two doughnuts on a desk.
4   A reverse shot revealing that the secretary seen earlier is eating at her desk as Dongwoo returns and is told by her that he should return later for the meeting.
5   The interior of a car from the point of view looking forward from low on the back seat toward the windshield as the car stops at the curb and Dongwoo gets in.

Not only does the editing of this sequence omit indications of the spatial relationships between shots, camera placement further denies other traditional elements of continuity. The shot of the restaurant kitchen could be a traditional master shot establishing the overall geography of the restaurant. However, because there is nothing in the second shot that shows any of the restaurant's interior, the shot that follows, of Dongwoo standing by a window, has no necessary logical or spatial connection with it. The close-up in the third shot of the milk carton and doughnuts on the desk top is the opposite of the restaurant kitchen because it lacks enough detail for viewers to identify the locale as one that they have already seen. That it is in the secretary's outer office only becomes clear with the reverse shot. The final shot of the interior of a car seen from an unusual point of view is the most disturbing shot of the series because the intervening telephone call Dongwoo must have made asking his friend to pick him up has been omitted entirely. By freeing the narration from the strictures of traditional editing that normally show every step in a process, Hong creates a world of spatial and temporal uncertainties that demands that viewers be extra-attentive.

Crash and *The Day a Pig Fell into a Well* are strikingly different in how each presents story information to viewers. Of the two, *Crash* is considerably more omniscient, its narration moving smoothly from character to character as it interconnects their actions based on racial discrimination and suspicion into a broader cultural pattern than any single character could know. Narration further heightens the impact of their actions by restricting our depth of knowledge about their motivations almost solely to their thoughts and feelings about racism. In contrast, *The Day a Pig Fell into a Well* employs a considerably more restricted narration punctuated at times by passages of unrestricted omniscience; both kinds of narration severely restrict the depth of our understanding of the main characters' motivations. As a result of these narrational differences, viewers are puzzled by little in *Crash*, while there is much that mystifies viewers in *The Day a Pig Fell into a Well*.

The shifts back and forth between restricted and omniscient narration in Hong's film are an important element in the program to guide the viewers' perceptual reeducation because the omniscient passages reveal explanations to them about situations that the film's characters either believe unquestioningly or misconstrue. For example, once Dongwoo reaches his friend's apartment, the friend tells him he will have to take a bus to return for his meeting. The friend explains that he cannot drive him back because if he left the apartment he might miss an important fax that he is expecting. After a shot of showing Dongwoo walking to a bus stop, however, Hong shifts to omniscient narration, cutting back to the apartment to reveal the friend's real reason for not leaving as he calls his wife into their bedroom to have sex. Though without any significant consequence, this brief shift to omniscient narration in order to reveal the friend's true intentions serves as one cautionary warning to viewers, among many, to be wary of accepting at face value what they hear and see during restricted narration elsewhere in the film.

Often the shift to omniscient narration helps viewers correctly construe information otherwise missing because of gaps caused by restricted narration. For example, the first shot of Minjae surreptitiously leaving work to apply for a job dubbing videos shows her walking on the sidewalk and waiting at the curb for the traffic signal to change so she can cross a street. With the next shot a shift to omniscient narration shows Minsu, her coworker, seated in a restaurant, eating (the narration is omniscient over Minjae). After he happens to turn his head to look toward the window, a shot from behind him reveals that that Minjae is visible to him through the restaurant's window as she waits for the traffic light to change. A return to restricted narration in subsequent shots shows Minjae's visit to the dubbing studio (the narration is therefore restricted to Minjae). However, nothing of her return to work is shown. Instead, immediately after a shot of her receiving payment in the dubbing studio for her work, a return to omniscient narration shows Minsu's arrival in the theater lobby and his cryptic statement to the theater owner that he has something to tell him. In the next shot, a return to restricted narration shows Minjae seated in the theater's ticket office as Minsu knocks on the door and tells her, somewhat diffidently, that she needs to make up an excuse for her earlier absence because the theater owner knows that she went out without permission. From these shifts in narration, we can construe, retrospectively, that Minsu has told the theater owner about her absence. Consequently, we can construe, as well, that he has done this self-servingly, so he can warn Minjae as though he were watching out for her best interests.

The alternations of restricted and omniscient narrations have a considerably more important effect after Bokyung leaves the note wedged in Hyosup's apartment door asking him to telephone her after he returns. Once Bokyung leaves, a shift to omniscient narration shows Hyosup's neighbor some time later as she retrieves the note and takes it into her apartment to read. Restricted narration is reestablished when Bokyung returns to Hyosup's apartment that night and sees that the note she had carefully wedged into the door is no longer there. She knocks on the door, but gets no response and leaves. After her departure, omniscient narration reveals the scene inside the apartment that Bokyung – and the viewers because of restricted narration up to this moment – could not see: Minsu has killed Minjae and Hyosup.

Consequently, we know why Hyosup failed to meet her at the bus station that morning or return her messages as well as what, most likely, Bokyung will mistakenly construe from the disappearance of the note. While we know that Hyosup is dead, Bokyung is likely to conclude from the disappearance of her note that he has read it. And from this will follow, probably, a chain of mistaken conclusions: that he no longer cares for her, that he has changed his mind about going away with her, and, as a result, that he has spent the day avoiding her rather than admit all of this to her. And, quite likely, these mistaken conclusions will lead her later that night to stop resisting her husband's sexual assault. (In the film's first part she assured Hyosup that she no longer had sexual relations with her husband. If she has mistakenly concluded from the missing note that Hyosup did not love her, she might just as easily conclude after the momentary resistance that we see that she might as well give in to her husband because she was no longer has any reason to resist his sexual advances.)

This oscillation between a restricted and less knowledgeable, less communicative, less self-conscious narration on the one hand, and an omniscient and more knowledgeable, more communicative, more self-conscious narration on the other, suggests a much more complicated diegetic world that is considerably more difficult to interpret correctly than the world depicted in *Crash*. At certain points, Hong heightens the difficulty even further for viewers by ending the depiction of an action before it reaches its conclusion. For example, after Bokyung leaves the bus station and begins her day of wandering through Seoul, a shift from restricted to omniscient narration shows her from the inside of a convenience shop as a man notices her walking by. He leaves the shop and follows her to where she is standing, waiting for a taxi. He stands behind her with his hands in his coat pockets and looks to his right and left. A cut to a taxi slowing as it approaches the curb turns out not to be a continuation of the omnisciently narrated sequence, but a return to restricted narration some time later, as a cab in which Bokyung is a passenger stops to let her out. As she goes to find money in her purse with which to pay the driver, she discovers that her wallet is not in her bag and wonders where she may have left it. How is a viewer to interpret what has happened? Has Bokyung lost her wallet or forgotten it somewhere, as she wonders? Or was the man who followed her a pickpocket who stole her wallet in the moment we did not see because of the abrupt cut that reestablished restricted narration? The man's glances suggest he may be scanning the area to see whether anyone might observe him pickpocketing her wallet, but we cannot be sure that this is what he is doing because the sudden cut prevents us from seeing what happens in the moment after his sidelong glances.

All together then, rather than deconstruct the traditional concept of reality as Min, Joo, and Kwak assert, the structure of *The Day a Pig Fell into a Well* presents viewers with a narrative whose uncertainties of meaning and motivation mirror the limits of understanding that viewers encounter in everyday reality. By refusing to allow viewers to escape briefly into the highly interconnected alternative to reality presented in a classical narrative like *Crash*, Hong redirects viewers to an alternate cognitive model applicable to their everyday experiences. Rather than an escape from reality, the film offers viewers a method of escape from the perils of jumping to conclusions based upon insufficient evidence.

The revelation of Minsu's murders of Hyosup and Minjae reveals to viewers what has been impossible for them to discern up to that point: though
Minsu has seemed to be merely a fleeting presence, he has actually been a
hidden force driving the narrative in unperceived ways. His presence has
been so hidden that his first appearance as another prisoner at the end of
the film's first section will never register on first-time viewers since he is
not formally identified until the film's third section. Those who recognize
Minsu's early appearance on a second viewing may well wonder what interaction he will have had with Hyosup during the five days they were in jail.
Whatever it may have been is as impossible to know as is what happened
between the end of Minjae's section and the end of Bokyung's section that
drove him to kill Minjae and Hyosup.

The certainty that first-time viewers will be unable to recognize Minsu
at the end of the film's first section, or, for that matter, to recognize the
also as yet unidentified Dongwoo when he and Hyosup stand side by side
in an elevator earlier that day, defines how Hong has fashioned the film's
narrative structure and visual style to continually force viewers to struggle
to construe the uncertainties of motivation. Unlike *Crash*, in which the motivations and experiences of the film's characters are reduced to the easily
understood consequences of racial discrimination and suspicion, *The
Day a Pig Fell into a Well* revels in a complexity created though narrative
gaps and nontraditional editing that suggests conversely how difficult it can
be to interpret motivation or understand experience. Quite the opposite
of traditional, mainstream narrative films, as well as of the films of the Korean
New Wave which preceded it, *The Day a Pig Fell into a Well* demands that
its viewers engage in an exercise in epistemological realism that asks them
to ponder the nature of knowledge, it presuppositions, the extent of its
validity, as well as its inevitable uncertainties. To reduce the film, as some
critics have done, to nothing more than a reflection of sociological malaise
is to miss the experiential richness that it offers those willing to perceive
its possibilities with heightened attention.

Bibliography

Cheever, J. 1978. "The day the pig fell into the well," in *The Stories of John Cheever*.
New York: Knopf, pp. 219–35.
Kim, J. 2002. "Cinephilic nation, minimal film: South Korea's Sangsu Hong and
his *The Power of Kangwon Province.*" *Utah Foreign Language Review*, 11, 1: 10–24.

Kwak, H. J. 2003. "Discourse on modernization in 1990s Korean cinema," in J. K. W. Lau (ed.), *Multiple Modernities: Cinemas and Popular Media in Transcultural East Asia*. Philadelphia: Temple University Press, pp. 90–113.

Min, E., Joo, J., and Kwak, H. J. 2003. *Korean Film: History, Resistance, and Democratic Imagination*. Westport, CT: Praeger.

Robinson, M. 2005. "Contemporary cultural production in South Korea: Vanishing meta-narratives of nation," in C.-Y. Shin and J. Stringer (eds.), *New Korean Cinema*. Edinburgh: Edinburgh University Press, pp. 15–31.

11

Looking for Access in Narrative Complexity. The New and the Old in *Oldboy*

Eleftheria Thanouli

South Korean cinema has become one of the central nodes in the debates about world cinema thanks to a flourishing domestic film market, on the one hand, and a remarkable presence in prestigious film festivals around the globe, on the other. The significant transformations that took place in the South Korean film industry in the 1990s, with the opening of the market to Hollywood competition and the investments of the local conglomerates, appear to have inspired a new turn in South Korean cinema (Paquet 2005, p. 33). Guided by the imperative of being both artistically innovative and commercially successful, South Korean filmmakers have reinvigorated their national filmmaking tradition and have accomplished a highly respectable performance equally in terms of box-office receipts and festival prizes. One prominent example of this new drive is Park Chan-wook's *Oldboy* released in 2003 as the second installment of a trilogy on the theme of revenge.[1] *Oldboy* is a typical product circulating in the networks of world cinema nowadays, stimulating questions such as "what makes a film travel or 'translate' to other cultures?"; "how can a filmmaker be original in the era of the 'already filmed'?"; and, above all, "how can one resolve the tension between Hollywood and national cinemas in this increasing phase of globalization?" My purpose in this chapter is not to address these issues head-on; instead, by focusing on the intricate narratological issues that the film's formal construction raises and by restricting my method to a consistent textual analysis, I will try to bring to the surface a set of tensions and contradictions that the film contains on a narrative level, hoping that my observations could offer an oblique answer to the aforementioned questions and hint at the developments that need to be addressed on other conceptual or cultural areas that relate to world cinema.

On first viewing, *Oldboy* leaves the spectator simultaneously enlightened and baffled. The secrets of the story are revealed, the masks of the protagonists are thrown off, and, yet, one feels the need to go over the facts once more, to double-check the connections among the characters and verify the premises of a particularly twisted narrative as it is transmitted through the channels of an equally twisted narration. And indeed, it was all intentional; as Park admitted at the news conference following the award presentations at Cannes Film Festival, he made the film with the DVD viewers in mind so that they could watch it several times and discover new elements each time.[2]

The young South Korean filmmaker, however, is not alone in the effort to cater for the needs and tastes of the DVD audience, which is not constrained by the limitations of the single viewing of a film in the theater. Since the late 90s, an increasing number of films have employed complex storytelling techniques that extend the classical rules of filmmaking and test the limits of the narrational capacities of the cinematic medium.[3] Some of them experiment with the treatment of narrative time, using time-loops and repetitions as in *Run Lola Run* (1998); others exhaust the possibilities of the screen by "exploding" the cinematic space as in *Time Code* (2000), while others create characters with impossible identities as in *Mulholland Dr.* (2001) and *Inland Empire* (2006).

Unlike these examples, however, *Oldboy* embodies an intriguing paradox for, on the one hand, it complicates the workings of all the narrative systems – causality, time, and space – while, on the other, it remains accessible and intelligible to the spectator even on the first viewing. The complexity in its narrative construction is so masterfully planned that everything is still within the viewer's grasp, everything is almost literally "in our face." In the close textual analysis that follows, I will try to uncover this meticulous narrative planning and explain the delicate handling of the various narrative devices in the film. My methodological and conceptual toolkit will primarily comprise the terms and concepts of the narrative analysis that David Bordwell has introduced in his contribution to the study of historical poetics (Bordwell 1985; Bordwell et al. 1985). More specifically, I will analyze *Oldboy* along the three main analytical axes – system of narrative logic, narrative space, and narrative time – and, consequently, I will examine the distribution and transmission of story information in the overall narration. The ultimate goal is to unlock the mechanisms of the film and reveal the constant and fierce negotiations that take place between the classical norms of narrative construction and the powers of innovation that stem from the highly self-conscious and multi-mediated cinematic practices all around the world.

Narrative Causality: Who, What, Why

The story is about an ordinary man called Oh Dae-Su (Choi Min-Sik), who becomes involved in an enigmatic game with tragic dimensions. After getting drunk one night, he is kidnapped by a stranger and wakes up to find himself in a private makeshift prison. Oh Dae-Su cannot understand who imprisoned him and why, and he anxiously wonders how long his ordeal will last. Time passes agonizingly slowly, as the hero is tortured not only by his questions remaining unanswered but also by the news of his wife's murder, for which the police blame him. The television set in his room is his only contact with the real world and the urge to take revenge on the person who destroyed his life becomes his sole purpose. Fifteen years pass and the hero is finally released in a suitcase on the rooftop of a building. The film dedicates almost 20 minutes of its screen-time to establish a highly intriguing narrative premise that poses several questions and triggers off a long chain of events until the final revelations. The mysteries that the hero needs to solve are three: who is responsible for the imprisonment, what is his motivation, and why the period of 15 years?

Yet, soon after Oh Dae-Su regains the right to walk around freely in the streets of Seoul, the villain returns at the helm of the story showing off his omnipotence. He hands Oh Dae-Su a wallet full of money and a cell phone through a passer-by and makes his first direct contact with him over the phone. During their brief conversation, he probes the hero to think back on his life and he poses an enigma, saying "Remember this: Be it a rock or a grain of sand, in water they sink as the same." This phone-call initiates a new trial for Oh Dae-Su, as he continues to be a pawn in the villain's game, the rules and goals of which remain obscure. However, he will not be alone in this game anymore; the narrative promptly offers him a young female partner called Mido who works as a chef at the restaurant where Oh Dae-Su walks in on his first night after his liberation. Mido immediately becomes his companion and then lover, as the two characters bond together in the pursuit of answers.

So far, the narrative of *Oldboy* contains some very classical compositional and generic motivations (Bordwell et al. 1985). As far as the former are concerned, the center of the narrative is a male protagonist whose fate and actions set off a cause-and-effect chain of events. Moreover, there is a series of clear and strong compositional elements, such as a victim of kidnapping, a string of tortures, the liberation, and the desire for revenge. The male protagonist builds a set of character traits during the years of imprisonment, which become his weapons as soon as he returns to the outside world. There he meets a woman and eventually forms with her a heterosexual couple, which is a staple of classical cinema. On the other hand, the generic identity of the film hinges on the trope of the mysterious villain, the investigation process, the solution of riddles, and the revelation of hidden secrets, all of which are part of the repertory of the thriller/suspense genre that allows for the revelations to take place only in the closing moments.

After the protagonist is contacted by his persecutor for the first time, he ventures on a quest for answers, following a rather classical narrative thread. First, he tries to locate the prison by tracing the Chinese restaurant that delivered the fried potatoes he ate for 15 years. Then, he interrogates the jailer for information and gets hold of a pack of audiotapes where he listens to the villain explain that "Oh Dae-Su speaks too much." This becomes another enigma that guides his investigation, as he collects clues and recollects his past. Gradually, after a number of trials and tribulations, he puts the pieces of the puzzle together, identifying both his torturer – the brother of an old schoolmate – and the deed that caused the latter's wrath – Oh Dae-Su starting a rumor that the two siblings had an incestuous affair. The final step for this classical male hero is to take revenge.

Nevertheless, the conventional narrative trajectory that the main character has traveled up to that point becomes radically subverted in the film's revelation scene. The key change regards the question that he was supposed to answer; instead of figuring out "why he was imprisoned for 15 years," he should have thought about "why he was *liberated* after 15 years." The narrative twist hidden in what seems a subtle shift of emphasis generates a complete breakdown of the classical plotline, leading us to a different reading of the events preceding it. The film is not about Oh Dae-Su seeking revenge on his imprisonment, but rather the entire story *is* an act of revenge on the part of the antihero, a young man called Lee Woo-Jin, who was in love with his sister and lost her because of the rumor Oh Dae-Su spread. From start to finish, all the depicted events were carefully orchestrated by Lee Woo-Jin with one single goal; to get even with Oh Dae-Su by causing him to have an incestuous relationship with his daughter Mido. Fifteen years had to pass for her to come of age and during that time the former had to remain secluded. The meeting with the young woman at the restaurant and their instant attraction were guided by the powers of hypnosis and the sinister planning by Lee Woo-Jin.

With these shocking disclosures, the film's narrative not only takes an unexpected turn but invites us to reevaluate the characters' actions in this new light. *Oldboy* acquires thus a Möbius strip structure that assigns its protagonists doubly coded roles with shifting qualities and dimensions.[4] Who is the perpetrator, who is the victim, which is the revenge, which is the punishment, who is in charge of the story, and who is finally vindicated are all questions that become ambiguous, as the positions of the hero and the antihero turn out to be doubly occupied by the two male protagonists. The classical character-centered causality that appeared in the first instance to be the foundation of this narrative becomes daringly challenged, as other powerful compositional elements enter the story, namely the theme of the double incest and the existential crisis that the two characters find themselves in. These two elements become catalysts in the film, complicating the narrative structure beyond any classical norms and, above all, preventing it from reaching a stable and clear closure.

Narrative Space and Time: Where, When

The complexity and density of the plot in *Oldboy* parallel the intricate treatment of the cinematic space and time in the overall narration. The three main narrational axes – causality, space, and time – in any given film are always interdependent but there are ways to handle them differently and adopt diverse principles for each one of them. For instance, films like *Sliding Doors* (1998), *Amores Perros* (2000), *The Hours* (2002), *21grams* (2003), or *The Three Burials of Melquiades Estrada* (2005) feature two, three, or more separate plotlines that complicate the shape of the narrative logic of the film but the spatiotemporal dimensions of each thread remain particularly classical. On the contrary, Park Chan-wook's choices in the handling of the space and time on the screen mirror the twisted nature of the story and enrich the classical options with a long list of new stylistic devices.

Starting with the cinematic space in *Oldboy*, one is easily impressed by the filmic universe the characters inhabit. Contrary to the classical prerogatives that dictate the construction of an unobtrusive visual space to accommodate the story (Bordwell et al. 1985), the South Korean filmmaker has taken full advantage of the graphic qualities of the filmic image to manipulate in an expressive manner the spatial coordinates of the action. Both at the level of shot composition and editing, he experiments with techniques that frequently offer impossible views of the narrative events and allow the camera to take a life of its own. Instead of the classical staging in depth, the linear perspective, and the central positioning of the characters in the frame, he opts for overhead shots, slanted angles, fish-eye lens distortions, extreme long shots, and extreme close-ups. In Figure 11.1 the overhead view of Oh Dae-Su's release on the rooftop is immediately followed (Figure 11.2) by the extreme close-up of his eye reacting to the daylight. This type of framing and editing in some cases becomes particularly demanding, as the viewer is required to adjust swiftly to the changes in distance and perspective, as shots come and go in a fairly fast tempo. On the other hand, the scenes that are shot in longer takes rely exclusively on fluid camera movements that generate a floating experience of the narrative space. Thus, it seems that Park follows the trend of several contemporary filmmakers who have moved from the classical continuity to the intensified continuity that

Figure 11.1   *Oldboy*

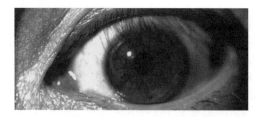

Figure 11.2   *Oldboy*

Figure 11.3   *Oldboy*

embraces a mannerist and self-conscious staging and shooting approach (Bordwell 2006).

  Complicating matters further, Park explores the possibilities of the movie screen by frequently relying on the use of "spatial montage," as that is defined by Lev Manovich (Manovich 2001). This type of montage allows various images of different origins and with complex relations with one another to coexist in the same frame, breaking down the logic of one screen/one image and adding enormous density to the composition of the shot.[5] For instance, in Figure 11.3 we have a composite shot made of several layers superimposed on top of each other. Lee Woo-Jin is placed on the right supposedly looking through the mirror. Oh Dae-Su is seen in the background on the left holding up a picture in front of a wall covered with framed photos. This intricate arrangement of characters and props in the shot emulates rather blatantly the classical staging in depth, while playing with a *mise-en-abyme* display. Even more explicit, though, is the spatial montage in Figure 11.4, which belongs to an extensive sequence consisting exclusively of split-screen shots. On the right, Lee Woo-Jin with a smirk on his face reveals the role of hypnosis and replays some of the key events of the plot on the left, such as the ringing of Oh Dae-Su's phone in the restaurant. The presentation of the flashback with the help of spatial montage in this case replaces the options of the traditional temporal editing, which would place the shots in a linear fashion, one after another, in order not to break the transparency of the frame and, by extension, the realistic effect of the device.

Figure 11.4　*Oldboy*

The breakdown of linearity becomes even more obvious in the construction of the cinematic time in *Oldboy*.[6] The complexity of the narrative with the plot twists and riddle-solving is largely supported by the complex temporal order in which the story events are presented on the screen. A closer look into the first 20 minutes of the film could illustrate the nonlinear chronology that characterizes the entire narration. A pre-credit sequence welcomes us *in medias res*, as the silhouette of a person appears to be holding another one off a neck-tie on the ledge of a rooftop. The one holding the rope is Oh Dae-Su who introduces himself by initiating a flashback. The story events follow in the order below:

a.　Cut to a police station where Oh Dae-Su has been arrested for being drunk and disorderly. He is bailed out by his friend, Joo-Hwan.

b.　Oh Dae-Su calls his daughter from a phone booth. Joo-Hwan takes over the phone and as he speaks, Oh Dae-Su is kidnapped by persons unknown.

c.　Credit sequence with various types of clocks ticking and turning.

d.　Oh Dae-Su is held captive in a private prison resembling a shabby hotel room. He has been held captive there for 2 months with no word of who is holding him there or why.

e.　He describes his routine, which includes regular visits by his holders who clean the room and cut his hair. During those visits he is gassed into unconsciousness.

f.　A year after his imprisonment, he watches on the news a report of his wife's murder and finds out that the police consider him as the prime suspect. He has a nervous breakdown.

g.   A montage sequence compresses the time Oh Dae-Su has spent watching television, using it as a watch and a calendar and relying on it as the only friend and companion.

h.   One day he begins to write an autobiographical diary in his attempt to maintain his sanity and trace his captor. He fills several notebooks.

i.   As time passes his boiling anger forces him to train by shadow boxing, punching at the walls of his prison until thick calluses form on his knuckles.

j.   After the first 6 years, he decides to mark the passage of time on his hand by tattooing one straight line for each year that goes by. At the same time he begins to slowly dig a hole into one of the walls with the help of a metal chopstick.

k.   A montage sequence compresses the years from the sixth to the fourteenth. With the use of a split-screen, the film shows us in the right half of the frame some of the key historical moments that took place in those years, such as the 9/11 attacks or Korea's participation in the football World Cup, while in the left half Oh Dae-Su is seen carrying out his daily activities.

l.   By the fifteenth year Oh Dae-Su manages to dig through the wall and feel the rain in his hand. Filled with excitement, he estimates that it will take him another month to escape.

m.   Not before long, though, a woman enters his room and hypnotizes him.

n.   Oh Dae-Su is set free on a rooftop with a new suit of clothes and his prison diaries. He sees another man sitting on the edge of the building with a small dog in his lap and he tries to communicate with him by touching and smelling him. That man is suicidal and attempts to jump off the edge, but Oh Dae-Su grabs his neck-tie, saving him from death. He asks him to postpone his death in order to listen to his story. This takes us back to the exact opening moment of the film and sheds new light on the scene.

This segment is typical of the overall temporal construction in the narration of *Oldboy*, which contains an intricate handling of the chronology of the events, on the one hand, and an inventive use of temporal devices, on the other. The long flashback that contains the phase of imprisonment is fragmented into various episodes, which evolve at different speeds and with various stylistic devices, such as extensive jump-cuts (fragments a. and i.), masterful long prowling camera movements (fragment b.), fast motion (fragment f.), and split-screens (fragment k.). Finally, the return to the opening scene not only completes the temporal loop but it also helps us reinterpret the event before our eyes: the man holding the neck-tie does not try to kill the other one, as it appeared the first time; instead, he tries to forestall his death. This deception results from the staging of the action and foreshadows the broader sense of deception that the narrative performs, as regards the relations of the characters and their goals. Thus, the temporal ordering of the events becomes an ally in twisting the story and withholding its key secrets.

Moderating the Complexity

The complex narrational choices I have examined so far in the systems of causality, space and time serve Park's avowed goal to present his viewers with a dense and demanding film that would require several viewings on a DVD in order to unravel all its dimensions. And yet, there is an organizing principle underlying the various levels of complexity and maintaining a high degree of intelligibility even for those who see it only once. I believe that the mechanism that holds the film together and attributes to it a considerable measure of coherence is related to the way the narration controls the transmission and the flow of story information.

At the broadest level of inquiry, the narration of a film can be defined as a vehicle for information of different sorts. The sum of the causal and spatiotemporal elements aim at transmitting varying amounts of information and distributing the knowledge about the story at various paces from the beginning till the end. This multifaceted process of conveying data to the spectators is moderated by three properties: "self-consciousness," "knowledgeability," and "communicativeness"[7] (Bordwell et al. 1985, p. 25). Firstly, the self-consciousness refers to the degree in which the film acknowledges its constructed nature and breaks the illusion of being a segment of reality. More specifically, a narration can be *self-conscious* to different degrees, depending on how much it flaunts the actual transmission of information to the audience. When we want to evaluate the element of self-consciousness in a film, we ask questions such as "how aware is the narration of addressing the audience?" or "which aspects reveal the artificiality of the narrating act?"

Secondly, the knowledgeability is related to the amount of information that the narration possesses about the story. Depending on the range and the depth of knowledge, a narration can be either knowledgeable or restricted. To measure the degree of knowledgeability, we have to investigate the sources of information on which the film relies; if, for instance, the narration confines itself to the knowledge and actions of one character, then it is bound to be restricted and ignore other sides of the story. If, on the other hand, the film switches from character to character and rises above the subjective level, then it acquires a sense of omniscience.

Thirdly, the communicativeness determines the extent to which the narration communicates the information it has at its disposal. An omniscient narration is not necessarily obliged to share its knowledge with the spectators and may choose to suppress it until the very end or even indefinitely. Alternatively, a restricted narration could be entirely communicative, sharing all its knowledge with us no matter how little that may be. In other words, the question we seek to answer in regard to the aspect of communicativeness is "how willing is the narration to tell us what it knows?" or "how open and talkative is the film about its story?"

Looking at the narration of *Oldboy* through this prism, one is immediately struck by the ubiquitous presence of self-consciousness that constantly reminds us of the fabricated quality of the film. All the elements of complexity that I previously detected – from the use of the voiceover to the mannerist *mise-en-scène* and the regular manipulations of the chronology – bring forward the very act of narration, defying the directives of the classical model that dictate the suppression of the aspect of self-consciousness. What is intriguing, however, is that the extreme self-consciousness does not block our engagement with the action, no matter how it foregrounds the artificiality of the filmic texture. This is paradoxical, given that a high level of self-consciousness is not usually a sign of easy access to the characters and the plot. Rather the contrary, as the traditional bearers of self-conscious devices, the modernist and experimental films, favored the obscurity and the ambiguity of their signifiers. Nonetheless, in the case of Park's film, what tones down the effects of self-consciousness and mitigates the sources of complexity is the amplified knowledgeability and communicativeness of the narration.

More specifically, the presence of an omniscient narrator who continually comments on the action functions as a navigation tool in a diegetic world that would otherwise seem chaotic. For instance, in the first scene where Oh Dae-Su appears locked in a room screaming at the guard and asking for how long his captivity will last, his voice in the form of a nondiegetic narrator informs us right away that he would remain in the room for 15 years. This is a piece of very crucial information that, on the one hand, helps us understand and position the entire phase of imprisonment within the story, while, on the other, it reassures us that the narration is in hold of all the necessary information. Moreover, the long and fragmented episode of captivity, despite its complex temporality and, by extension, the high degree of self-consciousness, is held together by the regular intrusions of Oh Dae-Su's comments, offering detailed explanations regarding the methods and practices of his prisoners, such as the fact that he was drugged with the same gas that the Russians used on Chechnyan terrorists.

At the same time, the voiceover soundtrack becomes a parallel diegetic space where the protagonist's emotional and mental life can unfold. It is an ambiguous narrative realm where the most extreme levels of narration[8] are welded together; on the one hand, Oh Dae-Su operates as a non-diegetic narrator who reveals his omniscience, while, on the other, internally focalized sounds give us insight into the innermost workings of his mind.[9] For example, as soon as Oh Dae-Su is liberated, he promptly shares with us the realization that his enemy left him on exactly the same spot from which he was abducted 15 years before; the rooftop of a building constructed where the telephone booth used to be. This information immediately explains the bizarre choice of location and reveals the meticulous planning of the villain's game. Moreover, the narration often grants us complete access to the character's inner dialogue and allows us to hear his thoughts as he encounters a new world, walking down the streets of Seoul. In one instance, he hears a new slang word and thinks to himself that television could not teach him such things, while later on he wonders if 15 years of imaginary physical training can be effective. After beating up a gang of young hustlers, he realizes that it can indeed.

In addition to the safety of this omniscient narrator who not only possesses information but also shares it with the viewers, the film employs multiple other devices to transmit information. The selection of the television images in the secluded room indicate with precision the passage of the years, while the presence of clocks and calendars reminds us of the various deadlines that punctuate the action. Moreover, through the extensive use of cell phones, internet chat rooms, audiotapes, and photographs, the characters exchange information and communicate their plans and goals. There is one particularly decisive piece of the puzzle, for instance, which is added through the tapes that Oh Dae-Su violently detracts from his jailer; the recorded conversations reveal the instructions given to the jail manager, they describe the treatment that was prescribed by the villain, and they give us a hint regarding the latter's motivation. This impersonal source of information, along with several others, increases the communicativeness of the narration and helps us slowly unravel the mystery of the story.

Finally, the resolution of this twisted narrative comes in a long chain of sequences where all the plot twists are revealed and the knowledge gaps are filled, fully satisfying the curiosity of the viewer. In fact, the final confrontation between the two male protagonists lasts for more than 25 minutes, in the course of which several earlier scenes are replayed in order for them – and for us – to reconsider our initial assumptions. This delayed expository segment takes the aspect of self-consciousness to the highest level, while it strives to reassemble the chronological and causal chain of events. Apart from the diegetic exchange of information in the conversation between the two men, the narration employs extensive cross-cutting as well as flashbacks in the form of split-screens, as I have previously mentioned, which communicate in a blatant manner the information regarding the characters' past actions. This point constitutes the peak of all three qualities of the narration and becomes an exemplary case of how the extreme self-consciousness can be paralleled by an extreme knowledgeability and communicativeness.

With such lengthy denouement the film draws to a close after a series of very intense and dramatic revelations that can only lead to death and destruction; a physical death in the case of Lee Woo-Jin and mental one for Oh Dae-Su. The increased omniscience and communicativeness of the narration, especially during the closing moments, succeeded in finally neutralizing the complexity of the story and relieving the tension that the secrets and the reversals had built.

Conclusion

My analysis of Park's film has given us the opportunity to detect some of the key workings of narrative complexity in contemporary cinema. In a way, it has helped us tame the forces of complexity and demystify its secrets by analytically describing the functions of causality, cinematic space, and time in the overall vehicle of narration, which transmits and distributes story information. On all narrative levels, *Oldboy* appeared to deviate in a considerable degree from the classical rules of filmmaking, trying out different formulas and looking for new solutions to the problems of dramatizing a particularly intense story of double incest and violent revenge. The construction of its characters and the causal chain of events borrowed some of the compositional and generic elements of the classical narrative, such as the role of the male avenger or the motif of the investigation, only to subvert them by entailing them in a Möbius strip structure that allows every person and every event to be doubly coded. Similarly, the cinematic space enriched the options of the classical *mise-en-scène* and continuity editing with spatial montage and intensified continuity, respectively. Moreover, in the axis of narrative time the filmmaker employed several breaks in the chronology of the events and manipulated the temporal signifiers quite freely, resulting in a sense of a continually mediated progression of time. All these innovative elements created a complex narrative that discovers new possibilities for the storytelling capacity of the cinematic medium.

On the other hand, the thread that holds this narrative together is the unremitting transmission of story information through an extensive network of sources that range from the characters' diegetic interactions to a very "talkative" voiceover commentary and a long chain of old and new media. The film invests a great deal on the increased knowingness and communicativeness of the narration in order to offer the viewers a coherent account of the action and to allow them to access its secrets. Therefore, by latching onto the classical principles that dictate the gradual exposition of the story and the complete filling of the knowledge gaps by the closing credits, *Oldboy* manages to combine the forces of innovation with some solid and reliable classical mechanisms.

However inventive Park's narrative choices may appear, they are not path-breaking; rather, they seem to fit in with a wider trend in current filmmaking that strives to outgrow the classical norms and experiment with new tools and new territories. Elsewhere, I have argued about the existence of a post-classical paradigm of narration that offers international filmmakers[10] a new set of constructional options that do not radically subvert the classical model but imbue it with the logic – and the corollaries – of a highly mediated mode of representation (Thanouli 2006). What is intriguing for me in the case of *Oldboy* is to see how a South Korean filmmaker has, on the one hand, mastered the rules of this new post-classical mode, while, on the other, he has instilled it with a particularly South Korean sensibility evidenced in the thematic choices and the approach to physical violence. Perhaps it was the negotiation between the international codes of post-classical cinema and the local story material that secured the film a successful performance on all the fronts. Perhaps not. I am afraid that secrets of world cinema will require more investigation in hidden places, other than those of narrative analysis, before they reveal themselves to us.

Notes

1   The release dates for *Oldboy* span almost 3 years; from the South Korean release in November 2003 to the latest one in Venezuela in September 2006. http:// www.imdb.com/title/tt0364569/releaseinfo

2   *Oldboy* won the Grand Jury prize at Cannes Film Festival in 2004 and Park's statement is reported on the festival's site: http://www.festival-cannes.fr/ films/fiche_film.php?langue=6002&id_film=4182985

3   By the term "classical narration" or "classical filmmaking," I refer to David Bordwell's account of the narrational norms and principles of the Hollywood cinema during the studio years, namely from 1917 to 1960. See Bordwell et al. (1985).

4   For the cognitive issues that the Möbius strip narrative structure raises, see Buckland's analysis of *Lost Highway* (1997) in Elsaesser and Buckland (2002) (reprinted in this volume).

5   From a similar perspective, another new media theorist, Yvonne Spielmann, describes this type of digital images as "clusters." Spielmann seeks to capture the aspect of density by borrowing the term "cluster" from music theory to characterize the images that are produced from processing. She notes: "Transferred to media, in particular visual media, the term cluster means the simultaneity of different images or elements effected through multiple layers. The cluster results in spatial density or fusion." See Spielmann (1999, p. 139).

6   According to David Bordwell's narrative theory, the cinematic time in the filmic narration consists of three variables: order, duration, frequency. See Bordwell (1985, pp. 74–88).

7   Bordwell borrows Meir Sternberg's (1978) terms from literary theory in order to be able to analyze the way a film controls the filmic information in relation both to the story itself and the audience.

8   I am using the term "level of narration" in the way Edward Branigan defined and developed it in his work on narrative analysis and comprehension. See Branigan (1992), ch. 4.

9   Branigan refers to "internal focalization (depth)" as the fully private and subjective level of a character's experience that consists of thoughts, dreams, memories, hallucinations, etc. (1992, p. 103). I should note, however, that Branigan mostly focuses on the internally focalized images and much less on sounds, which is an issue that perhaps requires further elaboration in his over- all scheme.

10   The origins of the post-classical mode of narration cannot be traced solely in one filmmaking tradition, as the narrative pattern emerged in films that came from all directions; the United States, Europe, and Asia. However, it is undeniable that the post-classical paradigm has certain prerequisites such as

a good knowledge of the classical norms, a technologically advanced production environment, and a hypermediated sensibility. These elements would be harder to find in underdeveloped countries and, thus, their film products would be unlikely to incorporate the post-classical narrational choices in their repertory.

Bibliography

Bordwell, D. 1985. *Narration in the Fiction Film*. London: Routledge.

Bordwell, D. 2006. *The Way Hollywood Tells It: Story and Style in Modern Movies*. Berkeley: University of California Press.

Bordwell, D., Staiger, J., and Thompson, K. 1985. *The Classical Hollywood Cinema: Film Style and Mode of Production to 1960*. New York: Routledge.

Branigan, E. 1992. *Narrative Comprehension and Film*. New York: Routledge.

Elsaesser, T. and Buckland, W. 2002. *Studying Contemporary American Film: A Guide to Movie Analysis*. London: Arnold.

Gombeaud, A. 2004. "*Old Boy*. La cloche de verre." *Positif*, 524 (October): 29–30.

Manovich, L. 2001. *The Language of New Media*. Cambridge, MA: The MIT Press.

Paquet, D. 2005. "The Korean film industry: 1992 to the present," in C. Y. Shin and J. Stringer (eds.), *New Korean Cinema*. New York: New York University Press, pp. 32–50.

Spencer, L. 2004. "Revenger's tragedy." *Sight and Sound*, 14, 10 (October): 18–20.

Spielmann, Y. 1999. "Expanding film into digital media." *Screen*, 40, 2 (Summer): 131–45.

Sternberg, M. 1978. *Expositional Modes and Temporal Ordering in Fiction*. Bloomington: Indiana University Press.

Thanouli, E. 2006. "Post-classical narration: A new paradigm in contemporary cinema." *New Review of Film and Television Studies*, 4, 3 (December): 183–96.

Index